D1133203

Urban Life and Form

Contributors

F. STUART CHAPIN, JR.
University of North Carolina

WERNER Z. HIRSCH
Washington University

LEE N. ROBINS
Washington University

LEO F. SCHNORE
University of Wisconsin

JOSEPH R. PASSONNEAU
Washington University

RICHARD C. WADE
University of Chicago

WILLIAM L. WEISMANTEL
Washington University

MORTON WHITE
Harvard University

ROBERT C. WOOD
Massachusetts Institute of Technology

URBAN LIFE AND FORM

Edited by WERNER Z. HIRSCH

Papers presented at the Faculty Seminar on Foundations of Urban Life and Form (1961–1962) sponsored by the Institute for Urban and Regional Studies, Washington University, St. Louis, Missouri

HOLT, RINEHART and WINSTON, INC.
NEW YORK · CHICAGO · SAN FRANCISCO
TORONTO · LONDON

Library of Congress Catalogue Card Number: 63–10967
23647–0113
PRINTED IN THE UNITED STATES OF AMERICA

Contents

Introduction

WERNER Z. HIRSCH, *Editor*

Cities give us collision—RALPH WALDO EMERSON

Urbanization is a quite recent phenomenon. Its advance in the United States was most rapid and powerful; only at the end of World War II did we become aware of its scope and begin to show concern for its consequences. Our tardiness in realizing the magnitude of urbanization is accompanied by the free dispensation, and almost universal acceptance, of shallow and pat explanations and answers, usually based on little sound research.

The opportunities that cities appeared to offer in the nineteenth century were attractive to many Americans. Once aware of them, they responded rapidly and the massive flow into our cities has continued ever since. Interestingly enough, few of those who moved into cities stayed there long. Perhaps no other country has had a similar experience. The great urge to move into cities, where good working conditions were sought, and cultural and educational opportunities were ample, was soon replaced by a desire for the amenities of life only available in suburbia, which in some respects is more similar to the rural life Americans had abandoned than the city life to which they had aspired. Many explanations can be offered for this phenomenon but a clearly important contributing fact has been the automobile.

What are the opportunities that are offered by cities and suburbs? What kind of life do American urbanites and suburbanites want to live? What objectives should we plan and help our cities to attain? Can we at least identify alternative objectives and programs? And which are the more attractive policies for executing promising plans?

These are some of the key questions that our society faces. They are significant and relevant, and deserve thoughtful, judicious answers. For, when we show concern for American urbanites and suburbanites, we are actually dealing with the vast majority of Americans; and when we examine urban and suburban life and form, we are touching on many of the fundamental issues facing America, present and future.

For these reasons, a group of scholars came together under the auspices of the Institute for Urban and Regional Studies of Washington University, for the express purpose of improving our understanding of the foundations of urban life and form.[1] It was hoped that as these foundations became more clearly identified and comprehended, it would be easier to carry out high quality work on specific urban questions. For example, an examination of the foundations of urban life and form and its evolution can be expected to help identify basic values and attitudes of today's society. Once uncovered, they may be reexamined critically and related to alternatives before they are made the basis of plans and policies for the future. Let us not forget that on a decent diet, man can produce daily about one horsepower hour of work with which he must also replenish his exhausted body. With whatever is left over, and in an affluent society this amount can be substantial, he is free to build a civilization.

Both architect and lawyer are highly influential in developing the environment in which the urbanite works and resides, as well as concepts of that environment. From the standpoint of pure form, it is not altogether clear what makes a city. Pierre DuColombier in his book, *Sienna and Siennese Art*, makes the thoughtful statement, "A collection of houses does not become a town on exceeding a given population. For example, San Gimignano in its existing enceinte, that is, the great thirteenth-century wall, has only 3,000 inhabitants and is a town; whereas Boggibonsi is much more populous and remains a village. San Gimignano, even within its first line of walls, still marked by a gate and no more than three-quarters of a mile around, must have already had an urban flavor. Its towers bear witness to what astonishes us in these miniature Italian cities, their ardent municipal feeling.''[2]

Joseph R. Passonneau defines a city as an inhabited place which rises above some minimum level of ''imageability.'' The cities abroad that project the most vivid images are Paris, Florence, Rome, and Venice, and those in the United States are New York, Boston, San Francisco, and New Orleans.

It is useful to view a city as a living organism which has a past, present, and future. Most of the cities of recent vintage are spiritless and lag in image. The function of the architect and artisan is to provide for the translation of society's social needs into physical form and thereby into lasting images. Architects can make their contribution in this regard and can create public taste.

The conventional view of land is related to ownership considerations. William L. Weismantel advances a new prospect—land, and especially urban land, as an artifact of society. A greenbelt, a park, a city square, are all artifacts. This new conception of land must be integrated with the long-held theory that the owner exerts dominion over the land. Reconciling the two points of view will not always be easy, since an individual is often likely to have a distinctly different attitude towards the same piece of land, depending on whether he considers it an artifact or property. But such a novel view can greatly revolutionize the planning and zoning of urban land.

An examination of the evolution of urban life and form in America could be carried out by scholars of various disciplines. The urban historian might stand at the top of the list, but as Eric E. Lampard, himself an urban historian, points out, ''. . . After more than half a century of problem-oriented research on cities, it is surprising how little we know about the phenomenon of urbanization. . . . Until recently historians have had little cause for satisfaction with their contributions to the field. American urban history—what there is of it—is largely the history of cities and their 'problems,' not the history of urbanization.''[3]

With this criticism in mind, Richard C. Wade takes a new look at America's urban experience. Obviously much of the thinking and direction of inquiry of many American historians since 1893 has heretofore been dominated by Frederick Jackson Turner's famous "Frontier Thesis." Turner looked westward and thus overlooked the city and its institutions. Later in his life he became aware of this omission and, in 1925, agreed on the desirability of an urban reinterpretation of our history. Wade undertakes such an effort. He finds that the cities were the centers that guided and shaped American economic, social, political, and cultural life ever since the days of the Revolution. Rivalries between businessmen in different cities brought about the building of roads, canals, and railroads, leading ultimately to the transportation revolution of the nineteenth century. In their role as cultural and educational centers, points of entry for immigrants, and places where funds and leadership could be found, cities experimented with new ways of life. They were seedbeds of progressivism. When the core city and surrounding suburbia started to evolve into distinctly separate units, each with its own interests, progressivism shifted its emphasis from intracity to intraurban conflicts. The twentieth century saw the mass introduction of the automobile, which soon was to modify America more, perhaps, than any other single invention.

For the longest time, Americans have been taught that their most cherished institutions and ways of life were uniquely shaped in a rustic mold. Morton White looks carefully into the origin of these ideas and attitudes. Examining the writings of the most influential philosophers, White concludes that the majority of them lament the growth of cities and the accompanying changes in the character of the population. Although not all for the same reasons, American philosophers on the whole have viewed cities and city dwellers with mistrust and extolled the so-called rural virtues. And there is evidence that the history of the philosopher's reactions to the city is not an isolated phenomenon. Apparently, in other fields of intellectual and literary endeavor much the same line has been pursued. This is an important fact to keep in mind. A predominantly urbanized society whose intellectuals are anticity is subject to many strains and stresses.

Following this historical perspective, an effort is made to identify distinctive contributions to the study of urban life and form which three of the key social sciences have already made or possibly might make. Robert C. Wood examines the contributions of political science to urban form. He finds the urban political scene so complex and torn by diversity of interests that it has been almost impossible to attain the political power that would permit formulation and execution of an intelligent public policy. As a result, one of broad scope has rarely been formulated and the impact of political decisions on the development of urban form has been relatively minor. He calls for the establishment of a series of urban observatories that would collect data in a coordinated manner and carry out an integrated research plan. Such a proposal is most attractive to all social scientists. For example, it would offer many unique possibilities for research to the economist who is interested in the study of urban government services and their financing. The economist is concerned with the problem of which goods and services urban governments should render and how they should be priced. In a mixed economy it is the government's function to create an environment conducive to efficient and desirable private economic activity. Thus, urban government activities are means toward the creation of an appropriate private decision-making climate. For this reason, then, economists have attempted to develop a generalized decision-making model which closely relates the urban government and private sector.

Another area of concern involves intergovernmental relations under our federated political and fiscal systems. Three key motives can be identified—intervention and encouragement, equalization, and responsibility. At the moment we have almost no intergovernmental fiscal relations system that is consistent with all three motives. The economist is also interested in the issue of metropolitan consolidation, which has mainly been argued in terms of efficiency, equity, and opportunity for offering better and more varied services. There is evidence that urban governments, unlike private firms, probably will not benefit from major-scale economies when they grow and consolidate.

Human ecologists among the sociologists, concerned with the interaction between man and his environment, have directed attention to urban form. Their emphasis has been on spatial structure. This approach treats the metropolitan community as a functioning whole and permits an understanding of some of its morphological features in space and over time. The most promising ecological research, according to Leo F. Schnore, looks at the metropolitan community in a larger setting, placing it within an external system that has major effects upon it, and then studies the interaction.

One of our most challenging problems today centers around the Negro who is trying to find his place in a rapidly urbanizing society. Most observers will agree that the "Negro problem" enters into more urban decisions than perhaps any other single issue. But we know very little about the basic human behavior pattern of Negroes, the social factors determining its expressions, and the full range of social consequences. Lee N. Robins finds that the sociologist who examines this problem is often handicapped by his own weaknesses. His liberal political leanings have tended to shift the blame for the social problems of the minority group to the attitude of the majority. It is, however, important to ask, whenever a minority's behavior is frowned upon by the majority, whether this represents a violation of standards shared by both groups, or rather indicates that the minority group has a different set of values and norms. But perhaps urbanites must of necessity exhibit more social problems. The high density of population and goods offers increased opportunities for aggression and theft. Urbanites are also more exposed to the ills of unemployment, which in turn can lead to social problems. Alleviation of such conditions among Negroes could proceed, possibly simultaneously, along two paths. We could seek the causes of the high incidence of social problems and develop means to intervene; we could also tend to improve the social and economic status of the Negro. Robins considers the second as offering an easier solution in the short run. It would require improved education, more skill-oriented and white-collar positions, and easier access to capital for investment in small enterprises.

Finally the role of the planner, perhaps somewhat ambiguous in a democracy, is considered. The one area where planning has been broadly accepted is city planning. F. Stuart Chapin looks upon city planning as the integrating discipline bringing together the social sciences, the arts, and architecture; thus it can provide for orderly progress and innovation. The great challenge faced by modern city planning is the identification and articulation of planning objectives, hand in hand with improved means of attaining them. This brings us back to our first question—what kind of life do our city dwellers seek in their surroundings?

I would like to think that in a democracy the single most important issue in relation to the creation and modification of urban life and form is to provide a large variety of opportunities and experiences from which people can choose with relative ease. Quick and comparatively effortless communication and transportation are of the essence. While society must permit horizontal and vertical mobility, it must also offer a large diversity of jobs, housing, educational experiences, services, facilities, and amenities of life from which a choice can be made. Planning must therefore be open-ended in many dimensions. It should permit great flexibility and as its objective, must permit us to choose the kind of habitat and institutions we prefer. It is most desirable to have different kinds of cities, some large, some small, but all containing within them sufficient diversity to permit the enjoyment of varied experiences and thus improve the citizen's chances for judicious choices in public and private goods. Within limits, such diversity enhances the opportunities of citizens to live in an environment most consistent with their individual aspirations.

A setting of such variety can be consistent with the esthetic growth of the city or the larger areas. It should be visually vivid and well structured and thus project a clear and satisfying image.

Yet, variety and proliferation of alternatives can be at odds with efficiency considerations and social consciousness to provide every citizen with life's essentials. International as well as domestic considerations have persuaded the United States that in the sixties it must grow rapidly. There are exciting prospects for rapid efficiency increases and economic growth. They stem from our post–World War II investment in research and development and the revelation of new fundamental knowledge at a scale never envisioned before. The federal government alone, in the fiscal year, 1962, spent about $12 billion on research and development. While defense and outer space were the major motivating forces for these investments, the new knowledge that is being discerned does not know these boundaries.

Urban America will be the key to the translation of new fundamental ideas into applications which can enrich our lives and enhance our economic growth. They can be developed and introduced into industry. But they can also produce new methods for the planning and operation of our cities and the hardware to accomplish these objectives. Thus the scientists and engineers who are creating a sophisticated system designed to take man to the moon and back to earth, are engaged in an effort that should also help to disclose new systems of automatic urban transit, waste disposal, city management, etc.

The problems of urban living in American cities and suburbs have multiplied and are becoming increasingly complex. The challenge is to plan for an open-ended and free society that is replete with esthetically beautiful communities and offers maximum variety and flexibility without undue loss of efficiency.

Notes

[1] Valuable comments on the papers presented by the authors appearing in this book were made by A. Theodore Brown, Ralph E. Morrow, Fumihiko Maki, Roger Montgomery, Carl A. McCandless, Robert H. Salisbury, Peter N. Riesenberg, Werner Hochwald, Elbert Segelhorst, Joseph A. Kahl, David B. Carpenter, and John A. Stern.

[2] Pierre DuColombier, *Sienna and Siennese Art* (London: Nicholas Kaye, 1957), p. 73.

[3] Eric E. Lampard, ''American Historians and the Study of Urbanization,'' *The American Historical Review*, 67:1 (October 1961), pp. 49 and 50.

The Emergence of City Form

JOSEPH RUSSELL PASSONNEAU *is Dean of the School of Architecture, Washington University, St. Louis, Missouri. He has made notable contributions to urban design in various sections of the United States, including design of a new downtown for Oak Ridge, Tennessee, over a billion dollars in industrial buildings for the Tennessee Valley Authority, and the summer auditorium for the Chicago Symphony Orchestra.*

What is a city? Boston in 1760 (population about 20,000) and Lexington, Kentucky, in 1820 (population about 10,000) were cities, but Kankakee, Illinois, in 1960 (population about 250,000) is not a city. To an economist, a city is a large, complex, input-output device. To a sociologist, a city is distinguished from a village by its higher degree of social differentiation and by the wider opportunity it offers for fruitful interaction between diverse individuals. To a political scientist, a group of compact, contiguous, but separately governed suburbs might not be a city, while a sprawling series of communities under a single government might be a city with a distinctive personality.

A physical designer might classify a city as a community with highly differentiated building types, and might even list the requisite buildings; but this would be an extension of the definition of a city as a socially differentiated community. To provide both a check on other disciplines and a spur to the imagination, we should search out a formal definition of the city independent of other definitions and rooted in the meaning of form itself.

To say that a "thing" or "event" has form is to say simply that we know that it exists. Conversely, to say we "know" or recognize a "thing" is to say that it has form.

Recognition of "form" is at the root of all intellection, and association of certain experiences with the recognition of certain forms must be the essence of thought in the animal sense. When the mind associates with forms experiences (or meanings) that do not inhere in the forms themselves, this is probably the beginning of uniquely human intellection—of symbol making and, therefore, of language.

If we understand the form say, of snowflakes or of cities, from fragmentary information about an individual snowflake or city we can make accurate predictions about the nature of other parts of that individual. A typical grid street pattern, for instance, gives a kind of physical form to most American cities. From street numbers at any location we can estimate our direction and distance from the downtown area. If we examine the buildings around us and have studied the form of other American cities, we can guess rather accurately the size of the city. At another level, if we can ascribe form to the physical configuration of a city, we can tell a good deal about its inhabitants, their history, and the structure of their values.

CITY SPACES

This is an essay on architecture, thinly disguised. Architecture deals with building elements and the relationships between building elements, and with buildings and the relationships or spaces between buildings. Geoffrey Scott, in *The Architecture of Humanism,* says that ". . . architecture . . . uses space as a material and sets us in the midst . . . The habits of our mind are fixed on matter. We talk of what occupies our tools and arrests our eyes. Space is nothing—a negation of the solid. And thus we come to overlook it . . . Even from a utilitarian point of view, space is logically our end. To enclose a space is the object of building; when we build we do but detach a convenient quantity of space, seclude it and protect it . . .

But esthetically, space is even more supreme. The architect models in space as a sculptor in clay."[1]

To think about the form of architectural spaces helps us to avoid fruitless arguments about such concepts as "beauty" and "functionalism." Whether we think the cathedral beautiful or ugly, to stand in the choir of Beauvais is a moving experience. It is also apparent that eliminating the upper 150 feet of space would not affect the function, in the narrow sense of the word; nevertheless, the true function of the church, somehow imbedded in the void in which we stand, would be destroyed.[2]

To think of architecture as the forming of spaces as well as the forming of solids also directs our attention to the activities that spaces contain and that, to a large extent, shape spaces. It emphasizes that architecture does not stop at the building line, that a building is not isolated from its surroundings, that there is an architecture of interior spaces and an architecture of exterior spaces, an architecture of rooms, of groups of rooms, of paths, of plazas, an architecture of cities, and even of regions.

THE EVOLUTION OF THE FORMS OF THE CITY

By cataloguing in a gross way the buildings and spaces common to most cities in history, we can develop an Aristotelian definition of cities as a class of things including certain formal elements and contained within recognizable boundaries.

Most early cities were contained within perimeter walls. In turbulent times—Mesopotamia in the third and second millennia, the Mediterranean towns of the first millennium before Christ, and in the cities of medieval Europe—the wall dominated the city. During peaceful periods or in protected regions, the wall was less important. When the Roman Empire was strongest and during most of the dynastic periods in Egypt, walls played a small part in shaping cities. After the invention of gunpowder, cities were surrounded by star-shaped ramparts that permitted enfilade. These ramparts in vestigial form still shape parts of many great European cities—Turin, Vienna, Copenhagen—and persist unchanged to create the beautiful pattern of such a village as Naarden in Holland. The edges of later cities were more negatively defined by the thinning out of dwelling patterns. As modern American cities coalesce, the boundaries persist as political fictions with no meaning in architectural form.

Within its perimeter, the city is a more or less continuous set of spaces shaped by a welter of buildings. All human settlements, from rude villages to noble cities, have contained three types of spaces: dwellings, paths, and places of assembly. The city's dwellings provide its texture, the paths give it a structure, and the places of assembly, particularly those with a ceremonial function, create focal points or local perturbations in the city's texture.

As the social organization of the city becomes stratified, the types of dwellings multiply; as institutions differentiate, places of assembly multiply. There will be places for production, for government, for instruction, for commerce, for leisure, for defense. The more complex the life of the city, the more varied the individuality of the citizens; the more directly this complexity and individuality can find expression in the city's spaces, the richer will the form of the city become.

This definition of a city as a settlement containing differentiated spaces for family life, for movement, and for assembly is a reasonable dictionary definition, but it is not very useful for our purposes. We need a definition that tells us more about the form of cities, that reveals that there is some threshold of urbanity at which a village becomes a city and that there is a hierarchy of city form.

Those needs that unite all human societies create the common elements in city form; family life shapes and is shaped by the dwelling spaces, communication shapes the city's paths, and social and political institutions shape and are shaped by places of assembly. These functions and their crystalization in the form of the city are continuously modified by ecology (geography, vegetation, climate, local building materials), by powerful individuals, by forces which we might lump together under the label of fate, and by the accumulating experience of the race. We must understand the way these forces modify city form, if we are to understand the unique qualities of cities separated by time and space: the early cities that emerged in Mesopotamia, Greece, China; a series of Romes emerging from Rome; the cities that grew or began in western Europe during the Middle Ages; and, finally, the emergence and coexistence of many twentieth-century cities distinctly different from each other and from any that preceded them.

Most early villages were groups of scattered shelters, each housing a family or clan. Each shelter was dwelling space and often storehouse, barn, and factory. As villages grew, the dwellings coalesced for economy in space and material. In the Indus Valley, in Mesopotamia, and along the border of the eastern Mediterranean, the texture of early cities was created by one- and two-story houses packed together, with common walls and interior courtyards. Similar communities persist today in North Africa and in the Hopi villages of the southwestern United States.

The social forces that pushed dwellings together also pushed them upward. Rome in the first century A.D. was composed largely of six- to ten-story *insulae,* the prototype of the modern tenement block. During the great period of city building and rebuilding begun in Europe in the Middle Ages, the requirements of defense and communication limited the area of cities. High, closely packed tenements were the standard dwelling in medieval Paris, the cities of Renaissance Italy, and the baroque cities of most of Europe; and the working-class quarters of such nineteenth-century industrial cities as Edinburgh and Birmingham may have formed the most depressing and unsanitary environment men have ever created. Dwellings in all of these cities were limited in size by the strength of materials and the height to which people could be forced to walk, with only marginal regard for light, air, and sanitation even in upper-class quarters.

Where freedom of choice has existed, wealthy and powerful citizens have generally lived either close to the center of the city in town houses built around gardens or courtyards, or in villas isolated in the countryside.

The modern American city includes all of these dwelling types. New York, for instance, has districts of large town houses and districts of fine, early nineteenth-century row houses. It has tenement districts, low apartment districts, and districts with the highest building densities of any city in history. The suburbs of New York, like the suburbs of most twentieth-century American cities, are formed by villas. For the first time since the earliest villages, we are building settlements in which most inhabitants live in detached dwellings.

The city's paths have become differentiated in much the same way as the city's dwellings. The footpath became a road for wheeled vehicles. Roads were later paved and, in such cities as Peking and nineteenth-century Paris, the boulevard became not only a path but a grand ceremonial space. The railroad shaped the nineteenth-century city both by cutting through its older fabric and by stringing suburbs out along radial rapid-transit lines. Canals shaped such cities as Amsterdam. In cities that grew over long periods of time, paths were the interstices between groups of buildings. In colonial cities, on the other hand, from the time of Miletus and Priene to the opening of the American West, the street pattern came before the buildings; the rectangular grid is, therefore, the mark of the colonial city.

As transportation in the twentieth century has increased in speed and decreased in cost, communication has become a less restrictive determinant of city form.[3] The modern superhighway, cutting through the city like a Parisian boulevard with little regard for the traditional dwelling patterns, makes new city patterns inevitable. We can now spread the city all over the landscape (Los Angeles) or concentrate parts of it in extraordinary densities (Manhattan). Modern Americans are in the enviable position occupied previously by the very rich and powerful: they can (if they are middle-class, Protestant, and white) live wherever they choose.

Institutions have generally been located at or have formed focal points in the city. The fork in the road or the intersection of the road and the stream became the market. In Greece, the market became the agora, in Rome, the forum. It persists today in the Italian piazza, the French *place*, the English square, and the New England village green. Such community open spaces have often been bordered by ceremonial enclosed spaces: the palace, the cathedral, the town hall.

As society grew complex, new institutions shaped the city. Greece developed the theater and the hippodrome, Rome, the basilica (which later became the cathedral) and the communal bath, and changed the scale and even the function of many Greek institutions. In the Middle Ages, new types of institutions—the alms house, the hospital, the monastery, and the university—added to the vocabulary of institutional forms. Most institutions have simply created local variations in city form. But the medieval castle, the Gothic cathedral, the baroque palace, and the American university have often been the major determinant in shaping the cities that grew up around them.

That public spaces in this country, at least since the beginning of the eighteenth century, have seldom been designed reflects the general neglect in America of the public sector of life. Our disregard for places of assembly (plus the rapid and simultaneous growth of large cities) has created cities, particularly west of the Alleghenies and east of the Rockies, similar to each other and with few internal variations in form. Gertrude Stein described such American cities succinctly, "There is no there there."

Distinctive geography has shaped many cities. Rivers have both given form to, and been dominant elements in, such cities as Stockholm, Paris, Rome, and Boston. Lakes and great rivers have barred growth in one direction, creating the fan-shaped street patterns of such cities as Chicago and St. Louis. The islands of medieval Paris, Venice, and modern Manhattan, and the hills of San Francisco, many Italian towns, Imperial Rome, and Buenos Aires have given these cities their special configurations.

Climate has, until recently, shaped cities: the open galleries of New Orleans (climate, warm and humid), the pitched roofs of Northern Europe (climate, cold and wet), the adobe buildings of the American southwest and of North Africa (climate, hot and dry) gave the cities of these regions their special character.

Local materials and the technology that grew up around them have always shaped cities. The reed construction of the Nile, the mud construction of Mesopotamia, and the wood construction of Greece not only shaped the early villages of these regions, but the form of such building elements persisted for thousands of years, often translated into buildings of stone. The masonry cathedrals of the thirteenth and fourteenth centuries and the wooden temples of Japan were created by artisans who had learned to shape ancient materials in extraordinarily ingenious ways. Later, more spectacular changes in technology influenced city form; today it is steel, reinforced concrete, the elevator, and the telephone that make the towering centers of modern American cities possible.

To the names of ancient kings was often added the phrase, "city builder." The Italian princes and French kings cut Renaissance squares into the fabric of medieval cities. Pope Sixtus V in Rome, and Haussmann, supported by Louis Napoleon, in Paris, carved out the boulevards that give form to those cities. The Chicago lake front is a magnificent and useful memorial to Daniel Burnham, though the city rejected most of the rest of his monumental plan. Such modern public works directors as Robert Moses in New York and the heads of urban renewal authorities are having a similar impact on the shape of the city. (Urban renewal is not a new idea. Joseph Hudnut has called Nero the first slum clearance expert and described his methods as "impetuous but thorough,"[4] and Notre Dame of Paris was almost destroyed during an "urban renewal project" in 1792.)

THE MANY DIMENSIONS OF "CITY FORM"

This brief description of the evolution of the elements of cities is a subjective selection of bits of objective data. We could elaborate the description but we would soon prove to ourselves that we have not yet found how to capture the *gestalt* of city form or learned to describe the city geometry in any satisfactory way.

While a city is inanimate, in the sense that the skeleton of a living animal is inanimate, the forces that shape it are very much alive. Inanimate forms are identical and interchangeable. While living form retains its identity, it also changes (it has a history) and is at each instant unique. This means that a city is constantly changing and disappearing into itself and it is difficult to produce a record of the form of any city at any cross section through time. This is true of all history, but the fact that, at first glance at least, city form has a precise geometric nature makes its evanescence peculiarly frustrating.

Such disasters as the burial of Pompeii in 79 A.D., by the eruption of Mt. Vesuvius, or the destruction of Olynthus by Philip of Macedon in 348 B.C., cut short the growth of a few ancient cities, leaving us a rather complete record of their physical form at the last moment in their history. But, because of the persistence of cities on a few locations favored either by myth or geography, the physiognomy of most cities is lost forever and what data remain are not assembled in any systematic way.

The cities about which we have the best information are those of which we are now a part. In the present state of our art, it seems logical to find out first what we can say with precision about the form of cities we can observe directly, then watch how they evolve, and finally try to work backward in history, using those descriptive tools that prove to be most useful. This should improve both our understanding of the nature of city form and of those variations in form that make classification useful.

If we try to treat the description of a specific city, St. Louis for instance, as a restricted problem in descriptive geometry, we still have difficulties. Do we describe a city at some instant? Even if we so decide, the data gathering process takes time—when we are half through, the form we started with will have changed. Perhaps we should "average out" the form over, say, a year.

Other problems remain. Do we describe spaces formed only by inanimate objects? Trees and shrubs are such important objects shaping city spaces that we can hardly ignore them. If we include living trees, do we also include people? Even if this is simply an exercise in descriptive geometry, people are objects and they are part of the "shape" of the city in the strictest sense of the word. Automobiles, if we include moving objects, are also important elements of city form.[5]

As we study St. Louis there emerges, not the form of a city, but rather a new set of problems, problems of understanding and interpretation. Consider an old avenue that is now a downtown commercial street. The two-dimensional, "map forms" of Olive Street in 1860 and Olive Street in 1960 are identical. Even the three-dimensional form of Olive Street did not change significantly in 100 years. But from sketches and photographs, it is obvious that the nature of the street, and the way it was seen by its inhabitants, has changed profoundly. In 1860, the street was filled with children playing, neighbors gossiping, mothers wheeling perambulators and shoppers riding by in carriages. In 1960, the street was filled with automobiles and pedestrians hurrying elsewhere.

Similar problems appear when we compare areas separated not by time but by distance. The map forms of Forsyth Boulevard (a fine old residential street) and Manchester Road (a typical suburban commercial slum) are identical. In model form, the streets are similar and in some areas the buildings on Manchester are more orderly than those on Forsyth. Yet the two streets are quite different. Manchester is a chaotic waste land into which few people would venture except through economic necessity. Forsyth is a magnificent outdoor public room enjoyed by many people. The difference is in detail: Manchester is shaped by disorganized signs and by automobiles; Forsyth is shaped by beautifully organized trees.[6] These details are crucial to the form of the city as understood by its citizens.

Even if we think of the city in simple geometric terms, it is soon apparent that the city changes even its gross physiognomy while the description is in progress; that important elements (people, cars) change position constantly; that significant aspects are so subtle that they can be revealed only by a geometry too complex to be useful; in short, that the city is a living organism, that it has a history, and the form of the city at any moment is both a description of its present life and a record of its past. It is also apparent that when we ascribe form to a thing or event, we describe a relationship between the observer and the thing observed. The "form" of St. Louis is not simply its physiognomy but an image in the observer's mind or, more accurately, the many images that exist in the minds of many citizens.

How people "see" their cities is the subject of Kevin Lynch's study, *The Image of the City*. Lynch compares parts of Boston, Jersey City, and Los Angeles through analyses, professional field studies, and sample interviews with their inhabitants. For most of a city's inhabitants, the image is predominantly one of paths, though outsiders tend to see a city as districts organized around topography, and older natives see their city as a network of small landmarks.[7]

The image of the city varies with the geographic and social location of the viewer. It will be a kind of mirror image of the viewer's total experience, dependent on his sensitivity to his environment.[8] Profoundly affected by the intensity with which he lives, the nature of the image may also affect his capacity for living intensely.

I will choose to define a city as an inhabited place which rises above a here unspecified level of "imageability." [9] A way to examine, if not to test, this definition is to compare it with competing definitions of the city. The most "imageable" cities in this country —New York, Boston, San Francisco, New Orleans—stand high in the hierarchy of cities by any definition. Paris, Florence, Rome and Venice project vivid images. Their images are vivid because of their history, but their historic significance may also be a function of the quality of their image. By this definition, Chicago is partly city and partly anticity. Such sleepy towns as Chartres, Portofino, and Williams, Massachusetts, are higher forms of cities than many a metropolis, as witness Los Angeles, Jersey City, Detroit. By our definition, the recent history of St. Louis is a story of the submergence of urban form; St. Louis in 1860 probably had a much higher degree of imageability than St. Louis in 1960.

There is apparently a general, though not a one-to-one, correspondence between urbanity measured by imageability and urbanity measured by other standards, such as physical size, degree of social differentiation, political unity, "culture."

Verbal descriptions of the geometry of the city deal with city form at second hand; they bear the same relationship to the form of the city that program notes bear to the form of the symphony. The image of the city deals with form directly. Geometric descriptions of the city all founder on the fact of change. The "image of the city" not only embraces its changing form, but the vividness of the city's image is a function of the extent to which the form of the city is a record of its history.

Thus city form has temporal as well as spatial dimensions. From this dual organization stem most of our difficulties in describing city form. Our distrust of subjective criteria makes imageability suspect as a criterion of cityishness.[10] But it is only in our image of the city that we unite the temporal and spatial dimensions of city form.

This duality is also the locus of the architect's dilemma. A true Janus, the architect must have a vivid image of "the city" (he must face the past), but he must also elicit an image of the emerging city (he must face the future). We are today in most American cities, in the suburbs of European cities, and in the new cities of Asia, building what may be the most spiritless cities in history. If this is true, it reflects qualities in our societies, but it may also reflect a misunderstanding of the possibilities in city form. In the rest of this essay we will add to Kevin Lynch's concept of imageability some guesses about the symbolic function of architecture and speculate on conditions under which we might once again create noble cities.

CITY FORM: A LANGUAGE OF HUMAN BEHAVIOR

The architect and the artisan who imitates him are the agents through whom society translates, however imperfectly, social needs into physical form and, therefore, into new images. The great cities were produced by "articulate" societies—and their architects were the "voice" of these societies. Conversely, when the architect is out of touch with society or when society misreads its own deepest needs, the city becomes inarticulate.

We have long recognized that the architect, at the command of a prince or a building committee, constructs a building that is a reflection of forces that exist in society. When buildings have been grand enough, we have often called them symbols of the society that produced them. We should expect such monumental buildings to create imageable cities, and that such buildings should be "symbolic" of vigorous societies. This is not always the case. Some monumental cities (Brazilia, Leningrad, modern Athens) have a low degree of imageability; some vividly imageable cities (Amsterdam, probably Elizabethan London, San Francisco, early nineteenth-century New Orleans, even New York) have had little monumental architecture. All of these cities, however, were built by vigorous and creative societies.

That we label monumental buildings symbolic reflects, I believe, both a misunderstanding of the way a city speaks through its architecture and of the creative function of symbolic systems. Suzanne Langer, in *Philosophy in a New Key,* distinguishes between signs, which she calls proxies for objects or events, and symbols, vehicles for intellection, and she speculates on "the use of symbols to attain as well as organize belief."[11] It is clear, for instance, that mathematical systems have contained and revealed ideas unknown to the societies that created the systems. We also sense that words can combine in such ways as to adumbrate the possibility of human experience that could not be revealed through direct experiment.

Monumental architecture is not, in the strict sense that Langer uses the word, *symbolic* at all, but is simply a *sign* of the existence of an independently developed social pattern. The pyramids were built after the great dynastic periods; the Acropolis was finished as classical Athens disintegrated, and before the Hellenistic city; the baths, the Coliseum, and the great forums were built long after the end of the Roman Republic; the Gothic cathedrals during the Albigensian heresies and other schismatic movements, and after the flowering of the church. When St. Louis was looking confidently ahead to the day that it would be the leading metropolis of the

United States, it did not feel it necessary to build a 650-foot high arch.

Norris Smith argues that (monumental) architecture is the most conservative of the arts, that architectural forms are not produced by socially creative societies, that architectural form is "concretized" only after the social pattern begins to disintegrate.[12]

Architectural historians and architects themselves have conspired to focus attention on monumental architecture (many would not even give the name "architecture" to nonmonumental structures) and, therefore, on the servile role of spatial images. However, it may be that a creative function for architecture can be found only if one looks also at humbler structures.

Lewis Mumford asserts repeatedly that cities created social forms. He suggests, for instance, that city walls, designed for protection, served a more important role. "Under pressure of one master institution (Kingship) a multitude of diverse social particles, long separate and self-centered, if not mutually antagonistic, were brought together in a concentrated urban area. As with a gas, the very pressure of the molecules within that limited space produced more social collisions and interactions within a generation than would have occurred in many centuries if still isolated in their native habitats, without boundaries." [13]

But while we sense, with Mumford, that architecture at its best must play a creative role, we should be able to go further and demonstrate that there are architectural images that are true symbols—in Langer's words, "vehicles for expression and *conception*." We should expect that where such architecture existed, it should have created cities with a high degree of imageability, and that such cities should have played significant roles in history.

This coincidence between moments of historic significance and imageability indeed exists, though only fragments of many of the most significant cities have come down to us. The Italian towns of the early Renaissance, London of Elizabethan England, sixteenth-century Amsterdam, both the villages and cities of Revolutionary America, and even fragments of nineteenth-century St. Louis, are all vivid cities, though they produce few architectural monuments. The image is created—both words are powerfully suggestive—not by *monumental* (read: "cenotaphic"?) but by *vernacular* architecture.

The vernacular elements were: in Amsterdam, red brick, brightly painted wood, stuccoed gables; in the Italian hill towns, the local stone and brick, tile roofs, and round arches; in New England, cedar shingles, white clapboard, native carpentry; in colonial Boston, red brick, multiple chimney flues, small paned windows, and simplified Georgian cornice door and window details. While each vernacular was different, each was formed from a few simple elements. The elements had multiple uses; they combined in diverse and rich ways to produce socially useful (and socially creative) spaces. The elements could be used in artful ways by artisans uninitiated into art. The cities created from these elements had diversity within unity—the common architectural language expressed common values, and the multiplicity of possible combinations made possible the expression of a rich, varied, and highly individualistic society. Finally, in many of these cities public ceremonial architecture grew naturally over many generations from vernacular forms and, therefore, had deep roots in the cities' history.

THE EMERGING CITY

In the twentieth century, the logic of mass production technology argues for an esthetic based on permutations of simple building vernacular. History also argues that from such a repetitive vernacular we could create a family of form flexible enough to embrace the constant change and infinite variety of modern society.

The fact is that for the first time in history we go to great pains to avoid the appearance of repetition. We are wealthy enough to indulge our most capricious tastes, and the builder's and layman's preoccupation with novelty reflect similar preoccupations among architects. The reaction against historicism in architecture can be partly explained by the history of the modern movement, but while novelty very occasionally can be equated with quality in city design, it is difficult to explain the continuing preoccupation of architects with such a transient virtue.

While architects design only a small percentage of all buildings, their attitudes establish public taste. To Daniel Burnham and most of his architectural contemporaries, the nineteenth-century American city had a low imageability. The image of their "ideal city" bore striking resemblances to baroque Rome, Versailles, and Haussmann's

Paris, and they projected this image on American cities, with varying results. This baroque image of the ideal city persists in the minds of most laymen and many "city planners."

The leaders of the modern movement in architecture rejected the baroque image of the city along with most of the paraphernalia of the architectural past. The Cartesian images of *Broad Acre City* and *La Ville Radieuse* were the answers of Wright and Corbusier to the chaos and disintegration of the modern city.[14] But despite the fact that Wright and Corbusier rejected traditional forms, their images of the city were still classical and static.

The most creative contemporary architects now find vivid the same city images that arrest the average traveler: the image of the medieval city, the New England town, the Georgian suburb, and many primitive villages. These are images of cities highly differentiated but uncontrived, formed from simple vernacular, and therefore with a visual unity in marked contrast to the modern city.

Jakob Bakema, for instance, is profoundly moved by the imageability of Hopi pueblos (in our terms, Hopi "cities").[15] To Aldo van Eyck, the natives inhabiting the region near the confluence of the Missouri and the Mississippi rivers live in rude settlements; the preliterate Dogon tribes of North Africa live in noble cities.[16] And the hypnotic image of the Alfred Newton Richards Medical Research Building of Louis Kahn is probably the image, not of a building, but of a city in embryo. Roger Montgomery explains the compelling imageability of primitive towns and of Kahn's laboratory to modern eyes by the fact that they are, as opposed to monumental "closed" forms, formally "open-ended" and therefore suggestive in a time of extraordinarily rapid and violent growth and change. "Built-in change is characteristic of indigenous buildings and settlements. Here is an esthetic based on change, open always to the possibility of addition, subtraction and modification."[17]

Fumihiko Maki is trying to establish a theoretical formulation for an open-ended architecture and a systematic basis for action. He contrasts what he calls compositional form, the product of the classical approach to form making, with group form, or "a vocabulary of group forms, i.e., a set of definitions of functional relationships [in which] many types of linkage are conceived [and] which may become a great many forms."[18]

The classical forms and the classical methods by which we attempt to order cities may be dead weight, or worse. For our open society we must create an open city form. History tells us that the significant forms of this emerging city will not grow from historic monuments nor will they spring full blown from the brow of avant-garde architects. They will take shape as our new technology is applied simply and directly to our new social problems to create a new language of city forms.

The evidence lies all around us. Where architects deal in self-conscious ways with frivolous issues (in the spurious individuality of the suburb or the shopping center) or when they create monuments without recourse to familiar and useful forms (whether in the Jefferson Memorial or the Roosevelt Memorial), they produce nothing that will meet the test of imageability. The contemporary forms to which men respond, whether they are laymen or artists, are the elemental shapes of farms and factories and, at another scale, the office towers of Chicago or Manhattan.

The usefulness of language lies partly in the nature of words themselves. Words link freely into complex and often unsuspected and fruitful combinations. Words are evanescent; the spoken word disappears as it is formed, making room for new words. A study of vernacular architecture suggests an approach to form making close to language itself, by which elements can be freely combined and discarded and recombined to satisfy needs previously unsuspected either by the people who dwell in the forms or by the men who created their elements.

What we regularly describe as architectural symbols are simply signs of past events. The artist is interested in an architecture that is true symbol, a vehicle for conception. If city form is, as Jakob Bakema asserts, "a language for human behavior," and if language does have a creative function, then architecture may reveal to a society that is fragmented and unfulfilled, healing patterns of human behavior that could be revealed in no other way.

Notes

[1] Geoffrey Scott, *The Architecture of Humanism* (New York: Doubleday & Company, Inc., 1954), p. 168.

[2] If all the capitals, piers, vaults, and statuary were dismembered and reassembled at eye level (as has been done with the mosaics of several of the Ravenna cathedrals) we would understand the elements more clearly, but we would not have a cathedral. Herbert Feigel, in a lecture many years ago at the University of Minnesota, put it in more homely language, "Take my liver, my fingers, my heart, all of the pieces of Feigel, throw them in a pile—that's not Feigel."

[3] I owe this idea to informal discussions with Melvin Weber.

[4] Joseph Hudnut, *Architecture and the Spirit of Man* (Cambridge, Mass.: Harvard University Press, 1949), p. 187.

[5] Roger Montgomery has suggested that the city may be so complex that it cannot be described in any useful way. But our capacity to store and process data is increasing far more rapidly than is the data to be processed. The problem lies in assembling the data. Here techniques from military intelligence, electronic mapping, etc., may prove useful.

[6] Most of the objects (signs, buildings, used cars) that shape the ugliest street were designed, some by very good architects. The trees that shape city streets were planted by semiliterate laborers directed by a petty government official, possibly the nephew of a corrupt alderman.

[7] Kevin Lynch, *The Image of the City* (Cambridge, Mass.: Technology Press, M.I.T., and Harvard University Press, 1960), p. 46.

[8] Lynch argues that in the developing image of the city, education in seeing is quite as important as the shaping of what is seen. Art and audiences grow together. Ours has become largely a verbal society, and while most instructors think that freshmen in college are verbally crippled, their verbal skills are highly sophisticated compared with their visual skills.

[9] Lynch, *op. cit.*, p. 9: "Imageability: that quality in an object which gives it a high probability of evoking a strong image in an observer. It is that shape, color, or arrangement which facilitates the making of vividly identified, powerfully structured, highly useful mental images of the environment." Fumihiko Maki has pointed out that the modern city is so vast and varied that we cannot really speak of the image of the city, but only of the image of its parts.

Lynch's investigations have been limited to discrete parts of cities with a special configuration. David Crane, however, is trying to find organizing principles for complete cities and would probably argue that the success of city design must finally be measured by the success with which we can uncover ordering principles strong enough to embrace entire cities.

10 George Santayana, *The Sense of Beauty* (New York: Modern Library, Inc., 1955), p. 6: "Man has a prejudice against himself: anything which is a product of his mind seems to him to be unreal or comparatively insignificant. We are satisfied only when we fancy ourselves surrounded by objects and laws independent of our nature. The ancients long speculated about the constitution of the universe before they became aware of the mind which is the instrument of all speculation. The moderns, also, even within the field of psychology, have studied first the function of perception and the theory of knowledge by which we seem to be informed about external things; they have in comparison neglected the excusively subjective and human department of imagination and emotion. We have still to recognize in practice the truth that from these despised feelings of ours the great world of perception derives its value, if not also its existence."

11 Suzanne Langer, *Philosophy in a New Key* (New York: The New American Library, 1958), p. 33.

12 Professor Smith is not enthusiastic about my development of this idea. "I have some reservations—first and foremost about your dismissal of monumental architecture as mere sign, divorced from the realms of thought and idea . . . In the Egyptian necropolis, the Roman bath, and the Gothic cathedral he (the architect) has given form, it seems to me, to an 'imageable' vision of a beneficient, stable, and enduring pattern of social order, or mode of relatedness, which, as an imaginative avowal, is on the same level as the best works of painters, poets, and other kinds of artists.

"I would argue, for instance, that the Parthenon was built in response to more or less the same situation that prompted Plato, a few years later, to write his Republic . . .

"In the same way I'd contend that the Gothic cathedral resulted, at least in part, from a backward-looking collaboration between the French monarchy and the French church, both of which institutions were probably somewhat taken aback by some of the new-fangled developments taking place in the new-fangled cities (see Haskins on Renaissance of Twelfth Century) and conceived that perhaps things had been better in Charlemagne's day, when church and monarchy had had things more firmly in their own hands . . .

"Moreover, I cherish a dark suspicion, with regard to this matter of monumentality, concerning the motivations of the modern architect. Iktinos could build a temple to the patron deity of Athens, and Robert de Luzarches could put up a cathedral at the heart of Amiens which represented an institution of which virtually everyone was a member. Today we lament the fact that there is no institution, such as the medieval church, in reference to which the architect can set forth his ideal vision. There remains only the city itself—but not the city as a government or as a human institution, as a society of fiercely loyal and deeply committed members, taking pride in their own city and holding others in contempt. No, only the city as an 'input-output mechanism' or as a complex pattern of paths along which great numbers of relatively unrelated persons may have a great variety of personal experiences. But if that's all there is left, then, dammit, we'll make *that* monumental! Isn't the urban designer trying to present an ideal and monumental pattern of the same order as that of the cathedral builder—except that the poor soul no longer has a cathedral to build? Isn't his rear-guard action even more rear-guard than that of Plato and Iktinos? At least there was still in Athens a strong conservative party which could influence policy; at least in the Middle Ages the church was immensely powerful, even though its hegemony was being challenged. The modern planner, it seems to me, looks back to the medieval town and to a unified and organic social order at a time when virtually *nothing* survives of the shared beliefs and traditions and social structures that made that order of things possible. (For isn't it the case that the unity of Sienna, say, depends in the last analysis not upon the appearance of the streets and buildings but upon a fabric of understandings among families and among neighborhoods that has been woven together over a period of some twenty-five hundred years? And does not the anti-historicism of modern style strike a deadly blow at the very notion of such a fabric, by denying the importance of all such understandings that are shaped by history and maintained by tradition?) In short, I suspect the present-day architect of hiding his itch for the monumental under a spurious veil of scientific practicality—and of destroying, by means of his coldly impersonal scientism, the warmly human symbols (not signs) of urban relatedness which have been handed down to us in the traditional forms of western architecture.'' (from an informal letter)

[13] Lewis Mumford, *City in History* (New York: Harcourt, Brace & World, Inc., 1961), p. 34.

[14] These images have materialized in debased form, *Broad Acre City* in Suburbia and *La Ville Radieuse* in many ''slum clearance'' projects.

[15] In a public lecture at Washington University, November 13, 1959.

[16] In a public lecture at Washington University, October 30, 1961.

[17] Roger Montgomery, *The Sequential Theme,* mimeographed, Washington University, St. Louis, 1961.

[18] Fumihiko Maki, *Some Thoughts on Collective Form with an Introduction to Group Form,* mimeographed, Washington University, St. Louis, 1961.

A New Vision in Law: The City as an Artifact

WILLIAM WEISMANTEL *is an attorney and a city planner, currently teaching, lecturing, and engaged in research at Washington University, St. Louis, Missouri. His recent articles "Multi-Center Land Use and Transportation System for Greater St. Louis" and "Proposed Demonstration of Uses of the Design Plan in Urban Renewal" are among his contributions to city planning in general, and to that of St. Louis in particular. He was formerly connected with Harland, Bartholomew & Associates, City Planners.*

Something momentous is about to occur in our legal system, not only in the written body of appellate court opinions and the statute books, but in everyone's opinion about property. It is a new concept of land—land, especially urban land, as an artifact of society—a spatial view that recognizes the city as a physical arrangement and begins to make judgments about its plastic form, just as one recognizes a plow to be making a line, and judges that the line is too straight, or too irregular. The older view of land, as something an individual owns and exerts dominion over, is not inconsistent with the new concept, but they must be adjusted to one another. The new idea impinges on the old when a preferred spatial or plastic order tying together the parts of the artifact is recognized as a persuasion or obligation on the separate parts. For example, the city dweller's planning commission proposes to girdle his entire city with a greenbelt. As with a new possession, the citizen visualizes the greenbelt, and finds it satisfying. It joins his collection of pleasant ideas about his city, to be referred to occasionally for indulgence and elaboration. But almost the first time he reflects on this greenbelt concept, he substitutes himself for an owner of land in the greenbelt—such self-substitution for the owner has been one of his conventional ways of thinking about land—and discovers a terrible conflict.

This paper considers five areas where the spatial, artifact idea of land is emerging. The first is the mind of the typical city dweller. His opinion of the city as either something you live in and own a small parcel of, or as something to be fashioned and enjoyed, is described as The Popular View. Next, the reader is led through three time corridors of land law: Landowning As An Office—is being a land developer some kind of public trust? From Word Law to Map Law—can one draw law, or can it only be spoken and written? And Great Planners of History—showing that land law evolved slowly through the centuries but made great strides through certain decades. Finally, American Zoning is examined as an advanced form of map law, though it is a rather bad art form. *Artifact* is used in this paper as an ideal for city building. A city, or part of it, is an artifact when people are willing to look at it and use it and enjoy doing so, without regrets or explanations. The place should be satisfying for its own sake, as matter, without having to borrow its reason for being from a real estate theory, a social theory, or a style idea from architecture or city planning doctrine. It must be so satisfying that the users and viewers accept it as perfect, within its own context, just as one accepts a Goya and does not say, "Goya made the eyes too hollow." The residents of most parts of the city only live there; they do not look at the buildings except for other reasons, such as geographic or social orientation. The esthetes do not look at these areas either, or accept their own presence within them. They pass through in conversation, in transit between large-scale objects of art whose existence they deign to accept. So, in a real sense most buildings are the buildings nobody sees, nobody lives in. To correct this, city building must be more than a useful art, as difficult as this is. It must become a fine art as well.

THE POPULAR VIEW

In the United States, an idea is frequently known and accepted by the public long before being defined and recognized by courts and legislatures. This is the case in the concept of the city as an artifact whose lines should be traced, therefore, from popular sources, to see just what can be expected to emerge from the law before turning to legal sources to see it emerge.

With over one third of interregional travel occurring by air, it is becoming customary for average people to discuss how land looks from above. From 10,000 feet in the air over the rural areas of the midwest and west, it looks as if the U.S. Public Lands Survey is holding the land together, separating corn from plowed fields or pasture. Tiny country roads, viewed on the ground as part of an informal system, are seen from aloft to follow a formal, north-south range line, spanning the country from Canada to Mexico.

Furthermore, two kinds of mobility exercised by the average person within his metropolitan area strengthen his vision of the city as an artifact. First, the automobile allows him to travel throughout the city, gathering an understanding of the physical form of the city stronger and more accurate than his understanding of his own back yard. The interstate highways program precipitates a new concept of the city in several ways. A new radial, cutting the travel time downtown, lets the driver feel what the highway planner experienced—an Olympian dominance over what had been a different city for many years. Second, a completed circumferential expressway, like the ring road around Dallas or the tollroads around Chicago, permits the driver to experience the form of the city. He travels around its edge fast enough to gain the sensation of being all around it at once. The individual is also aware of sections with special character—Georgetown, Vieux Carre, Carondelet in south St. Louis. The idea that only certain land uses and certain colors, materials, and architectural styles (and certain types of people) are appropriate to such special areas, is a very popular one.

Contemporary city planning assigns a high value to such popular "imageability" in the design of cities. The discoverer of the concept of imageability has thus far disclosed its presence with convincing research to show that there are strong and consistent city images in the minds of a city's inhabitants.[1]

These impressions of the city, of Back Bay as something different, and of the outer drive as a public right allowing every Chicagoan to appreciate that his city is lineal and concave along a great body of water, is superior to an earlier vision of the entire American city still held by many lawyers, planners, and economists. That earlier view interprets the city as a competitive jungle, a lump, with the toughest and most aggressive activities piled up hotly in the center, and the most sensitive and least productive displaced out to the edge.

Cultural approaches foretell that the visual concept of the city as a whole is bound to emerge. Pictures are displacing words in books; television is crowding out an oral mass medium (radio) and a written one (newspapers); there is a movement to introduce mathematics into the wordy, great books-dominated, liberal arts education program.[2] And finally, ordinary people are associating city plans with law and government through zoning hearings, televised presentations of plans by city officials, and through graphic city plans published and distributed by cities. In the report of the President's Commission on *Goals for Americans,* Catherine Bauer, discussing cities, proposes some rather spatial goals for large centers, namely, that these areas recentralize, forming mature subcenters.[3] L'Enfant's plan for the Capitol is now displayed on library walls with the same reverence as are the Bill of Rights and the Constitution.

LANDOWNING AS AN OFFICE

In feudal times, the king and his courts looked upon the owner of land as an officeholder. In a sense, everyone in the kingdom was something of an officeholder. The owner's obligation to give service in exchange for holding the land held the kingdom together. The nature of common property can best be interpreted through the concept of ownership as an office. A villein, for example, fiercely defended his right to let his two oxen out onto the wasteland of the vill. This was not an early idea of corporate life, similar to the modern relation between the citizen and a public city park. The villein owned a parcel of land which had as an incidence of ownership the right to let the two oxen out onto the waste; the next owner of that parcel would succeed to the same right.

The arrangement whereby the landowner has responsibilities of office is attractive. But his duties had little to do with good land management and gradually they deteriorated. The responsibility of military service was eventually evaded by a money payment.[4] Office became associated too exclusively with particular families, until it was a man's position in a family that entitled him to land, rather than the services he carried out by his office. Royalty and aristocracy plotted to assemble estates by arranging favorable child-marriages, without regard to those who actually lived on the land, or to the children themselves.[5] The status or prestige of landholding lived on beyond feudalism, motivating aristocrats and the new rich alike to judge one's worth by the size of one's estate. But the office of landholding became so burdened with fantastic responsibilities and public obligations foreign to the economics of good land use that the lord of a fine estate found the job crushing. Heirs to land were burdened, while purchasers were more and more favored.[6]

During the early industrial period, when the concept of land as an office was disappearing, the courts identified the owner of land too closely with the land itself.[7] The owner was not an officeholder but an individual expressing himself, exerting his own will, through personality. This era, too, saw the first acceptance of profit seeking as a complete explanation of human conduct.

In 1916, when zoning was introduced in America, the owner was completely identified with the land, as was to be expected in the light of the preceding concepts of the law of real property. Bassett, an early authority, said that if one owner is allowed to build to ten stories, the owner of an adjacent tract should be permitted to do the same.[8] This premise is too limited because it exalts the owner over others, such as pedestrians and occupants. It is also too limited because it focuses on those who own land at the time of passage of the ordinance, excluding the whole succession of owners of each building. In other words, two equally tall buildings side by side, taking one anther's light and air, may be the best adjustment between two present owners, vis-à-vis one another, assuming the buildings' lives are coterminous in time with the owners' lives. But how should these buildings be reconciled objectively? It might be useful to consider each owner as holder of a different office, adding up the combined value of the two offices; or we might include in the formula the interests of all the future owners of both buildings, since buildings do outlast their builders or first owners. Then, perhaps, we would decide that the first building should be tall and the second one low and complementary, so that the light and air of which we have an abundance is not squandered.

There is another way of looking at the office-owner-land trichotomy in the contemporary urban situation. For some purposes one can separate the concepts of office and owner from that of the land, thinking of it only in relation to other land. Consider the feudal vill where, by their office as owners of specific parcels, landowners could graze a specified number of oxen on the wasteland. The parcels near the wasteland had a relation to it that can be separated from owners or officeholders altogether. Oxen (and feudal society needed oxen) were garaged on the small parcels at night but ranged over the common wasteland during the day. It was a street for cows. Similarly, the land planner today knows that land is owned but thinks more about it in relation to other land than in its relation to owners or officeholders. Innocent of his conceptual debt to feudalism, he also considers the interests of the buildings' occupants and of passing pedestrians, and such values as the skyline.

FROM WORD LAW TO MAP LAW

The city plan can be viewed as the culmination of ten centuries of property law and as the idealized, perfect form of that law. Once adopted, it establishes the pattern of public and private development. As a portrayal of how things could be, it is in more positive form that even such a classic instrument as the Bill of Rights, which, after all, is negative, admonitory: "Congress shall make no law . . ." etc.

The perfection of the city plan comes from its graphic form. It is not that graphic law is inherently better than word law but simply that map law is almost perfectly suited to what it governs, the arrangement of land. Word law is a clumsy description of what it frequently governs: conduct. The only standard comparable to the city plan is that of the "reasonably prudent man," a standard of good conduct conjured up by judges to help juries measure a defendant's liability for damaging acts. Even though he caused harm, if the defendant only did what the "reasonably prudent man" might have done under the circumstances, he would be free of liability.

But, despite its semantic perfection, the map as a form of law does not yet carry the prestige that words do. An observation of ten centuries of land law shows that customs, spoken words, written words, sealed instruments, and other communications media have flourished at various times. The prestige of map law has developed slowly through the years but will soon, perhaps, replace words as the best way of controlling land. Is it not obvious how the concept of the city as an artifact to be socially directed is bound up with map law's prestige? City building will not create artifacts until city builders freely use the language of art, which is graphic and plastic, more like a map, rather than verbal, like a law book.

Prior to the use of a map was the use of written words, and before that, custom—some symbolic way of treating land. Before the Norman conquest, ownership, to a large extent, was identical with possession (this is a very Roman idea, seen in the Latin word for property, *dominium*). Property changed hands by devices of custom, recognized in court as conveying interests in land, rather than by written instruments. There was little written matter that the law recognized and little written down of the property laws of the time. The Venerable Bede is one of the few sources. Written wills were used, however, and some types of land conveyance were recorded in books. This was "book land," large tracts conferred by the king on religious or lay nobles, with the consent of the occupants of the land.[9]

A tremendous advance toward map law was the Domesday Book, a comprehensive land inventory of the whole kingdom, made for tax purposes about twenty years after the Battle of Hastings. Our present land recording system can be traced to the Domesday Book.[10] In two volumes, it has been preserved in a chest built after the survey for the very purpose of storage for posterity. The book is spatial in that it is comprehensive, covering the entire kingdom, and in its separation of one county from another. But within the county, land is listed by name rather than location, and there is no map. Apparently, people were more conscious of where land was located socially, within the feudal structure, than where it could be found on the ground. A peculiarly British idea persisted, namely, that land was movable.[11] This geographical indifference can also be seen in the legal composition of a vill. It might contain land that was physically situated in the midst of another vill. Yet the hue and cry was required of each vill as a criminal ran through.[12]

Rules about sealed instruments heightened respect for all written documents and brought the day nearer when a map would be recognized as a form of law. A written obligation that was sealed was presumed to be binding, without showing that the debtor had received value for entering the obligation. The Statute of Wills of 1540 gave a deceased great power over land, if he had followed the requirements for a valid will. The will itself gained almost mystical prominence in portraying the decedent's intention. The "four corners" rules for interpreting wills required that only what could be found within the four corners of the document could be interpreted, rather than outside facts showing what the deceased probably had intended. The Statute of Frauds of 1677 associated land closely with documents, requiring that all land transactions be in writing. In the early centuries, the local, unwritten customs of each part of England were highly respected in court. This deference to geography and location delights a land planner but it fell to a greater deference to a jurisdiction-wide written law. As map law evolved from written law, so deference in the law can find its way back to that forgotten geographical sense. The beginning of written judicial opinions in 1194 is also important. Before such decisions were recorded, justices tried to recall fact situations from memory similar to the case before them, so that the previous decision could be applied again. The Statute of Enrollments of 1536 and subsequent recording acts gave the purchaser of land assurance that his seller really owned the land and had already made an effective conveyance, thus furthering the primacy of written records. It was a declaration that the government was a central intelligence over all the land within the jurisdiction. Admittedly, however, it was only an instrument enabling the central mind to remember land transactions, not to reason about all land.

Another foundation for map law was the emerging idea that land continued through time impressed with certain legal characteristics independently of who owned it. For example, a covenant between owner A and buyer B, declaring that the land be used only for agricultural purposes, could impress a character onto the land that obligated a subsequent owner, C, regardless of what B and C would rather do. This covenant "ran" (through time) with the land. That such characteristics could become attached to land, regardless of any deliberate intent or agreement between persons, helped courts think about land as a spatial quantity rather than as "a bundle of rights."

Three types of land description available in law can show the evolution toward map law now in existence. Most primitive is a metes and bounds description. This is a list of points (stones, iron pins) marking the corners of a tract, with distances between points spelled out, as well as the compass bearing of each line. Only by plotting the description, either mentally or on paper, can a reader understand the shape and location of the parcel being described. With this type of description it is difficult for the subdividing land owner, or anyone else, actually to visualize the land. Where such methods of subdividing land are permitted, a chaos of ill-shaped tracts along the existing roads, with no access to interior pieces of land, is the usual result.

When, instead, a plat in map form is prepared by a surveyor, land is cut more rationally than with metes and bounds description because (1) a professional, the surveyor, is brought in, who can advise the seller about the wisdom of his proposed slice and can usually improve upon it; and (2) the plat permits the seller and surveyor to visualize what they are doing, and perhaps either cut up future tracts for sale or at least plan future cuts. (See Figure 1.) Covenants that run with the land are often created at the same time a plat is prepared showing lots and streets. Courts exercised an advanced form of spatial law when they proved willing to scrutinize carefully such plats to infer covenants that were not spelled out.[13] Given the limits of patience of businessmen and land conveyancers, many convenants or perpetual easements in subdivisions, such as the curved streets and building lines, could not be described at all, if it meant doing so with words rather than by a map. There are subdivision ordinances that require every land subdivision to be by plat rather than metes and bounds description, foretelling abolition of future metes and bounds description altogether. Manchester, Missouri recently adopted such an ordinance. Use of record plats to subdivide land, and the enforcement of graphic and written covenants, enable a landowner to make a mandatory plan for a large

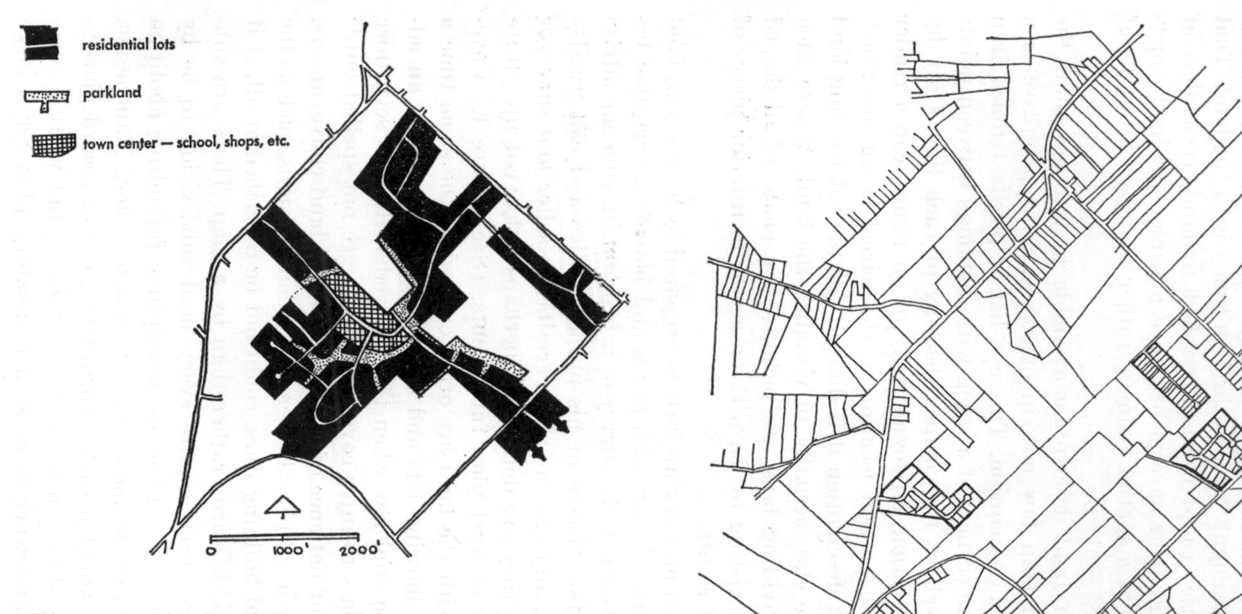

Figure 1. At the right, word law surveying cuts up a section of St. Louis County by aspatial metes and bounds divisions. Such land description wastes land and roads, causes chaos and isolation.

Above, a plat being recorded in the same area by map law surveying. It makes possible the assembling of small parcels into a complete community for 750 families.

area. Most of the outstanding examples of land planning in England and America rely on a recorded plat for description and stability.

The third method of describing land is the U.S. Land Survey. In 1785, Congress ordered that public land henceforth be laid out in a giant north-south, east-west grid, with lines one mile apart, capable of being further divided into smaller and smaller squares until a forty-acre tract could be described for conveyance just by reference to the U.S. Survey system. This is a striking case of early awareness that land arrangement is public business. Yet, the U.S. Survey system was so much less than it might have been. It was inexorable, like the compass itself or like a mercantile grid street system in establishing a line. It was spatial, but used mathematical space rather than man-land space. It disregarded many natural boundaries between future uses and ownership of land, such as streams or ridges, and was more concerned with easy land sales than land use. Nor did it attempt to anticipate the future public needs for land. The surveys might have reserved 100 feet in width for future public roads one mile apart and have retained flood plains and riparian land in the public domain. Had this been done, current public road and public recreation programs would be billions of dollars richer. (See Figure 2.)

There are other doctrines within the law itself that can be applied to city plans to give them the prestige in courts that they deserve as legal media. From the law of evidence comes the best evidence rule. It might be applied to advance a city plan over verbalized policies of the planning commission, on the theory that since a map describes land better than words do, map control over land is better than word control. Under other disciplines than the law, semanticists such as Korzybski influence teachers of future lawyers and judges to look for the best media for describing a thing, with perhaps a bias in favor of mathematical over prose description. A map is more akin to mathematics than to prose.

In summary, then, of whether map law will be accepted by courts and lawyers as the best medium for controlling cities, history gives an affirmative answer. There has been an evolution away from custom, ritual, and oral lawmaking, toward written law: the seal or attested signature took on accepted meaning, then notice was given through public record rather than by individual pronouncement, and, finally map law has been accepted in survey plats and in the

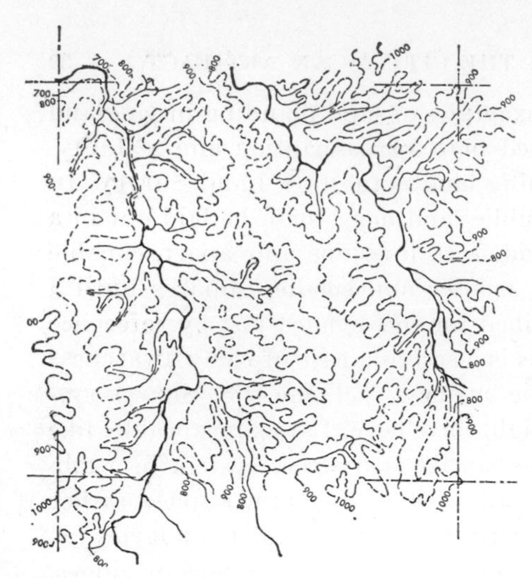

Figure 2. Land Surveying.

Figure 2a. Township 35, Range 2, west of the fifth principal meridian in Crawford County, Missouri. It is six miles square, with two streams and wooded hills.

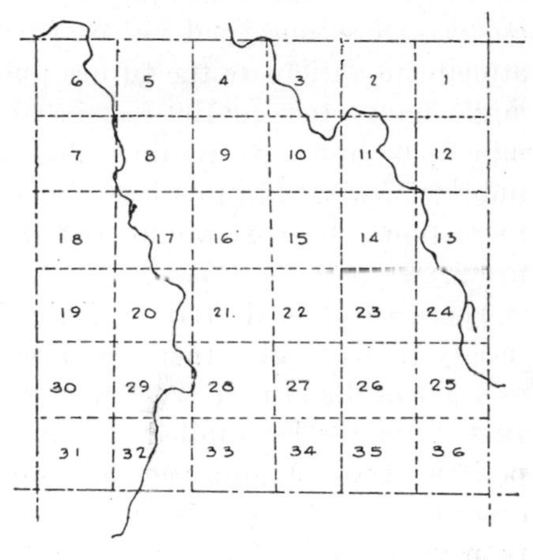

Figure 2b. The United States Survey system. Each 640-acre section (one square mile) was surveyed and numbered last century for land description purposes. A trace as small as a quarter-quarter section (forty acres) can be described by reference to it.

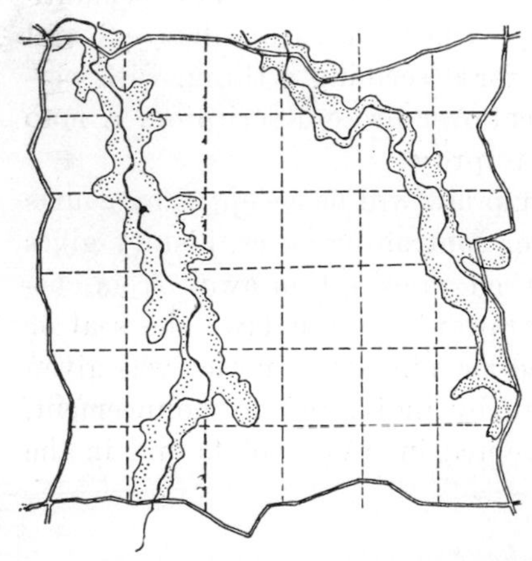

Figure 2c. A future public land survey might follow this system. It reserves a 200-feet wide road right of way, generally along section lines, but seeking flat topography; stream valleys are also for common use. Development would begin with trapping, go on to grazing, then later, hiking trails and parkways.

zoning district map. The U.S. Survey system, which places a reference grid on the ground ahead of development, is another demonstration that lawmakers have a spatial sense.

This history shows a factual evolution toward map law qua map law. But, more important, it shows that the media—spoken words, written words, signs—most appropriate to the subject matter being governed is generally accepted by the law. Since a graphic plan is the most appropriate way to govern a city, its acceptance as the exalted law form, superior to case-by-case decision making or to written word policies about building the city, should be positively encouraged, and its eventual triumph expected.

GREAT PLANNERS OF HISTORY

If the city plan is a form of land law evolved from ten centuries of property law, then great city planners are not only Sir Christopher Wren (seventeenth-century architect and planner), John Wood (designer of Bath), Ebenezer Howard (creator of garden cities), Sir Patrick Geddes (planner throughout the British Empire), and Patrick Abercrombie (author of a plan for London), but also those known and anonymous writers, judges, and parliamentarians who, at various times, have had a unified or unifying view of real property law. There are strong relations between organizing all the land in a jurisdiction according to a graphic plan and a comprehensive organization of the whole spectrum of private land law. One is this: a common-law real property system can more easily accept organizing the physical land within a jurisdiction according to a graphic plan after it has accepted periodic reorganization of the tangled ends of the law.

Early courts settled the problem before them with little help from Parliament. Later, statutes were passed to correct abuses that did not arise as much because of man's perversity as because a changing society had different land problems, or was advanced enough to allow more freedom with land. The Statute of Wills, Statute of Frauds, and Statute of Uses were all progressive, but were written to meet specific problems. By contrast, the Magna Carta of 1215 was a rather comprehensive statute since it set out to adjust a wide range of land problems. Finally came the codification of real property law accomplished in England in 1922–1926—a most comprehensive task.[14] Many American states now have property codes,[15] and the Restatement of Property by the American Law Institute [16] is another example of the comprehensive approach.

These codes are written in the spirit that land ownership is a human institution to be manipulated—designed—for human purposes. Its goals are to make conveyancing predictable, certain regarding effect, easily learned. Codes are written to spell out public policies such as free alienability of land, with limits on an owner's desire to create perpetual interests, to create a nuisance, etc. Without such a code, court-made land law tended to become arcane, metaphysical, complex, its sources scattered through too many cases in too many books. The effect of a decision was as difficult for a judge to visualize as a metes and bounds description of land. By contrast, the property codes display all the basic rules together, so that conveyancing and real property as a workable institution can be totally visualized, just as a plat of a subdivision of land shows the shape of the tracts in the scale of their spatial reality on the ground.

Getting back to the great planners of history, between the Magna Carta and the 1922 property code there were several individuals with a comprehensive view of real property who exerted a tremendous influence Their way of looking at the law consistently won over slow, self-directed evolution.

Henry Bracton was a most creative writer of the mid-thirteenth century who drew on Roman law, and who anticipated future problems and suggested solutions, at a time when so little was settled in the law. By contrast, Edward Coke, three centuries later, was introverted in his sources, using as his authority the early written decisions, the Year Books, rather than the continental sources of Bracton. Yet Coke was progressive, searching the old cases for rules that could be applied to then current problems. He personified the common law itself and used its method of internal progression rather than a comprehensive, stated code. He saw himself hurrying the common law along in its mission. But under the fire of his erudite use of Latin and Norman French, and his voluminous citations of early cases, scholars have found as much Coke as common law.[17]

About the time of Coke, the serfs of England, the copyholders, who through the years had lost the protection of the courts, had this protection returned to them. This meant the land was theirs again, they were owners rather than tenants, and one of the great land reforms in history had occurred without bloodshed, revolution, or attention.[18]

Some view this quiet revolt of the peasants as a great victory of the common law—something that emerged. But it can also be seen as a victory of two comprehensive writers, Bracton and Coke. Using the Roman idea that the man in rightful possession of land is its owner, Bracton played down tenure and was a champion of the copyholders. Coke, several centuries later, found certain authority in the law for returning rights in land to the serfs, and relied for this on Bracton.[19]

A great reformer whose academic approach differed greatly from Coke's was Jeremy Bentham (1748–1832). He ridiculed the complexity of land law and the mumbo jumbo of land lawyers, and helped establish the code approach to contemporary problems.

The vulnerability of land law to a comprehensive approach is demonstrated by Sir William Blackstone. He drew a picture in his *Commentaries* of the whole of English law. Although conservative in property matters, many progressive innovations were suggested by Blackstone, and he did much to establish law as a subject of formal education. Eighteenth-century lawyers and influential laymen were seldom up to reading Coke, whose books were organized with all the depth and mystery of the common law itself. Coke's approach was apparently also too much for Blackstone, who wrote down the simple, middle-class, mercantile reasons that occurred to him for each common-law real property doctrine. The idea that landownership meant absolute control, subject only to the same rights of adjacent land owners, is strong in Blackstone.[20]

That idea of Blackstone did not underlie the feudal landholding institution that equated land with a social hierarchy. It did not underlie the postfeudal fashioning of estates in land, and the elaboration of rules about the form required for conveyances or the limits of what one could do with land. Change in land law through the centuries carried the implication that the law was granting another privilege to private land owners, not that rights in land were primarily and originally individual and absolute, to be curtailed by law only where necessary for an adjacent owner's similar right. Coke described fee simple ownership as "the most highest [sic] and absolute estate that a man can have," implying that public interests in land were original and paramount.[21] However, they conceded to individual owners, as occupants and users of the land, a bundle of rights known as fee simple ownership. Blackstone helped squeeze out the public interest altogether in a quiet revolution as far-reaching as the revolt of the peasants authored by Coke and Bracton.

Notice Coke's, as compared with Blackstone's, use of a Latin maxim that means "who has the soil, he has to the sky." Coke used it in a very beautiful passage describing land and how mankind depends on land as on the air itself "The earth [as distinguished from heaven] hath in law a great extent upwards, not only of water, as hath been said, but of air and all other things even up to heaven; for: *cujus est solum ejus est usque ad coelum.*" This appears under a description of the word "Land" in Coke's *Commentaries,* Ch. 1, Sec. 4a. Blackstone uses this expression in discussing the law of nuisance, to define one owner's rights against another's, and ends with a snipe at esthetic values. "The rule is, *sic utere tuo, ut alienum non laedas.*" ("So use yours, that you do not harm another's.") "So that the nuisances which affect a man's dwelling may be reduced to these three: overhanging it, which is also a species of trespass for *cujus est solum ejus est usque ad coelum.* . . . But depriving one of a mere matter of pleasure, as of a fine prospect by building a wall, or the like: this, as it abridges nothing really convenient or necessary, is no injury to the sufferer, and is therefore not an actionable nuisance."[22]

In the great tradition of cosmic writers—Bracton, Coke, Bentham, Blackstone,—is Edward M. Bassett. This lawyer, who reported and apparently invented zoning in New York in 1916, was able to transform ideas from word law into space law. Actually, the first New York zoning ordinance was the work of a committee appointed in 1913, of which Mr. Bassett was chairman. His writing and consulting after 1916 helped establish the New York style of zoning throughout the country, and helped establish his reputation as "the Father of City Planning." His writings on zoning show such a deep understanding of the subject that one can infer authorship of its mystique. Bassett wrote that "City Planning is the determination by public authority of the legal quality of land areas. . . ." He then supposed that the city was devastated. "They thought all was lost" until someone found the plans and maps. But, he continues, "Even if the maps had been destroyed, the city plan would have been intact because the different land qualities were the same after the devastation as before."[23]

Bassett resembles Bracton in that with little to go on, he had to create to solve future problems, but he resembles Blackstone more. The works of both Blackstone and Bassett achieved great popularity through an appeal to "common sense" and middle-class values. Like Blackstone, Bassett's system squeezed out the public interest, as if the planning of a city were simply the problem of adjusting theoretically unlimited rights of property owners. Bassett was a three-dimensional Blackstone. The following, from the report of the 1913 New York Committee on Building Heights, is typical of the concern for property values and land owners: "The natural result of a poor utilization of its land areas by a city is high rents for occupiers and low profits for investors. It may seem paradoxical to hold that a policy of building restriction tends to a fuller utilization of land than a policy of restriction; but such is undoubtedly the case. The reason lies in the greater safety and security to investment secured by definite restrictions."[24]

Besides personalities in the law's development, the influence of entire professions can be seen. Lawyers so dominated property law that there was a reaction against them after the American Revolution. But American courts are final arbiters of property matters, and American judges are robed lawyers. The British planning program, in contrast, is little controlled or interpreted by law courts.[25] Perhaps Parliament knew that Her Majesty's courts were not ready for spatial land law.

When Bassett introduced zoning there was no articulate, coherent city planning profession available to which the power to design cities could be transferred. The first professional school for city planning was not opened until 1929, at Harvard University. Such a profession might have blended the entire discipline and tradition of city planning into the law. In actually drawing zoning district maps, such a city planning profession might have underplayed the common-law, nuisance doctrine approach together with Blackstone's view that a man could do what he wanted with his land. Instead, the post-Bassett city planning profession accepted Bassett rather than earlier city planning principles. In fact, Bassett-style zoning is so simple that it was caught up in the do-it-yourself movement.

Much zoning is done by amateurs, working over official district maps with colored pencils, usually after dark in a poorly lighted city council chamber. Carl Feiss calls this "The Amateur Hour."[26]

Landscape architects, members of a profession responsible for eighteenth-century gardens and housing layouts, have kept alive a tradition that the city, or a large part of it, can be laid out and organized as an artifact, a work of art, like a garden. In 1927, a criticism of Bassett, the lawyer who had invented do-it-yourself city planning, was voiced by Crawford, a landscape architect. He spoke out against Bassett's definition of city planning with these words: "The Essence of City Planning is City Designing. That is its fundamental ingredient. It is landscape designing in a larger phase."[27] One thread of a similar tradition can be seen in American architecture today, carrying through Bulfinch and Jefferson to Burnham, repudiated or at least ignored by Wright and Sullivan, and found again in a Clarence Stein or a Pei.

Many landscape architects, imbued with their tradition, and many architects, carrying on the tradition of civic design, are now the planning directors of American cities. Almost twenty universities today grant degrees in city planning; the 1963 graduate pictures himself in ten years as the planning director of a large American city, usually San Francisco, Philadelphia, or Honolulu. Although not mentioned at all in most planning statutes and ordinances, planning directors hold influential positions. They are assisted by an army of professional help, are granted a big budget besides a federal subsidy, and can rely on designs by consultants. Through their influence on members of the planning commission (front men who hardly have time to read all the reports issued by the planning directors' offices) and through their beautiful city and site plans personally defended in court, they are finally designing American cities. They have entered the Hall of Justice with maps and diagrams to sketch city shapes for a black-robed, land law judge who is fascinated with the idea that law can be drawn, that the city is an artifact.

A survey of ten centuries of land law in search of the artifact concept is not conclusive. One force has been clear throughout history, namely, the comprehensive planning approach to land law. It was exercised by individuals, committees, or deliberative bodies who assembled, organized, or codified all the property rules, who dominated the material and manipulated it. At first, there were centuries of slow evolution, of case-by-case erection of a legal edifice. But the work of such spatial, private law planners was more valid and influential than all the cautious filling in between the peaks of their creativity. Finally, in our day, this comprehensive approach to the whole range of land law problems is no longer exceptional but is accepted. And what of the city as an artifact?

An analogy might be made between (1) the total complex of private land rights of individuals, and (2) all the physical land in a city. The point of view that a code or treatise, supplemented by case law, best governs private land relations, manages all the land in the city by using graphic designs and three-dimensional models. There are a thousand bridges between a rational code governing private land law and graphic land planning. A good land description system for conveyance purposes results in orderly subdividing, whereas metes and bounds description butchers the land. A simple, fluid land market moves the ideal tract of land to that developer whose intention corresponds with the graphic plan. The urban freeways now under construction do not allow access from abutting land owners, contrary to a custom of centuries; they owe their success to this property law innovation.

AMERICAN ZONING

L'Enfant's plan for Washington, D.C., may be a symbol for treating the American city as an artifact, but it is a late symbol. That plan, with its long boulevards leading from one hilltop public building site to another, had almost no influence on other cities. Before the twentieth century, the amorphous gridiron of mercantile cities adopted by New York in 1811 was the prototype for city layout. This is the kind of gridiron system that lacks a hierarchy of grids to look and act as a public frame for the privately owned city, that lacks systematized, terminal open space where the public can stop its movement along the public lineal places, the streets.

Permanent voids were punched into the dense, expanding, urban building masses through the post–Civil War public parks programs. New York was again the leader with its Central Park. Landscape architects, such as Olmstead and Vaux, drew plans for major parks in big cities all over the country. But these were not integrations with private land use, as much as they were places where one could hide from the sight of buildings. The concept of city planning did not grow out of such park programs, except perhaps where continuous park systems were built and their structure permeated the entire city. This is true in sections of Kansas City and the idea is also mirrored in miniature in Kansas City's Country Club district residential development.

Private real property law in America began with British common law and statutes whose interpretation was influenced by Blackstone. American statutes and cases built on this import, simplified and made adaptable to pioneer conditions by American jurists. This, of course, went on separately in each of the states. Federal courts could not unify property laws since most real property questions were beyond their jurisdiction. Law sometimes became more archaic and complex in a simple agrarian state like Illinois than it ever had been in England.[28] Yet there are cases where common law was successfully adapted to American conditions. Rules for sharing streams, appropriate to wet England, were discarded and new rules, workable in an arid region, were created by the good sense of western judges.[29]

American judges tended to be impatient with rules that restricted the individual's dominion over his land; in this, they were encouraged by Blackstone. The doctrine of ancient lights, holding that a new building cannot invade the light and air of an existing building, was discarded on the theory that there is plenty of space for buildings on this continent.[30] (It is not clear why this geographic insight was not applied against the would-be builder of the second building discussed above.)

The "city beautiful" planning movement that began with this century dealt only with the public sector—parkways, civic centers, continuous parks, public open spaces at key points, such as the Lake Michigan waterfront. But the 1905 Plan for Chicago,[31] or even better, the 1907 Civic League Plan for St. Louis,[32] proposed a strong structure of public improvements whose realization might have established the American city as a beautiful artifact in a grand way. Ironically, although these plans dealt with public land almost entirely, they were prepared, not by the city government, but by private organizations. They were not adopted by the cities nor could cities of that period have financed them.

Present planning discipline has descended not from that movement as much as from a control over private land use exerted by the city according to the invention of that spatial Blackstone, Edward M. Bassett, and adopted in New York City in 1916. It has been copied in thousands of cities since. Mr. Bassett, the lawyer, examined New York and found that its space problems and conflicts were of two kinds: (1) incompatible uses interfered with more sensitive use; and (2) even where uses were similar, as in skyscraper districts, they crowded one another.[33] Some land owners, he concluded, were ruining the institution of private property by locating intense uses where they did not belong, or by exploiting their land to the detriment of their neighbor's right to exploitation. Bassett made an almost complete identification of the owner with the land, tacitly assenting to ownership for profit.

What kind of control could prevent abuses among land owners? The skyscraper case was easy. The nuisance doctrine, that one could not interfere with his neighbor's right to use land, was put into spatial form by fitting a space envelope around each building. The owner could go through whatever contortions he desired with the shape of his building, but he must stay in his envelope. If life is a jungle, and the city is life, and if property owners are jungle creatures and buildings and property owners are identified, then the analogy is complete between each building in its zoning envelope and wild animals in separated cages of the zoo.

Would it be fair to make smaller envelopes in more remote areas, where there were smaller buildings, or would a uniform rule for the entire city be necessary? What of the problem of incompatible uses, the factory in the residential area? The solution to both these problems dawned when it was observed that:

1. Similar uses tended to be together. It was the errant minority, a few radical, bad-acting buildings, out of place, that caused trouble.
2. There was a gradient of uses, by intensity, with building height lower and lower as one moved from the center of the city, or back from the edge of a busy street.

The more intense uses, the ones that made the most money per square foot of ground and also threw off the most noise, shadow, and glare, tended to be in the center; the less intense but more sensitive uses, such as detached dwellings, tended to be at the edge of the city or several blocks back from the busy streets and transit routes. It was as if the more competitive uses had fought their way to the center of the city, or to the brink of the main communication lines.

Without control or regulation of any sort, the natural law of man's behavior had wrought the city's very shape. Each parcel of land tended to be used for its "highest and best use," that is, for the most intense activity and the most profit that such a location in the city could command. An established order was seen: the giant battlers, the skyscrapers and factories, had won the prime central locations; stores had edged out apartments along the busy street; bulky, profitable apartments were drawn in a ring around the central areas, crowding the detached dwelling to the outside edge where there was less competition for land.

Mr. Bassett reasoned that this competitive system would be perfected if the few mavericks were herded into their appropriate area, thus separating incompatible uses. Detached dwellings would not be excluded from factory areas, but would merely be warned by a map showing where they would be protected. He believed that the right way to control land use was by a map that places the intense uses in the center (where they are) and along the major streets, with a gradual lessening of intensity, from factory to store to apartment to detached dwelling, in concentric rings of decreasing intensity out from the center, where the heavy weights are. It also showed how to impose a smaller and lower envelope on one area than on another. Building height and percent of land coverage was observed to decrease naturally with distance from the center of the city. Therefore, rings of envelopes allowing greater and greater height and bulk as they approached the center might be put in map form. Since the regulations in one district tended to be only slightly more or less intense than those in the adjoining district, the system viewed from any one point in the city appeared to treat everyone almost equally. Such a zoning system appeared to Bassett as a discovery of the natural law itself, since it so perfectly corrected both *intermingling* and *overcrowding*, the two flaws in the city's process of natural selection.

The district map drawn to carry out such a zoning scheme is map law, enacted as an ordinance and considered as equal in prestige to the word ordinance that accompanies it. But does it show the city as an artifact? Classic zoning shows something very different. It recognizes a form of the city created by individualism, endorses it, and modestly regulates it so that it will work more smoothly by calling a graphic limit to each owner's freedom to exploit land.

Zoning made spatial the common-law nuisance doctrine, but without advancing the idea that lawmakers can impose a greater graphic order on land to obligate the parts. Such an idea might have been found within the common-law real property tradition itself, by learning how the eighteenth-century jewels of land planning, the Georgian housing schemes, were carried out with their common open space, common circulation system, and protection of view. Graphic plats were drawn to impose such order on subsequent owners of allotments within the schemes. Covenants prohibited subsequent development of the common land, since it was somehow a part of each separate tract.[34] These schemes were successful in those courts where map as well as word covenants were upheld. A planning system springing from such a precedent would have brought together the civic design and the common-law property traditions, that is, the designing and legal professions.

Time reinforces the judgment that zoning should have used covenants and graphic plats of housing schemes for its wellspring, rather than the nuisance doctrine. The American city is in shambles. Those few housing schemes professionally designed and using recorded plats are incredibly superior. They are monotonous only in the number of references made to them.[35] They represent hope of what could happen to the American city.

Economists now study the city formed by four decades of classic zoning. They rediscover the zones of increasing intensity that the lawyers found in 1916.[36] They have developed spatial economic projection methods in the same way that lawyers introduced spatial aspects to the nuisance doctrine. Both lawyers and economists have been spinning webs alone, without benefit of the designing professions. Economists can predict and graphically demonstrate that natural economic forces will cause the future city to be bigger and intenser in the center, and ever quieter at its distant edges. (See Figure 3.) Planners, accepting these projections, make enforceable plans in the tradition of classic zoning to assure that they will occur. But the 1963 city, built through zoning in the image of the 1916 city, is much more complex than the zoning lawyers or projection economists declare it to be. The 1916 city, with its ''commercial streets'' leading to the center, its streetcars, its dependence on a

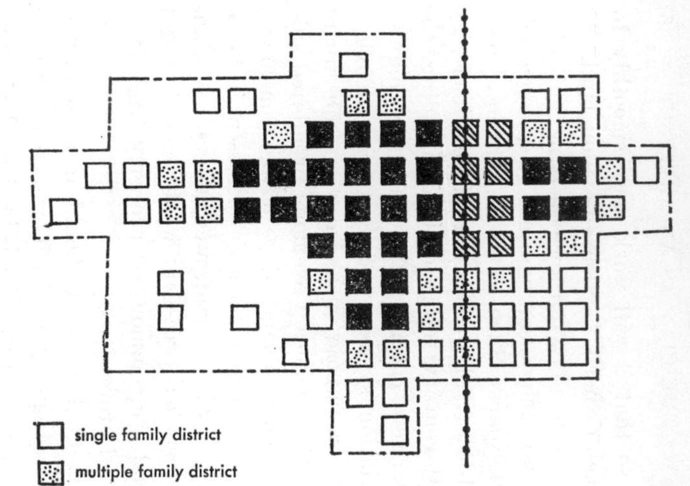

Figure 3a. *Plan of the zoned city. This is map law, an impressive conversion of the common-law nuisance doctrine to graphic form. But it is bad art and bad city planning.*

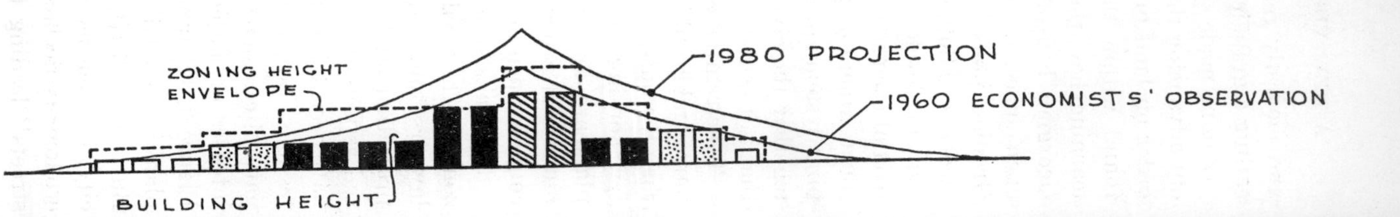

Figure 3b. *Profile of the zoned city. By growing upward into its zoning mold, the city takes on a lump shape. Projected by economists using J-curves, its three-dimensional form makes spectacular economics. But it is bad art and bad city planning.*

compact water system, its direct current energy, is breaking up. Personal mobility in a radial or any other direction has been conferred on every adult through a driver's license. Such technical advances as trucking and package sewer plants have added mobility to many uses of land. It is difficult to draw a zoning map to describe what is happening. Therefore, many zoning maps are left dynamic, uncommitted, while local governments give or refuse planning permission for each proposal as it comes along. This is in the British tradition but, unlike British planning, these jurisdictions do not have the benefit of graphic development plans to guide them. Rather, the local authorities and the reviewing courts rely on their own judgment as to whether the proposal conforms to some subjectively conceived natural law of the city.

The practice of requiring construction to follow a predictable, Bassett-style zoning map has almost disappeared, both in the central city and the suburbs. In the early sixties, the real power centers are playing it by ear. Although the lawyers and economists who were able to convert their disciplines to graphic form were great powers, their graphic work is now under fire. A new professional class of civil servants trained as economists, social scientists, lawyers, and urban generalists, with little or no spatial or design training, is entering the arena. Criticism of spatial planning in favor of a social scientist's type of program is given by Harvey S. Perloff in the following contrast between two forms of planning: [37]

Undesirable	*Desirable*
The Master Plan....	A general strategy of development....
A series of maps and drawings....	Broad standards....
Emphasis of the Grand Design....	Fitting departmental programs into a coherent pattern.

Not only are the aspatial, Perloff-type urbanists, armed with "broad standards" and "a general strategy," overcoming the bad graphics of Bassett's zoning, but good graphic plans at the scale of the urban renewal project, the neighborhood rehabilitation scheme, the shopping center, or the garden apartment project, are winning skirmishes all over the zoning map. The city that judges these designs on their merits, that is, as art forms, and encourages duplication of the best schemes and improvement of others, will be a beautiful mosaic. The city that adds its own graphic designs to the mix at the greenbelt, freeway, or continuous parkway scale builds even better.

SUMMARY AND CONCLUSIONS

Landownership now changes frequently. Subsequent landowners, therefore, as well as occupants and spectators, must be considered when land is developed. Rules against wasteful practices by those who hold a life estate were evolved centuries ago to protect the inheritor of the remainder. Today, the best practice must be required from that infrequent owner who decides the architecture or use of land.

To protect the combined interests of all subsequent owners of a particular parcel of land, improved controls must be imposed on a present improver. Gone is the day when the use of land was so fixed that it was generally outside the public's concern. Then the typical owner not only stayed on the land for life, but had to be restrained from so limiting its future ownership that only his male line, or some other limited class, could ever live there.

Under feudalism the user of land had few rights. He fared better in agricultural centuries. He became more farmer than serf and, as he came to this new status, property law evolved with him, giving him the powers and protection he needed. In the early industrial period, he was tenant, trespasser, business invitee or employee, but seldom owner. Now he walks in the shadow of a dead owner's building, turns his eyes from another man's billboard, drives to the end of a road, named by somebody else, to the little house he is buying. What can the law do for him, landless and alienated? Today, a land use arrangement between lot A and lot B by which these parcels together are worth 12 is preferred over one that gives a value of 10, even though the first involves an 8 to 4 internal distribution of value, and the second, a 5 to 5.

Thus property law goes on as it always has, adjusting rights between subsequent owners, giving certain users the status of owner for particular purposes, inventing new glories to add to the bundle of rights that compose title to land, laying to rest with fitting eulogy archaic rules, redefining "public" and "private." But there now looms a beautiful standard for testing possible changes in these relations of people (owners, users, tenants, private citizens, public officials, etc.) to land: Will the change help the art product of city building? Will the change help the creation or maintenance of inherently satisfying places, corners, spaces, shelters, temples, ways, and gardens? Will the change satisfy the growing number who are hunters of the perfect place, and only incidentally owners or tenants or mortgage holders or builders, seeking perfect justice?

The graphic plan, or map law, has emerged as the best medium for city planning; the law's ability to change media and use the most appropriate form promises the success of map law. A spatial sense that comes only from working with graphic media must develop in many officials, lawmakers, and citizens, however, before the full power of graphics will be absorbed by the law. The power that a legal concept, for example, the nuisance doctrine, assumed when put in the spatial model of the city, shows that for better or for worse the city responds to the language of graphics. But a visual inspection of these cities built according to the zoning mold and those that verify the economist's gravity models, is a dismal reminder that there are good graphics and bad. Within the law's own experience, the classic housing schemes that were designed and recorded as drawings demonstrate good graphics. A glimpse at the city planning tradition, in terms of landscape architecture or civic design, shows that traditional city graphics have been an art form, a design. A city can only be an artifact if, among other things, its plans are works of art.

Many problems faced in achieving the good city are best resolved by manipulation of the real property tradition. The comprehensive work of great men, or even committees, has had a far reaching influence on real property law. Today, great planners are needed who, in the tradition of Edward Coke, will look over the entire fabric of real property law, that part imprinted with medieval heraldry and that part with VA mortgages, and weave into it the design of a city.

American planning experience finds the zoning map a recognized form of map law. Ironically, this has hardened most people's inclination to view American city form as dictated by natural law, that is, by the invisible hand of the free market. This has occurred because zoning maps are not designs in the tradition either of art form or city planning, but are graphic representations of mass individualism. Planners should fold up their zoning district map but retain their sketch pencils. They should draw new plans as art forms in the tradition of city planning and architecture, not as diagrams of the rights of contentious property owners.

The idea that graphic or plastic designs best control cities says nothing about the so-called freedom versus planning question. It says nothing about the scale or explicitness of the graphics. A city with no public plan whatever, but with a composite of outstanding developments, each privately made according to designs—a city of Radburns, Regents Parks, Rockefeller Centers—is the city as an art form, a mosaic. Though unrehearsed and discursive, such a city would be testimony of the exquisite propriety of graphic plans. Or a city might have a detailed public plan, yet provide easy procedures for the land owner who has a superior scheme for his part of the city. The opportunity to create, propose, and build schemes that outdo the official intelligence of the rest of the plan is one not to be suppressed in the name of city planning.

Notes

1 Kevin Lynch, *The Image of the City* (Cambridge, Mass.: Technology Press, M.I.T., 1960).

2 Morris Kline, *Mathematics in Western Culture* (London: George Allen and Unwin Ltd., 1954).

3 Catherine Bauer, "Framework for an Urban Society," in U.S. President's Commission on National Goals, *Goals for Americans* (Englewood Cliffs, N.J.: Prentice Hall, Inc., 1960).

4 Sir Frederick Pollock and Frederick William Maitland, *The History of English Law* (2d ed.; London: Cambridge University Press, 1909), I, p. 276.

5 J. H. Jeudwine, *The Feudal Foundations of Society and the Land* (London: Williams & Norgate Ltd., 1918), p. 360.

6 Theodore F. Plucknett, *A Concise History of the Common Law* (London: Butterworth & Co. Publishers Ltd., 1948), p. 685.

7 Roscoe Pound finds the replacement of the eighteenth-century theory of natural rights by Kant's notion that property is inviolate, an extension

of personality. *An Introduction to the Philosophy of Law* (New Haven: Yale University Press, 1959), p. 117.

[8] See Edward M. Bassett, ''Zoning,'' in John Nolen ed., *City Planning* (Des Moines, Iowa: Appleton-Century-Croft, 1932), p. 415.

[9] Pollock and Maitland, *op. cit.*, pp. 28, 60.

[10] Plucknett, *op. cit.*, p. 12.

[11] Frederick William Maitland, *Domesday Book & Beyond* (London: Cambridge University Press, 1897), p. 10.

[12] Pollock and Maitland, *op. cit.*, p. 12.

[13] *Taylor v. Hopper* 62 N.Y. 649 (1875). (Streets shown on plat could not be closed though never dedicated.)

[14] Stat., 1922, 12 & 13 Geo. 5, c. 16; Stat., 1924, 15 & 16 Geo. 5, c. 4, 5 (effective 1926).

[15] See, for example, New York, Real Property Laws §§ 1, § 602 (1951) covering over 300 pages; or the Missouri Probate Code, Chap. 473, Mo. Rev. Stat. (1959).

[16] American Law Institute, *Restatement of Property*, Proposed Final Draft (1936).

[17] Plucknett, *op. cit.*, p. 267.

[18] *Ibid.*, p. 295.

[19] Coke cites Britton, an anonymous codified version of Bracton written about 1290. Edward Coke, *Commentary on Littleton* (18th ed.; London: Hargrave & Butler, Luke Hansard & Sons, 1823).

[20] ''The third absolute right, inherent in every Englishman, is that of property: which consists in the free use, enjoyment, and disposal of all his acquisitions, without any control or diminution, save only by the laws of the land.'' Sir William Blackstone, *Commentaries on the Laws of England*, Chitty ed., (Philadelphia: J. B. Lippincott Company, 1888), I, p. 100.

[21] Coke, *op. cit.*, Chap. 1, § 42 on Fee Simple.

[22] Blackstone, *op. cit.*, II, p. 172.

[23] Bassett, ''What is City Planning?'' Quoted in Charles M. Haar, *Land Use Planning* (Boston: Little, Brown & Company, 1959), p. 44.

[24] Quoted in Harold M. Lewis, *Planning the Modern City* (New York: John Wiley & Sons, Inc., 1949), p. 260. It is from the Report of the Height of Buildings Commission of the City of New York, December 23, 1913.

[25] Beverley J. Pooley, *The Evolution of British Planning Legislation* (Ann Arbor: University of Michigan Press, 1960), p. 64.

[26] See Carl Feiss, ''Planning Absorbs Zoning,'' *Journal of the American Institute of Planners*, 27 (1961), p. 122.

[27] Quoted in Haar, *op. cit.*, p. 45.

[28] In that state, many subtle questions were settled on the basis of which side first got to Kales, a master of all the subtleties. A. M. Kales (1875–1922) taught law and was the outstanding authority on future interests in Illinois. He argued appellate cases. See Albert M. Kales, *Estates, Future Interests and Illegal Conditions and Restraints in Illinois* (Chicago: Callaghan and Company, 1920), and his ''Should the Law Teacher Practice Law?'', *Harvard Law Review*, 25 (1911), p. 253. Rules that had been discarded centuries before in Britain were applied with vigor in Nebraska. An 1878 Nebraska case followed a New York rule based on a 1601 English decision. But the British themselves had rejected the 1601 rule in 1815. See ''The Running of Covenants for Title,'' *Nebraska Law Journal*, 1 (1922), p. 36. The idea that the whole field

of real property law can be compressed into a code, as the British did in the twenties, has still not been applied in many American states.

29 *Whitmore v. Salt Lake City,* 89 Utah 387, 57 P 2d 726 (1936). (Common law riparian rights rule rejected in favor of right to appropriate for beneficial use.)

30 *Parker v. Foote,* 19 Wend. 308 (N.Y. 1838); *Cherry v. Stein,* 11 Md. (1858). But see *Clawson v. Primrose,* 4 Del. Ch. 643 (1873).

31 Daniel H. Burnham and Edward H. Bennett, *Plan of Chicago* (Chicago: Commercial Club, 1909).

32 *A City Plan for St. Louis* (St. Louis: Civic League, 1907).

33 See reasons for zoning in New York City in Edward M. Bassett, *Zoning* (New York: Russell Sage Foundation, 1936).

34 Leicester Square—a seventeenth-century London open space, surrounded by town houses—was protected from invasion and its maintenance guaranteed through covenants. These were held to run with the land, enforceable against subsequent owners—*Tulk v. Moxhay,* 2 Phillips 774, 41 Eng. Rep. 1143 (Chancery 1848). See the discussion of the historic use of covenants by Charles S. Ascher in Coleman Woodbury ed., *Urban Redevelopment: Problems and Practices* (Chicago: University of Chicago Press, 1953).

35 See twelve modern American classics of site planning in Clarence S. Stein, *Toward New Towns for America* (New York: Reinhold Publishing Corporation, 1957). A few of the twelve started as government projects. Probably all are now controlled by deed restrictions.

36 See John R. Hamburg and Roger L. Creighton, "Predicting Chicago's Land Use Pattern," and Arthur Row and Ernest Jurkat, "The Economic Forces Shaping Land Use Patterns," in the *Journal of the American Institute of Planners,* 25:2 (May 1959), pp. 67, 77.

37 Harvey S. Perloff, *Education for Planning* (Baltimore: The Johns Hopkins Press, 1957), p. 30.

The City in History—Some American Perspectives[1]

RICHARD C. WADE *is Professor of History at the University of Chicago. He helped found the Urban History Group, an organization of historians in the American Historical Association, and served as a resident scholar on the Kansas City History project. He is author of "The Urban Frontier, the Rise of Cities in the West, 1790–1830," and numerous articles dealing with urban development.*

"The existence of an area of free land, its continuous recession, and the advance of American settlement westward, explain American development." Thus Frederick Jackson Turner introduced his famous "frontier thesis" to Americans in 1893. For over sixty years this perspective has provided the broad framework within which historians have viewed our nation's past. Turner's essay included both an *interpretation* and a *description* of American history. The interpretation set off a lively debate among scholars, the end of which is not in sight. Generally, historians now believe that many of Turner's notions are no longer tenable, and even disciples have dropped large portions of his original argument. In fact, at first glance it appears that Turner has lost every encounter with subsequent authors, and that his general thesis has been riddled

by a hundred monographs. Yet Turner remains; the "frontier thesis" is rediscovered by successive generations of historians even if they ultimately decide to reject it.

The persistence of the controversy stemmed in part from the widespread acceptance of Turner's description of the occupation of the continent and the nation's growth. Critics of the interpretation seldom questioned the broad narrative; indeed, they assumed its general validity. Hence, they could nibble away or, better said, hack away at this or that notion without doing fundamental damage to Turner's historical reputation. In the naval idiom, he kept control of the seas even while losing individual engagements. So long as the debate concerned his conclusions rather than his description, the dialogue moved generally within Turner's framework.

This framework contained the familiar elements. The continent was occupied in a series of waves. "It begins with the Indian and the hunter; it goes on to tell of the disintegration of savagery by the entrance of the trader, the pathfinder of civilization; we read the annals of the pastoral stage in ranch life; the exploitation of the soil by the raising of unrotated crops of corn and wheat in sparsely settled farming communities; the intensive culture of the denser farm settlement; and finally the manufacturing organization with city and factory system." [2] The emphasis of the story rested at the thither edge of population movement where whites contended with the primitive life of wilderness and savage. Slowly, in this evolutionary scheme, the area was rescued from the redman and, from simple beginnings, a fully developed, complex society emerged. Thus, Turner concluded, "the true point of view in the history of this nation is not the Atlantic coast, it is the Great West." [3]

Moreover, this "Great West" was agrarian. If, as Turner contended, "to study this advance, the men who grew up under these conditions, and the political, economic, and social results of it, is to study the really American part of our history," then the significant clues would be found in the cabins, sod huts, and farmhouses of the newly won country.[4] "From the time the mountains rose between the pioneer and the seaboard, a new order of Americanism arose. The West and the East began to get out of touch with each other." [5] In this Turnerian perspective, the distinctive phases of American development are seen as shaped by a rapidly growing rural West colliding with the older forces and institutions of the East.

Turner thus urged historians at least to look West, if not to go there. And a great many scholars took his advice, leading to a flood of articles, monographs, and books. In great detail, indeed almost step by step, historians followed white civilization across the continent. Some concentrated on the fur trade; others on ranching; still others on farming. The West and agricultural development became among the most intensively studied areas of the American past. The results were impressive, some of the volumes on these topics achieving the distinction of minor classics. This body of work, though informed by Turner's broader scheme, stands on its own very substantial merits.

Yet, the Turner framework involved significant distortions. In its Western emphasis, it overcompensated against the East; in its description of the occupation of the continent, it depended on a sequence that only occasionally occurred; and, most importantly, in its insistence on the primacy of agrarian elements, it neglected the importance of cities. Turner himself increasingly felt the inadequacy of this analysis, even if many of his students did not. By 1925 he could indicate that the time had come for "an urban reinterpretation of our history."[6] A total reworking of American experience with the city as the only focus would raise many of the same problems which sprang from an excessive reliance on the frontier framework; but an urban approach does furnish the historian with many valuable and interesting perspectives.

URBANISM IN THE COLONIAL ERA

Even in the areas where the frontier thesis seemed most compelling, this emphasis provides a necessary corrective. Tracing the rise of the Old West (the Ohio and the Mississippi valleys), one historian has recently written: "The towns were the spearheads of the frontier. Planted far in advance of the line of settlement, they held the West for the approaching population. Indeed in 1763, when the British threw the Proclamation Line along the Appalachians to stop the flow of settlers, a French merchant company prepared to survey the streets of St. Louis, a thousand miles through the wilderness. Whether as part of the activity of the French and Spanish from New Orleans or of the English and Americans operating from the

Atlantic Seaboard, the establishment of towns preceded the breaking of soil in the transmontane West.''[7]

Moreover, in the Far West, the last continental area to fall to white population and always pictured in full frontier regalia, the facts do not sustain the traditional image. In 1890, this region, though the most sparsely settled in the nation, was proportionately the most highly urbanized. Josiah Strong noticed this development several years before Turner presented his essay. Accepting the popular view about the Old West, Strong contended that a new sequence characterized the younger country. ''We must note also, the order of settlement,'' he wrote in 1885. ''In the Middle States the farms were the first taken, then the town sprang up to supply its wants, and at length the railway connected it with the world; but in the West the order is reversed—first the railroad, then the towns, then the farms. Settlement is, consequently, much more rapid, and the city stamps the country, instead of the country stamping the city. It is the cities and towns which will frame state constitutions, make laws, create public opinion, establish social usages, and fix standards of morals in the West.''[8] Strong's prophecy, though somewhat clouded, contained a better description of the growth of that area than the evolutionary one which saw urban centers appear as a climax to a mining, pastoral, and farming sequence.

Indeed, at nearly every point of American development the same kind of analysis can be made. For instance, Professor Carl Bridenbaugh's two books, *Cities in the Wilderness* and *Cities in Revolt,* demonstrate the crucial significance of urban centers in colonial life.[9] Historians had previously considered this early society in sectional terms—the appearance of two well-defined areas, the tidewater and the backcountry. Most of the important events and internal struggles were viewed as a dialogue between these regions. Professor Bridenbaugh added a third—and urban—dimension to colonial history by tracing the rise of Boston, New York, Newport, Philadelphia, and Charleston. In these young entrepôts, a kind of life emerged that was strikingly different from life in either the coast or the frontier. Their economic situation concerned trade and not agriculture; their life did not lean on the forests nor depend on the soil, but sprang from mercantile and simple industrial pursuits; their contacts were not confined to the colonies or even the empire, but extended over large portions of the globe; their face was towards Europe and the East rather than the wilderness and the West.

When the colonies revolted from the mother country, it was the cities that provided the impetus. Notions of the Enlightenment that informed the ideology of the rebel cause came to America through the cities that alone had the books, libraries, and newspapers to receive and spread them. Resistance to imperial reorganization policies found its leadership in urban classes, first the merchants and later radical politicians.

More particularly, Professor Bridenbaugh shows that Boston's declining fortunes furnished an atmosphere of growing desperation which made that city the special workshop of independence activity. Not only had the Hub fallen on bad times economically, but its position as the leading city in the North American colonies was snatched away by Philadelphia, and even New York had passed it by. "Boston's primacy as the 'Cradle of Liberty'," Arthur Schlesinger has written, "may well have sprung from her lagging progress in relation to other ports, inciting her at any cost to remove the obstacles that Parliament was thrusting in her way." [10]

The final phases of the quarrel revolved around the British attempt to chastise the Massachusetts port in the Coercive Acts of 1774. The role of Boston in these years suggests that there is no wrath equal to that of a rejected city. At any rate, in this perspective, the American Revolution began on the cobblestones of Boston rather than on the rolling greens of Lexington.

URBAN IMPERIALISM

From the earliest days, then, cities played a far greater role in national development than their numbers warranted. Though comprising about 5 percent of the population in 1790, they were the economic, social, political, and cultural centers of their regions. As they expanded, the towns created societies whose ways and habits differed sharply from those of the countryside. Most conspicuous, perhaps, were the complex social structures which emerged very quickly in young towns; they provided a striking contrast to the boisterous equality of farm life in the North and the simpler aristocratic divisions on plantations in the South. Though the stratification was primarily economic, immigration increasingly added new ethnic elements, giving the cities a much more cosmopolitan population than could be found in rural areas.

Like their European counterparts, American cities almost immediately became the intellectual foci for the scattered settlements around them. Enjoying a virtual monopoly of printing presses, newspapers, bookstores, and circulating libraries, they quickly established their cultural supremacy. The towns alone had the resources necessary for a rich and diversified life of the mind. Not only could they provide their own residents with wide opportunities, but they also became magnets for talented young people from the hinterland. As the cities grew, the contrast in cultures sharpened, deepening the cleavage between rural dweller and urbanite.

The economic power of the cities was even more pervasive. Nearly all the larger places owed their initial success to commerce. All sprang from it, and their great growth in the first half of the nineteenth century stemmed from its expansion. Each carved out large dependencies in its immediate area, but, never fully satisfied, reached out for more. These aggressive lunges into new regions led to collisions between the great metropolises as each sought to annex the growing market. The contests between urban giants were bitterly fought; and the outcome was often decisive. To the winner went trade, wealth, regional supremacy; to the loser, reduced opportunities, more modest prospects, even stagnation.

The rivals used every weapon available. Most importantly, they reached out with roads, canals, and railroads into the disputed areas. In so doing, they speeded up the transformation of the continent from a wilderness into a modern civilization. In trying to wrest the country beyond the mountains from each other, New York, Philadelphia, Baltimore, and Boston promoted all kinds of water and rail enterprises into the Ohio valley. Thus, their imperial ambitions ultimately created the basic transportation network which covered the area east of the Mississippi before the Civil War. It was not the demands of the farmers for access to markets as much as it was the needs of the cities that explain the appearance, location, and development of the country's railroad systems. It was the urban centers in search of new commerce that provided the funds and leadership, selected the routes, and, usually, reaped the largest benefits of the "transportation revolution."

Nor was this pattern of development peculiar to the North.

Southern cities, too, entered the railroad sweepstakes. Once again it was intense rivalry that explains the speed of construction and the final configuration of Dixie's network. Charleston and Savannah, locked in a desperate struggle for primacy in the southeast, reached with iron arms toward the cotton country of the black belt and the enlarging trade of the Ohio valley. Further south, New Orleans and Mobile, in a more unequal contest, competed with lines into the same area, adding a north-south ribbing to the railroad pattern of that region.

THE CITIES AND THE "PECULIAR INSTITUTION"

The clash of these urban imperialisms not only left the United States with a new transportation system, but it also shaped broad national events. For example, the acrid struggle between St. Louis and Chicago for hegemony in the Middle West had important consequences for the Union. Had the Missouri entrepôt been able to sustain its earlier supremacy in this area in the decade before the Civil War, the West might have been neutralized, thus enhancing the South's chances for independence. Instead, an aggressive and energetic Chicago not only conquered the Lake area, but raided St. Louis' nearby hinterland as well. By 1860, the self-proclaimed "Queen of the Lakes" had become the midcontinent's railroad center and had organized the immense area around it. The economy of the West now tilted toward the East where Chicago had its connections, rather than to the South and border areas which constituted St. Louis' historic orientation.

Moreover, the battle between these two cities was merely the last phase of a struggle which some contemporaries had seen on this same broad canvas before the startling rise of Chicago. "A contest has been going on between the North and South," wrote *De Bow's Review* in 1847, "not limited to slavery or no slavery—to abolition or no abolition, nor to the policies of either Whigs or democrats, as such, but a contest for the wealth and commerce of the great valley of the Mississippi—a battle for no principle of government, no right of human freedom in the abstract, but a contest tendered by our Northern brethren, whether the growing commerce of the Great West, shall be thrown upon New Orleans, or given to the Atlantic cities—which shall receive, store, sell and ship the immense products of that great country, lying between the Appalachian and Rocky Mountains.[11] Ironically, the outcome of the argument over slavery was importantly affected by the ambitions of the cities—ambitions which were unrelated to the ideological issues involved.

In fact, the relationship of Southern cities toward the issue of slavery had become quite ambiguous by 1860. Though they supported the "peculiar institution" as necessary and even desirable, their own experience with it had not been happy. Many townspeople in Dixie, of course, were slaveholders in the antebellum period, but their number declined drastically both totally and proportionately in the prewar decades. In 1820, Negroes comprised at least a quarter and often about a half of the population of Southern towns. The bulk of them were bondsmen employed as domestics, porters, draymen, gardeners, common laborers, factory hands, and in some instances, skilled mechanics. Bondage appeared to be as much an urban as a rural institution. Yet, by 1860 slavery was disintegrating in Southern cities.

Observers might disagree over the causes of this attrition, but few doubted that the urban milieu was inhospitable to the "peculiar institution." A Kentuckian who observed in 1848 that "slavery exists in Louisville and St. Louis only in name" explained that "there are two things that always, and under all circumstances, abrogates [sic] slavery. The first is a dense population, . . . the next [is] the intelligence of slaves. Both of these are silently and imperceptibly working their legitimate results." [12] A Louisiana planter, a frequent visitor to New Orleans, had noticed this same process. "Slavery is from its very nature eminently patriarchial [sic] and altogether agricultural. It does not thrive with master or slave when transplanted to cities." [13] Probably the best Northern student of the South, Frederick Law Olmsted, made the same point in 1857. "Servile labor must be unskilled labor," he wrote, "and unskilled labor must be dispersed over land, and cannot support the concentrated life nor amass the capital of cities." [14] Negroes who had known bondage in both town and country perhaps understood the problem best. One of them, Frederick Douglass, stated it simply. "Slavery dislikes a dense population." [15]

The reason for this is clear enough. The city in the South no less than the North created its own kind of world with a pace, sophistication, and environment that separated it from rural modes. In the process, it transformed Negro as well as white, slave as well as free man. Hence, it is not surprising that bondage as an urban institution differed greatly from its country counterpart. Initially, the greatest difficulty surrounded the utilization of the Negroes in a varied and constantly changing town economy where one owner "hired out" his excess bondsmen to another employer.

The more fundamental problem, however, was that the controls needed to maintain the "peculiar institution" broke down, and discipline became increasingly difficult. Soon urban communities began, though not consciously, to abandon the system. As slavery in its traditional organization disintegrated, the towns developed new race relationships. Indeed, the pattern of segregation that has since become so familiar had its Southern origins in the cities before the Civil War. In the last antebellum decades, urban slavery faced a crisis. The old arrangements were eroding and a new system was needed which would shed some of the ordinary requirements of bondage and yet preserve the historic line of deference between black and white. Segregation met these tests, and by 1860 its outlines emerged in Dixie's cities even though the "peculiar institution" had not yet been formally abolished.

POST-CIVIL WAR GROWTH OF CITIES

The four decades before the war had witnessed the most rapid proportionate expansion of urban population that the country would ever know. The nation's preoccupation with the impending crisis over bondage obscured this extraordinary growth. But the census figures told the story. The number of people living in cities jumped from 693,000 in 1820 to over 6,200,000 in 1860; the number of places containing over 100,000 inhabitants rose from one to nine; and those with at least 25,000 moved from five to thirty-five. Urban indices all showed at least fivefold increases, while rural growth only doubled in the same period.

This era of unprecedented expansion remade the face of American cities. Older municipal confines were trampled; population swarmed into unoccupied sections around the old periphery; hills were leveled, swamps reclaimed, waterlines extended by filling. Specialization, appearing as early as the eighteenth century in Atlantic cities, now dominated the building of the new urban plant;

whatever services remained in the household in an earlier period submitted to the continual differentiation of the urban economy. Yet, in a curious way, the city somehow managed to contain the mounting numbers, the new enterprises, and the additional functions. These were still "walking towns"; with few exceptions it was still possible to cross the city on foot. Congestion increased, pressures rose, problems multiplied; yet, even New York in 1850 was more as it had been in 1800 than it would be in 1900.

About the middle of the century, the breakthrough began; by the last quarter of the century the modern city had everywhere appeared. Crucial in the change was the developement of mass transportation. First the horse car, then the motor-drawn vehicle, ultimately the elevated and subway made possible the physical expansion of the metropolis. Relatively cheap, these common carriers moved large numbers quickly from one part of town to another, thus meeting the insatiable demand of the urban order for saving time and cutting costs. These innovations also produced modern suburbs, since some people could now live outside municipal boundaries and still conveniently work within them.

The new cities were unlike anything that had come before. The numbers themselves created a scale of life that seemed to frustrate any attempt at organization. No previous experience suited men for this environment. Certainly the newcomers from the countryside, whether from Europe or rural America, could find few guideposts to help them. Even those from Old World cities were unprepared for what they found.

The most obvious characteristic of the new metropolis was its congestion. New forms of building, especially the tenement, were devised to house the increasing population. Yet these only emphasized the problem of density, they did not solve it. The household in the old sense crumpled; the integrity of the family unit was compromised; old religious and social organizations found the new setting inhospitable.

The new metropolis also demanded a new concept of time. "The complex interrelationships of life in the modern city," Oscar Handlin has observed, "called for unprecedented precision. The arrival of all those integers who worked together, from whatever part of the city they inhabited, had to be coordinated to the moment. There was no natural span for such labor; arbitrary beginnings and ends had to be set, made uniform and adhered to. The dictatorship of the clock and the schedule became absolute. No earlier human experience had made such demands.'' [16]

THE RISE OF THE "BOSS"

The first generation suffered the greatest shock. A large proportion of these people were new not only to cities but to the United States as well. Forced to take what housing they could find, they occupied the center of town. After filling up abandoned warehouses and commercial buildings, they then jammed into former one-family dwellings. Ultimately, the tenement made the congestion complete—even scientific. Strangers in a new land and a new environment, the recent arrivals struggled to keep some kind of social organization and identity. None of their old institutions seemed wholly relevant to their predicament; but they utilized what they could, and through voluntary associations they met some of their most important needs.

Weak economically and deprived socially, the newcomers found some protection in their numbers. These numbers had been, in most instances, a curse: housing never caught up with the demand, the job market was always flooded, the breadwinner had too many mouths to feed. Yet, in politics such a liability could be turned into an asset. Soon the ''city boss'' appeared to organize this potential. At once speaking for a particular neighborhood and a broader immigrant community, he became the distinctive figure of urban politics. Himself only a generation removed from the difficult situation of those just arrived, he understood their problems; having grown up in the city, he had come to know the ways and interests of the native population. For the able and shrewd, this strategic position could be parlayed into substantial power and influence.

The city boss soon became the most pilloried man in American public life. The familiar stereotype cast him as an uneducated, unscrupulous man who wielded his arbitrary power against the older residents and traditional interests of the city. By-products of his rule were municipal corruption, low civic morale, and wasteful government. In fact, however, his power was never absolute. If the boss did not respect the aims of the neighborhood and group, he soon disappeared. The precise limits of his leadership were never clear, but he could not take his people where they did not want to go.

However, so long as he could handle the group's interest, protect the neighborhoods, and administer to their various needs, the boss could count on consistent, even dedicated, support.

THE POPULIST PROTEST

The immense urban expansion of the latter half of the nineteenth century not only created a new range of internal problems, but also deepened the cleavage between country and city. The census figures still showed a rural predominance, yet every year it grew smaller. The future clearly lay with the metropolis. Farmers had long felt the economic power of the city, but now the challenge was broader. The status of country life slipped badly in the face of urban growth. All the technological advances that made the nineteenth the "century of progress" seemed to be going to the cities. Opportunities there were wider; the symbols of success all bore the mark of the metropolis; the bright young people on the farm all moved irresistibly into the urban vortex. The novelist Harold Frederic, who himself had been caught in the undertow, wrote bitterly of the process: "The nineteenth century is a century of cities; they have given their own twist to the progress of the age—and the farmer is as far out of it as if he lived in Alaska. Perhaps there was a time when a man could live in what the poet calls daily communication with nature and not starve his mind and dwarf his soul, but this isn't the century." [17]

The countryside, however, did not tamely submit to its inevitable decline. The farmers, using their political energy and power, organized to fight for the older ways. Their agitation, culminating in the Populist movement of the nineties, was a dominant phase of the politics of the period. Though the rhetoric of this uprising had led earlier historians to see the aroused farmers as precursors of twentieth-century liberalism, it is now clear that their aim was to rescue a fading past rather than to create a brave new world. In their desperation, rural dwellers compiled a long list of enemies, some real, some imagined—Wall Street, Monopolists, Bankers, Foreigners, Catholics, Jews, etc. These evil forces all found a special home in the city. Urban life was seen as artificial, dirty, vice-ridden, and parasitic. William Jennings Bryan's famous "cross of gold" speech caught the conflicting forces and embodied the Populist notion of the primacy of rural America: ". . . the great cities rest upon our broad and fertile prairies. Burn down your cities and leave our farms, and your cities will spring up again as if by magic; but destroy our farms and grass will grow in the streets of every city in the country."

If the older concept of the progressive content of the farm revolt is questionable, so too is the characterization of the movement as a "Western" protest against the East. Many Populist orators presumed to speak for the whole region, and Eastern politicians often took them at their word. Yet closer analysis suggests that critical divisions existed in Western opinion. The cities increasingly withdrew from the protest. By 1896, midcontinent urban leadership strongly opposed both the program and the candidates of Populism.

THE URBAN ROOTS OF PROGRESSIVISM

Urban discontent was better expressed in Progressivism. Indeed, this movement had its seedbed in the cities. In one metropolis after the other, worsening conditions led to a demand for reform. Initially, urban reform centered on an attempt to clean up municipal corruption and to find some better means to come to grips with a wide range of pressing local problems. Only later was this impulse translated into a national movement. The enemy of this civic uprising was the city boss and his machine. Local business interests which had working arrangements with this political system also came under attack, especially traction magnates, gas rings, and utilities companies. The connection between "bad" politics and "bad" business became one of the most significant problems for urban reformers; indeed, little was said later by national progressives on this question that had not already been argued in the metropolis. But, in the municipal context the central target was the boss and his control of city hall.

The drive for improvement began sporadically in the seventies; toward the end of the century reform administrations appeared with increasing frequency. Though this municipal agitation contributed to the general discontent of the period, it grew independently of rural protest. It addressed itself to different problems, produced different leadership, and sought different objectives. Moreover, when the agrarian revolt failed in 1896 and new conditions calmed the countryside, urban reform activity continued at an accelerated pace. The years between the failure of Bryan and the accession of Theodore Roosevelt, so often left dangling awkwardly between Populism and Progressivism, were in fact filled with significant successes on the municipal level. When the twentieth century opened, the basis for a new surge of national liberalism was present in cities all across the country.

Progressivism in this phase was an intra-urban conflict and, although not without economic overtones, it was essentially political. Reform found its major spokesmen and greatest support in middle-class residential areas on the outer ring of the city. These were the wards occupied by the older inhabitants who had abandoned downtown for the more pleasant, less congested spots. Ethnically these sections were white and heavily Protestant. The boss's strength was in the city's core where the newcomers had settled. These were the tenement, tenderloin, and transient precincts. Low income, irregular employment, and overcrowding prevailed. The people were predominantly immigrants; neighborhoods developed strong ethnic flavorings; large proportions of the residents were Catholic or Jewish. Hence, reform was a movement of the periphery against the center.

The two camps divided over many questions. The formal issues usually had to do with "charter reform" and attempts to change existing structures of municipal government. But the real cleavage went much deeper. The contest was to determine whether the older residents or the newcomers would shape the life of the metropolis. Behind the attack on the boss lay thinly disguised hostility to the hyphenated population of the central city. The drive for a civil service system always carried an implied attack on immigrant leaders and their modest educational qualifications for public office. Charges of corruption in city hall, whether true or not, usually suggested that natives and foreign-born had different standards of conduct and honesty. And the sporadic raids on vice and gambling, generally directed at saloons and beer halls, carried a judgment on the private habits of the downtown neighborhoods.

The attack usually strengthened the boss and the machine, permitting them to pose as the protectors of oppressed segments of the city's life and the defenders of persecuted minorities. Nor was this wholly a pose. At a time when others preached self-help and limited government, the boss practiced paternalism and municipal service. People in his area felt they needed help—getting housing, jobs, relief, leniency in court judgment, even exemption from the law. Reformers thought assistance in these fields was harmful both to those who received and to the public agency that provided it. The boss had no such inhibitions. He did what he could, and when successful he expected recipients to show their gratitude by support. When a city-wide showdown came, they seldom dissappointed him. To the people of the neighborhood he had become a symbol of both their predicament and their hope. His enemies were somehow theirs; his triumphs would also be theirs.

Political patterns in the Progressive era reflected this split between the middle of the city and its outer edges. Voting results could be neatly plotted on the map; reform majorities dwindled, then disappeared, as they crossed over the lines demarcating the oldest parts of town. The balance between the forces was close enough to afford victories for both sides and to make no defeat permanent. In the first decades, reform succeeded often enough to make improvements in municipal government. Boss rule, however, was so deeply rooted in the needs of the neighborhood and the requirements of newcomers that it could only be tamed, not killed. Yet, the battle itself had led to a valuable discussion of city problems. The competence of local government was greatly widened, and the standards of municipal service measurably raised.

These internal urban political struggles had a broad significance for national Progressivism. Reformers active in local affairs often moved onto a wider stage, and they carried the same attitudes into the national arena that informed their approach to municipal problems. Hence, Progressivism found it difficult to appeal to the crowded center of the cities. Historians have observed, usually with some surprise, that neither labor nor immigrant groups responded very enthusiastically to progressive programs or leaders. The answer to this riddle is not only that Progressivism was essentially a middle-class movement, but also that it was led by the same people whose local activities had been directed against the residents of the downtown neighborhoods. Having rejected such leadership in the city, tenement dwellers could scarcely be expected to embrace it in the nation.

DOMINANCE OF INTRA-URBAN POLITICS

The gap between the center and the periphery remained a constant factor in local and national affairs for nearly three decades. In fact, on the municipal scene the division became increasingly institutionalized. Early in the century, good government advocates and planners discovered zoning as an instrument to control the rapidly changing configuration of the central sections of the city. As newcomers crowded into the core, the older residents could move to the remoter edges; but commercial property never had that mobility. Moreover, what could prevent the low-income tides from inundating the greener, less populated areas near the municipal boundaries? Some system to stabilize the present and protect future use seemed essential to those who traditionally had shaped town life. It is significant that New York's first zoning law stemmed from a crisis on Fifth Avenue where merchants feared the encroachments of the garment workers into the buildings close to the fashionable shops on the great street. Subsequently, zoning ordinances across the country became a kind of proprietary gesture by the older inhabitants as they abandoned downtown. They hoped this system would contain the newcomers within defined limits and protect the commercial investments which represented their remaining stake in the historic heart of the metropolis. This attempt to fix the line between the center and the periphery, between the old and the new, however, merely established the battlelines, it did not create the terms of peace.

The first major figure to build a bridge across this chasm was Alfred E. Smith in New York. Himself a product of the tenement and immigration section, he had a claim on the support of the machine; but he also developed strong ties with the reform community. His extraordinarily successful career in New York reflected an ability to join the traditional antagonists. What Smith accomplished within one state, Franklin Roosevelt was able to accomplish on a national scale. Standing prominently in the famous New Deal coalition were the boss and the reformer, neither exactly comfortable, but together making very formidable what political scientists came to call the "urban consensus."

The central importance of intra-urban differences in the twentieth century signaled the decline of the earlier conflict between city and farm. The 1920 census indicated that a watershed had been passed: for the first time more people lived in urban areas than rural ones. The balance had shifted decisively; the country could still protest, but it could no longer control. The broad drive for national political power of the Populist epoch dwindled to the more modest, if more effective, lobbying of the Farm Bloc and the manipulation of state legislatures. Though shorn of much of their political strength, farm regions were not without means of expression. Prohibition, the drive to halt immigration, the Ku Klux Klan and, symbolically, the Scopes trial, all bore testimony to the feelings of "old America" and its capacity to harass newer influences.

THE EXPLODING METROPOLIS

The twenties, however, brought to the cities a much more disturbing element than any which exercised the public life of the decade—the automobile. Initially a plaything of the rich, then a mode of incidental travel, it ultimately created an explosion that broke the historic casement of urban life. Previously, metropolitan growth had a kind of controlled development, since the means of transportation had governed the shape of the city. The spread was concentric, or nearly so, depending on the capacity of public conveyances to handle increased demands. Even suburban expansion had hugged railroad lines that radiated out from the commercial focus. But the automobile destroyed even this semblance of order. Its great mobility permitted building well beyond the limits that common carriers had established. The old confinements burst; the age of megalopolitan sprawl had arrived.

But not quite yet. The depression of the thirties did not deprive Americans of their cars, but it did inhibit wide-scale building outside of the established cities. Later, wartime shortages further prevented any substantial residential construction. With the coming of peace, however, the pent-up pressure was suddenly released. Almost uninterrupted prosperity provided an affluent economic base; the automobile brought the remotest spots within reach of the bulldozer. A sharp rise in the birth rate gave an added impetus to these centrifugal forces. For fifteen years, virtually without interruption, suburban development dominated American economic, social, and political life.

The term "exploding metropolis" scarcely seemed to encompass the full range of changes. Not only did the surrounding countryside fall to the suburbs with all that meant, but the old city faced a series of drastic crises. Its physical plant needed repairs that bad times and war had deferred; public transportation no longer competed with the private vehicle; downtown had somehow to service an immensely increased area and population. Furthermore, all these problems had to be met on a shrinking revenue base, for many of the well-to-do had led the flight into the green ghettoes beyond municipal boundaries, taking shopping centers and even some industry with them.

To be sure, some of the old elements were still there. Particularly the historic antagonism of the center and periphery broke out again. Though it was somewhat obscured by the spillage of population outside the town's formal limits, the new battlelines were simply the older ones on a larger scale. Within the metropolitan area, the urban-suburban clash was essentially the one which had characterized the city alone for a half century. Now, however, the core had moved out toward the boundary. The flow of low-income newcomers from abroad had been stopped, but the movement of Negroes from the South and Latins from south of the border replaced it. As a result, the old ethnic bitterness was heightened by racial divisions. Dreams of metropolitan government became the analogue of the old charter reform hopes of an earlier time.

THE URBAN PROBLEM TODAY

Suburban growth reduced markedly the previous domination of the city in presidential politics. In the fifties, Republican majorities outside municipal boundaries overwhelmed traditional Democratic urban successes. Though Eisenhower's personal popularity magnified this shift, observers understood that the conditions which produced the Roosevelt and Truman victories no longer existed. Any Democrat who hoped to win now would have to penetrate the crabgrass curtain which surrounded every urban center. The genius of the Kennedy campaign of 1960 lay in its appeal to the inner ring of communities just beyond the city line where it either divided the vote with Nixon or contrived small margins. The New Frontier's domestic program, with its emphasis on urban problems, represented an attempt to consolidate and extend these gains. If the tangent suburbs could be joined for electoral purposes to the city, a new metropolitan consensus would be created which might become as successful as the urban coalition that had sustained Franklin Roosevelt and Harry Truman through two decades.

Immediately, however, municipal governments could look to Washington for help in attacking their increasingly vexing problems. Such assistance encouraged municipal leaders to adopt comprehensive and long-term programs of renewal, rehabilitation, and growth. During the fifteen postwar years the approach had been piecemeal. What passed for "planning" in the forties consisted largely of public housing; in the fifties the emphasis shifted to traffic control, parking, and expressways. Even where successful, these projects usually only revealed the wide range of questions awaiting attention and the magnitude of the job yet to be undertaken.

Concern had still to be translated into precise programs, but signs of urban revival were everywhere present. Newspapers swung behind city-wide planning, often bringing large portions of the business community with them; some suburbanites began to realize that there could be no prosperous periphery without a successful downtown; an historian was awarded a Pulitzer Prize for an eloquent appeal on behalf of the western world's urban heritage.

Nor was this all merely agitation. The changing skyline across the nation demonstrated that some people were willing to invest in the future of the metropolis. The improving political climate of many cities produced new and able leadership, while public discussion indicated a growing awareness of the need for action and, in a few instances, even audacity. Federal funds on an increasing scale made it possible to outflank the rural domination in state legislatures and the Poujadists within municipal boundaries, a combination which had historically kept city governments in financial strait jackets. Perhaps no urban renaissance was in the cards in 1962, but gloomy prophecies about the death of the American city were surely premature.

Notes

[1] The title of this paper is obviously drawn from Lewis Mumford's recent book, *The City in History* (New York: Harcourt, Brace & World, Inc., 1961), but its purposes are much more limited. I have tried here to explore only a few themes in American urban development. A fuller and more comprehensive treatment is contained in Arthur Meier Schlesinger's epochal essay, "The City in American Civilization," which can be found in his *Paths to the Present* (New York: The Macmillan Company, 1949), pp. 210–233.

[2] F. J. Turner, "The Significance of the Frontier in American History," in *The Turner Thesis Concerning the Role of the Frontier in American History,* G. R. Taylor, ed., *Problems in American Civilization* (rev. ed.; Boston: D. C. Heath and Company, 1956), p. 5.

[3] *Ibid.*, p. 2.

[4] *Ibid.*, p. 3.

[5] *Ibid.*, p. 8.

[6] Schlesinger, *loc. cit.* p. 210.

[7] R. C. Wade, *The Urban Frontier, The Rise of Cities in the West, 1790–1830* (Cambridge, Mass.: Harvard University Press, 1959), p. 1.

[8] J. Strong, *Our Country: Its Possible Future and Its Present Crisis* (rev. ed.; New York: Baker & Taylor, 1885), p. 206.

[9] C. Bridenbaugh, *Cities in the Wilderness; The First Century of Urban Life in America, 1625–1742* (New York: The Ronald Press Company, 1938); and *Cities in Revolt; Urban Life in America, 1743–1776* (New York: Alfred A. Knopf, Inc., 1955).

[10] A. M. Schlesinger, *Prelude to Independence, the Newspaper War on Britain, 1764–1776* (New York: Alfred A. Knopf, Inc., 1958), p. 6.

[11] 3 *De Bow's Review,* February 1847.

[12] *Louisville Daily Journal,* February 22, 1848.

[13] S. Walker, "The Diary of a Louisiana Planter, Elia Plantation," unpublished ms. Tulane University Library.

[14] F. L. Olmsted, *A Journey Through Texas; Or a Saddle-Trip on the South-Western Frontier; with a Statistical Appendix* (New York: Dix & Edwards, 1857), p. 37.

[15] F. Douglass, *My Bondage and My Freedom* (New York: Miller, Orton & Mulligan, 1855), pp. 147–8.

[16] O. Handlin, "The Modern City as a Field of Historical Study," Paper read at the Harvard Summer School Conference on The City and History, Cambridge, Mass., July 24, 1961.

[17] Harold Frederic, *Seth's Brother's Wife, a Study of Greater New York* (New York: Charles Scribners' Sons, 1887), p. 33.

The Philosopher and the Metropolis in America

MORTON WHITE *is Professor of Philosophy at Harvard University. His "Social Thought in America," "The Age of Analysis," and "Religion, Politics, and the Higher Learning" are among his many contributions to the understanding of philosophy and American thought. With Lucia White he has written "The Intellectual versus the City: From Thomas Jefferson to Frank Lloyd Wright."*

In a recent study, Lucia White and I advanced and documented the view that dismay and distrust have been the predominant attitudes of the American intellectual toward the American city.[1] This is true not only of famous American novelists, sociologists, social workers, and architects, but also of influential philosophers and philosophically minded writers from the eighteenth century to the twentieth. In our study, we tried for the most part to examine the views of philosophers side-by-side with those of social workers, sociologists, literary men, and other intellectuals who speak during the same periods, and to similar concerns about the American city.

Therefore, we devoted no systematic attention to the history of the philosophers' reactions to the city; we presented no continuous examination of what our major philosophical thinkers have said or felt about urban life in America. But, as a philosopher, I may be forgiven my special interest in what the American heroes of my discipline have said about the American city, and I am moved primarily by that interest to limit myself here to examining their words, thoughts, and feelings on urban affairs.

There are important reasons for lifting Jefferson, Emerson, William James, Josiah Royce, John Dewey, and George Santayana from the stream of American intellectual history, and focusing on them as a philosophical group. For one thing, they were all distinguished and influential minds, whose writings on urban problems often have intrinsic interest or value. But more important is the fact that they represent an extraordinary variety of philosophical doctrine and point of view, and therefore demonstrate that distrust and fear of the American city is not the exclusive possession of one system of thought or one *Weltanschauung*. Also, the fact that Jefferson, Emerson, Thoreau, Dewey, Royce, and Santayana reacted critically to the American city shows how deep and pervasive antiurban feeling has been in America, and that it cannot be identified simply with roughneck prejudice, ignorance, or philistinism. To see this critical reaction in the writings of our most sagacious and civilized Americans may help explain why the efforts of the contemporary city planner and friend of the city meet with opposition on so many levels of our national life. Not only farmers and their political spokesmen have criticized the American city, but also philosophers whom one might have associated with a very different set of attitudes on this question. On this issue, poet, peasant, and all sorts of philosophers have united.

MAJOR PHASES IN AMERICAN PHILOSOPHY

Before trying to show this, I must say a word about the different sorts of philosophies that Americans have produced or espoused since colonial times. The history of American philosophy has gone through four major phases: the age of Enlightenment in the eighteenth century, the age of transcendentalism in the early nineteenth century, the so-called golden age from the 1890's almost to World

War I, and the present age of analysis. I do not mean to say that these are the only phases or movements, for I have not mentioned the impact of Scottish philosophy in the nineteenth century, nor Hegelianism, nor the various species of realism that were advocated and criticized by American philosophers between the World Wars I and II or thereabouts.

In the age of Enlightenment, the empiricism of the eighteenth century predominated and expressed itself with vigorous practical intent in the writing and thinking of Jefferson. But his empiricism and, as it was called by its enemies, his materialism and agnosticism, were repudiated and scorned by Emerson, Thoreau, and their transcendentalist friends. They turned their backs on the empiricist philosophy that had nourished Jefferson and Franklin, and they built upon Coleridge's interpretation of Kantian idealism a romantic world view which was fundamentally antithetic to the empiricism of the Enlightenment. After the Civil War, the philosophical influence of these Concord pundits began to be undermined by intellectual forces that corresponded to more pervasive ones radically transforming American society. In New England, after the death of Emerson in 1882, the transcendental age gave way to what is sometimes called the golden age of American philosophy. It began with William James, who was later joined by Royce and Santayana to form at Harvard one of the most powerful academic triumvirates ever to dominate a single philosophical department. James spoke for pragmatism, Royce for idealism fortified by mathematical logic, and Santayana for materialism tempered by classical wisdom and good taste. James and Royce of the golden trio had been influenced by the erratic genius Charles Peirce, and all three had great impact on the dogged, monumental, scientifically oriented John Dewey. Partly under the influence of all five of these figures, the most recent age of American philosophy emerged, the age of the pragmatic, analytical, logical, linguistic tendencies which dominate America today.

In this essay I wish to confine myself to the views of certain major figures in the first three of these periods, and to ask the question: What views of urban life have been advocated, sponsored, or encouraged during these three phases of American philosophy? Let me begin by saying that the answer is "None" if we are thinking of the systematic analysis or description of urban life. That was left for sociologists. But, even though American philosophers, unlike Aristotle, did not think of the city as the fundamental political or social unit and hence did not concentrate their attention on it systematically, they certainly expressed deep feelings and thoughts about it, from 1784 when Jefferson's *Notes on Virginia* appeared, to John Dewey's *The Public and its Problems,* published in 1927.

JEFFERSON'S EMPIRICAL ANTIURBANISM

What were those feelings and thoughts? Let us begin with Jefferson. In the eighteenth century, the American city was too small and inconspicuous to cause any great concern to Jefferson. But when he looked across the Atlantic at the European cities he knew, he expressed his anxiety about having such things in America. In spite of his attachment to the values of civilization as conceived by the enlightened philosophers of the eighteenth century, Jefferson despised the manners and morals of the urban crowd and prayed that they would not be imported to America, the home of the brave and innocent farmer. Even when his concern for national interests led him to revise his views after the War of 1812, Jefferson plainly showed that he was persuaded, not because of any change of heart about the ways of the urban crowd, but rather by a rational respect for the value of urban industry to a new country faced by threatening powers across the sea. Jefferson's final acceptance of the American city was grudging and military rather than fulsome and loving. Moreover, Benjamin Franklin, of whom one thinks automatically when one thinks of the colonial American city, was not an ideological partisan of urban life, but rather a city-builder. Indeed, Franklin was an agrarian pamphleteer who was certainly not prepared to conduct an intellectual crusade in behalf of the city and against the country.

For those who think of the Enlightenment as a period of calm intellectual activity in which the values of reason and the graces of urban civilization were greatly admired, the reaction of Jefferson to the city may cause some surprise. But no matter how much a stereotyped view of the Enlightenment philosopher might lead one to think that the urbane Jefferson would have welcomed the urbanization of America, the fact is that he did not. It is true that he had to fight hard at times in order to convince himself that the nation should stay down on the farm. Especially after he had seen Paris and had been overwhelmed by its charm and its concert halls. But not even Parisian chamber music, which he dearly loved, could move Jefferson to change his mind about the defects of urbanization. While he admitted that the great cities of Europe encouraged the fine arts, he thought that the cities' elegance and elevating qualities could not outweigh the danger of their sapping or damming America's moral and spiritual strength. Even after he had demonstrated his practical wisdom by conceding that we needed cities for our national defense, he continued to express deeply felt horror at their spirit and style. In short, the philosophical representative of the Enlightenment in American thought was an antiurbanist in feeling who conquered that feeling only because his first concern was to keep the nation free from foreign domination.

Because Jefferson was an empiricist and an active political man, he could not assess the city in purely emotional terms. But the transcendentalists who came after him in the history of American thought were literary men rather than statesmen, and their metaphysical aspirations were more abstract than Jefferson's. They could not control their antiurban animus as effectively as Jefferson controlled his. The War of 1812, which had stimulated Jefferson to adopt a more conciliatory tone about the American city, had increased the similarity between the American city and the European city that had occasioned Jefferson's earliest fears about urbanization. The age of Jefferson had ended on an irenical note so far as the American city was concerned, but soon the trumpets of a more militant antiurbanism filled the intellectual air, played by romantic metaphysicians with little sympathy for colonial epistemology and with no inclination to serenade the American city.

EMERSON'S METAPHYSICAL ANTIURBANISM

While Jefferson was an empiricist, Emerson was in sharp reaction against the traditions of British empiricism and French materialism. With the details of Emerson's metaphysics and theory of knowledge we need not be concerned, nor need we trace his views back beyond Coleridge to Kant. But it is important for our purposes to note than Emerson explicitly linked his own epistemology to his distaste for the city. Emerson distinguished sharply between the Understanding and the Reason. The Understanding, according to Emerson, "toils all the time, compares, contrives, adds, argues; near-sighted but strong-sighted, dwelling in the present, the expedient, the customary," while the Reason, which was for him the highest faculty of the soul, "never reasons, never proves; it simply perceives; it is vision."[2] Reason was for Emerson the soaring faculty of the forest-philosopher and the peasant-poet, while the Understanding was that of the city-bound, lumbering scientist. Reason, Emerson asserted, is characteristically exercised in the country, while the Understanding is an urban faculty. The city, he declared, "delights the Understanding. It is made up of finites: short, sharp, mathematical lines, all calculable. It is full of varieties, of successions, of contrivances. The country, on the contrary, offers an unbroken horizon, the monotony of endless road, of vast uniform plains, of distant mountains, the melancholy of uniform and infinite vegetation; the objects on the road are few and worthless, the eye is invited ever to the horizon and the clouds. It is the school of Reason."[3]

Faith was another faculty that Emerson preferred to scientific understanding, and faith too was absent from the city. In 1840 he wrote to Carlyle: "I always seem to suffer some loss of faith on entering cities. They are great conspiracies; the parties are all maskers, who have taken mutual oaths of silence not to betray each other's secret and each to keep the other's madness in countenance. You can scarce drive any craft here that does not seem a subornation of the treason."[4] In 1854, he developed the same theme of urban deception in his *Journal:* "Rest on your humanity, and it will supply you with strength and hope and vision for the day. Solitude and the country, books and openness, will feed you; but go into the city—I am afraid there is no morning in Chestnut Street, it is full of rememberers, they shun each other's eyes, they are all wrinkled with memory of the tricks they have played, or mean to play, each other, of petty arts and aims all contracting and lowering their aspect and character."[5]

However much Emerson distrusted the city, Emerson was too sociable and too instinctively democratic to shun cities altogether. He was a great conversationalist and was always prepared to give up a night in the country for elevating talk at the Saturday Club.

For Emerson, the urban clubs encouraged good words in a naughty urban world. Like so many Americans after them, Jefferson and Emerson thought of cities as great places to work in or to visit, but not to live in. Jefferson saw them somewhat as arsenals for the young Republic, Emerson admired them mainly for providing hotel rooms in which the Saturday Club might meet. But their dominant reaction to the city was that of distrust.

The distrust that they felt, however, was differently related to their respective philosophies. Emerson's view of the American city was intimately linked with his world view and epistemology, but Jefferson's antiurbanism was more peripheral to his philosophical thinking as well as to the spirit of the Enlightenment of which he was such a distinguished American representative. Although in his *Notes on Virginia* Jefferson expressed his distaste for the ways of the artificer or artisan, Jefferson did not try to justify this distaste by referring to an elaborate metaphysics or system of values in which art was held to be inferior to untouched nature. As a child of the eighteenth century and as a Deist in theology, Jefferson did not disparage artifice as such, nor did he share Emerson's degree of concern about transcending the findings of empirical science. For a Deist like Jefferson, God Himself is the Great Artificer whose existence one can establish only by scientific induction from signs of design in the world. Therefore the sheer artificiality of the city, the fact that it was an artifact, could not have supplied Jefferson with the metaphysical objections to city life that it supplied to the romantic Emerson in his essay, *Nature*.

In spite of the fact that Emerson wove his anticity feelings more tightly into his metaphysics than Jefferson did, the more basic fact for our purposes is that they both disapproved of the idea of an urban America. The empiricist Jefferson and the transcendentalist Emerson could easily forget their philosophical differences as they made common cause against urbanism. If Jefferson was, in later life, prepared to encourage the growth of the American city, that was partly because he had not lived long enough to see it come to resemble the European cities he distrusted in 1784. But Emerson faced a more highly developed and more menacing American city, and his militant reaction to it set the tone of a great deal of American literature in the middle of the nineteenth century. Above all, it is certain that three famous American philosophers, or if one prefers, three famous philosophically oriented American thinkers—Jefferson, Emerson, and Emerson's comrade, Thoreau—did nothing to encourage the American to love the American city. They preferred life in Monticello, Concord, or Walden. From those retreats they looked with suspicious eyes at Philadelphia, Boston, and New York.

JAMES'S CRITIQUE OF BIGNESS

We have now traversed two stages in our story of the American philosophers' reaction to the American city. Both stages precede the Civil War, that great divide in our national history, and so, when we come to the period after it, we are minded to ask whether our philosophy, like so many other elements in our culture, was drastically altered. The answer is, of course, "Yes," but it applies more to matters of high philosophical doctrine and style than to attitudes toward the American city. A generation after the Civil War, William James, Josiah Royce, and George Santayana possessed a technical expertness, originality, and power in philosophy that had been absent in the period of the preprofessional sages, Jefferson and Emerson. The philosophers of the golden age were professors who lectured to future professors and their standards of rigor were raised far above those of their predecessors. While the love of wisdom continued, it was accompanied by a kind of analytic acumen that was missing from the writing of Jefferson and Emerson. Pragmatism came upon the scene in the wake of Darwinism; idealism was armed by Royce with logical weapons that Emerson was incapable of supplying; Santayana courageously called himself a materialist. Science, technology, and logic were no longer scorned, as they had been by the transcendentalists. After the Civil War, philosophers lived in an age that was becoming more and more urbanized, and they focused their attention on its characteristic intellectual products.

Yet once again we may observe the old refrain of fear, dismay, and distrust so far as the concrete American city is concerned. Of the three, William James was by philosophical and personal impulse the most sympathetic to what he called the new New York at the turn of the century, and, more than any single American of his generation, he won the love of all kinds of urban personalities, from immigrants to their patrons in the settlement houses. Unlike his brother Henry, he was not offended by what Henry called the primary stage of alienism, nor did he want to escape from New York into a cozier past. But, in 1899, William James penned a credo that served as a text for a whole generation of progressive reformers of the city. He wrote to a friend: "I am against bigness and greatness in all their forms, and with the invisible molecular moral forces that work from individual to individual, stealing in through the crannies of the world like so many soft rootlets, or like the capillary oozing of water, and yet rending the hardest monuments of man's pride, if you give them time. The bigger the unit you deal with, the hollower, the more brutal, the more mendacious is the life displayed. So I am against all big organizations as such, national ones first and foremost; against all big successes and big results."[6]

James's notion that the big unit was hollow and brutal inspired reformers like Jane Addams to try to fill the urban void, but that is a path that I will not here describe in detail because of my resolution to confine myself to philosophers. Later I shall describe part of it when I come to the views of James's disciple, John Dewey. But here I want to emphasize the fact that James's distaste for bigness was part of a more general set of attitudes that he shared with Royce, his idealist opponent, and with Santayana, his materialist critic. Once again we find the American philosophical mind united on the subject of the city no matter how it might have been divided on the questions of God, freedom, and immortality.

ROYCE'S PROVINCIAL COMMUNITY

While the reforming disciples of William James worked hard in the cities, doing their pragmatic best to restore in them feelings of local neighborliness and in this way to combat the bigness and hollowness of the post–Civil War cities, Royce proposed a different solution. Royce was an admirer of life in the provincial community, which, he thought, would help eradicate the three main evils he saw in America at the turn of the century. One evil was the presence, as he put it, "of a considerable number of not yet assimilated newcomers" who were often a boon and welcome but who constituted, he thought, a "source of social danger."[7] Another was the leveling tendency produced by centralization and consolidation in an urban society, the same leveling tendency of which Kierkegaard and John Stuart Mill had complained a half century earlier in the name of the individual. The third evil was the spirit of "the mob" as it had been described in Gustave Le Bon's popular work of the times, *The Crowd*.

Royce, in his *Philosophy of Loyalty,* which appeared in 1908, described the malaise of the times in more general terms with the help of Hegel's concept of alienation or estrangement, much as Karl Marx had earlier with a very different political goal in mind. Hegel, Royce recalled sympathetically, had pointed out that in certain periods of European history the social mind of the Spirit had become "estranged from itself," notably during the decline of the Roman Empire and during the period of political absolutism in Europe in the seventeenth and early eighteenth centuries. On the other hand, the social spirit had not been self-estranged, Royce said, in the period of our thirteen colonies, which were small provinces. "In the province," he said, "the social mind is naturally aware of itself as at home with its own."[8] By the twentieth century, however, America had become the scene of urban alienation, in which the individual saw himself confronted by powers that he could not understand and to which he submitted without love or loyalty.

This spirit of alienation might be overcome, Royce thought, if the American spirit were to come to know itself better, if Americans were to combat the forces leading to detachment and loneliness by repairing to the provinces. In the romantic era, the poet Schiller could hope to escape from a self-estranged world to a world of dreams, but Royce was not drawn in that direction. Instead he found hope in the province. "There must we flee from the stress of the now too vast and problematic life of the nation as a whole. There we must flee . . . , not in the sense of a cowardly and permanent retirement, but in the sense of a search for renewed strength, for a social inspiration, for the salvation of the individual from the overwhelming forces of consolidation. Freedom, I should say, dwells now in the small social group, and has its securest home in the provincial life."[9]

SANTAYANA'S ARISTOCRATIC ANTIURBANISM

Royce's pupil, Santayana, could not have been more different from him in philosophy. Royce was an idealist, Santayana a materialist.

One was a dialectician, the other a poet. One received his nourishment from Kant and the post-Kantian idealists, the other went back to ancient Greece for philosophical insight and practical wisdom. And while Royce was above all a learned professor who was admired by the young philosophical "pros" who looked forward to their own chairs in philosophy, Santayana was a cosmopolitan esthete, a fastidious man of culture, and a devotee of the arts who despised most of the eager professional aspirants who sat in his graduate classes. In spite of these differences, however, Royce and Santayana were both uneasy about urbanization.

Santayana resembled those mobile, unassimilated strangers whom Royce had in mind when he spoke with anxiety of the newcomers who were filling the American cities. Born a Spaniard and a Catholic, Santayana was hardly at home with the Protestantism of New England in his day. He was contemptuous of the commercial path to success that was characteristic of Boston in his youth; by temperament he was cool and detached. Throughout his writings, especially his autobiographical writings, he expressed his antipathy to the ideals of what he calls Judaism, Liberalism, and Positivism, all of which were heavily represented in the New York he knew. And therefore New York, in spite of the great admiration that its philosophers felt for Santayana's work, was always a source of disturbance to him. There, he said, everything was "miscellaneous, urgent, and on an overwhelming scale." There, he complained, "nothing counts but realization." [10]

The tendency to think of Santayana as urbane and antiromantic in his philosophy has perhaps obscured his hostile attitude toward metropolitan life in America. But the fact is that he thought of commercial towns as feeding on, and levying a toll on, everything transportable. "However much they may collect and exhibit the riches of the world they will not breed anything original." [11] Even London of the 1880's, which Henry James admired so much, was for Santayana a "Babel of false principles and blind cravings," and Paris to him was "false, cynical and covetous." [12] He said he loved the earth while he hated the world, and he thought that ideal communities, like moral ideals, should be rooted in the earth.

In the end, therefore, Santayana did not differ very much in his opinion of urbanization from Royce, his philosophical antithesis at Harvard. Santayana believed that the modern world had become monstrous in certain of its aspects, that a leveling tendency was abroad in the world, and even perhaps that the world was suffering from an excess of strangers and Hegelian alienation. Being so estranged himself from the modern world, and lacking Royce's reforming zeal, Santayana did not officially advocate a return to the provinces, but his views on the city were not far from Royce's. Just as Santayana's moral philosophy required that ideals be anchored in natural impulses, and that, as he says somewhere, one must be a beast in order to be a spirit, so his ideal city had to be rooted in the land. Once again we find a meeting of philosophical extremes against the city, an occasion for Royce the idealistic provincialist and Santayana the naturalistic alien to compose their differences, far from the madding urban crowd.

JOHN DEWEY AND THE CONCEPT OF COMMUNITY

So far I have considered every one of the major philosophers on whose views of the city I wish to concentrate, with the great exception of John Dewey. Dewey's views on the city, as one might have expected, resemble those of William James, his great predecessor in the history of pragmatism, more than they resemble those of any other philosopher I have been discussing. As a pragmatist, Dewey admired most of the forces that were urbanizing America at the end of the nineteenth century: technology, science, industrialization and the matter-of-fact outlook which they encouraged. And, as one who lived most of his adult life in Chicago and New York, he, more than any major American philosopher, knew at first-hand the spirit of the metropolis. It was unlike anything that Jefferson could have known or dreamed of in Monticello, immensely far from Concord and Walden, and a world away from the Cambridge of James, Royce, and Santayana. To the practical problems of the metropolis, political and educational, Dewey addressed himself with more vigor and courage than any major philosopher in our history. Like William James, he was free of all prejudice against its immigrant residents; like James, he opposed urban corruption and national departures from high ideals; and, like James, he loved the active quality, the hurry, the eagerness and even the miscellaneousness of urban experience. He was no agrarian, no transcendentalist, no absolute idealist, no snob, no antisemite, no esthete. And yet he was terribly worried by the forces that we associate with urbanization. This, of course, does not make him, nor anyone, for that matter, an antiurbanist in the sense of a city hater. But when one examines some of Dewey's ideas about altering, improving, or eradicating the external causes of his worries about the city, one becomes aware of his link with the tradition of antiurbanism that lies behind him in American thought.

Here Dewey converges with Jane Addams and Robert Park, those other disciples and admirers of William James. The essential point of agreement is their localism, their respect for the values of what the sociologists call the primary group, their notion that only by somehow regenerating these groups could one combat the hollowness of which James spoke when he attacked blind, brutal bigness. In contrast to Royce, who advocated a higher provincialism, the urban reformers—and here I mean Jane Addams, Robert Park, and John Dewey—advocated what Park called a new parochialism, a way of life that would recreate some of the values of an earlier world in the urban context. It is in this spirit that one may view the emphasis that Jane Addams put on the settlement houses and Dewey's notion that the schoolroom contained within itself the method for improving our way of life.

Perhaps the most articulate expression of this appears in Dewey's *The Public and its Problems* (1927). Echoing some of Royce's fears, Dewey wrote: "The Great Society created by steam and electricity may be a society but it is no community. The invasion of the community by the new and relatively impersonal and mechanical modes of combined human behavior is the outstanding fact of modern life." [13] An age that had expanded the physical means of communication had failed to use them properly. The revolution that had brought Bangkok and New York closer together had turned New York into a vast hotel in which neighbors did not communicate with each other in spite of having telephones in each room. And so *the* problem of America in 1927, according to Dewey, was that of converting the Great Society into a Great Community. How this was to be brought about he did not say in detail. But he outlined his proposal with sufficient clarity to make it possible to conclude that he, like Robert Park, was an advocate of the new parochialism. Dewey emphasized the need for increased communication, and communication, he urged, was essentially and necessarily face-to-face in character. *Immediate* community had to be established if the great society was to be successfully converted into a great community.

It should not surprise us, therefore, to find Dewey returning to two familiar figures in our story. He had always had a fondness for Emerson, whom he once identified as *the* moral philosopher of democracy, and he now called upon Emerson at the end of *The Public and its Problems:* "We lie, as Emerson said, in the lap of an immense intelligence. But that intelligence is dormant and its communications are broken, inarticulate and faint until it possesses the local community as its medium." [14] The second familiar figure is, of course, Jefferson. At the age of eighty-one, Dewey presented an exposition of Jefferson's political philosophy in which Dewey insisted that Jefferson was not merely a spokesman for states' rights as against the claims of the nation, but that he also attached immense importance to self-governing communities of much smaller size than the state or the county. Impressed as Jefferson was by the virtues of the New England township, he thought that the counties had to be divided into wards if democracy was to work properly, and it was his affection for the wards as immediate communities that captivated the aged Dewey.

Jefferson said that he might have concluded every speech with the words "Divide the counties into wards." And in a similar spirit, Dewey might have concluded every one of his with the words, "Divide the cities into immediate communities," just as Jane Addams might have declaimed, "Divide the cities into settlement houses," and Park, "Divide the cities into primary groups." The new parochialism was their proposal in the first quarter of the twentieth century for the solution of some of the problems created by urbanization. It was an effort to fill the emptiness of the great city in a nostalgic spirit. This was not a call to revive the unestranged spirit of the colonial provinces, but it shared with Royce's viewpoint the idea that the city was lacking something that older preurban American communities possessed, and which had to be *re*-created. As such, the new parochialism was not an effort to provide *new* forms of association for city dwellers, but rather an effort to revivify old ones and to plant them in a new urban context.

I have now completed my survey of the three major phases of

philosophers' reflections on urban life: the age of Jefferson, the age of Emerson, and the age of James, Royce, Dewey, and Santayana. My purpose has been exclusively historical, and I hope I have established my historical point, which is that in different ways and in varying degrees American philosophers of very different points of view have been distrustful of, or dismayed by, the American city. It would appear that our nation's philosophical history has been characterized by a persistent distaste for urban life, which has at times been more pronounced than at others. This distaste has been associated in different instances with different kinds of feeling—with a preference for the farmer's life, for the hermit's life, for life in the wilderness, for life in a provincial community, for life in a city rooted in the soil. And where the American city was not condemned or escaped by our philosophers, they made an effort to reform it in a nostalgic spirit.

TRANSCENDING ANTIURBANISM

I conclude with some more general remarks. First of all, I want to point out that the history of the philosophers' reactions to the city is paralleled in other fields of intellectual and literary endeavor: the philosophers have not been idiosyncratic. Secondly, the philosophers' reactions reflect the fact that they—even the youngest of them, Santayana, who was born in 1863—lived the formative years of their lives in a preurban phase of American history. They do not transcend the preurban ethos of their times. Thirdly, we cannot explain the phenomenon in purely ideological terms. Too many different kinds of philosophers have shared similar feelings about the city.

In connection with this last point, one special kind of nonsense must be avoided, and that is the idea that the intellectual critique of the American city may be explained by the allegedly inherent romanticism of the American mind. The fact is that of all our major thinkers only Emerson may be seriously interpreted in this way. Among the philosophical thinkers I have discussed, he alone tied his attack on the city to a romantic ideology in which the wilderness was superior to the artificial city. Jefferson's attitude was more a matter of practical political concern about the impact of urbanization on a democratic rural America, and the attitude of the philosophers following Emerson was also unromantic. Even the idealist Royce spurned the flight to a dream world, and both Dewey and Santayana made their criticism of the American city as *partisans* of civilization rather than as romanticists drugged by the love of untouched Nature. One of the most striking features of the history of intellectual criticism of the American city is the fact that after the Civil War it comes to be made more and more in the name of the civilized values of order, rationality, and communication, and not in the name of the wilderness. The urbanization of the nation after the Civil War brought about a decline of romantic ideology in the highest reaches of our intellectual life. Hence, the city was criticized for reasons that were the very opposite of those advanced by doctrinaire romantics. In the age of transcendentalism the city was too civilized for the intellectuals; in the golden age of American philosophy it was not civilized enough.

When the American city was found wanting by Royce, Dewey, and others who were not gripped by romantic metaphysics, it was criticized on grounds that cannot be brushed aside as the expression of irrational prejudice or metaphysical moonshine. And it is from the very fact that we cannot subsume all the attacks on the city under one alleged trait of the intellectuals, their romanticism, that we may draw hope. We are not all heirs of Natty Bumppo, not all worshipers of the forest. The forces of American intellectual history do not, of themselves, preclude the possibility that intellectuals will create a set of useful ideas for the improvement of the American city. Some day we may have a coherent philosophy of urban life, a philosophy based not on distrust of the American city but rather on affectionate, sympathetic concern for its well-being. In creating such a philosophy we shall demonstrate that we can overcome the persistent strain of antiurbanism in our philosophical tradition from Thomas Jefferson to George Santayana.

Notes

[1] Morton and Lucia White, *The Intellectual versus the City: From Thomas Jefferson to Frank Lloyd Wright* (Cambridge: Harvard University Press and M.I.T. Press, 1962); see also their "The American Intellectual versus the American City," *Daedalus* (Winter 1961), pp. 166–179, reprinted in Lloyd Rodwin ed., *The Future Metropolis* (New York: George Braziller, Inc., 1961), pp. 214–232.

[2] Quoted in Sherman Paul, *Emerson's Angle of Vision: Man and Nature in American Experience* (Cambridge: Harvard University Press, 1952), p. 38.

[3] *Journals of Ralph Waldo Emerson,* E. W. Emerson and W. E. Forbes, eds. (Boston: Houghton Mifflin Company, 1909–1914), V, pp. 310–311; see Paul, *op. cit.,* pp. 79–82.

[4] *The Correspondence of Thomas Carlyle and Ralph Waldo Emerson* (Boston: Houghton Mifflin Company, 1883), I, pp. 269–270.

[5] *The Heart of Emerson's Journals,* Bliss Perry ed. (Boston: Houghton Mifflin Company, 1937), p. 264.

[6] *The Letters of William James,* Henry James ed. (Boston: Little, Brown & Company, 1920), II, p. 90.

[7] Josiah Royce, *Race Questions, Provincialism and Other American Problems* (New York: The Macmillan Company, 1908), p. 73.

[8] Josiah Royce, *The Philosophy of Loyalty* (New York: The Macmillan Company, 1908), p. 239.

[9] Royce, *Race Questions,* pp. 97–98.

[10] *The Philosophy of George Santayana,* P. A. Schilpp ed. (La Salle, Ill.: The Open Court Publishing Company, 1940), pp. 560–561.

[11] George Santayana, *The Middle Span* (New York: Charles Scribner's Sons, Inc., 1945), pp. 25–26.

[12] *Ibid.,* p. 22.

[13] John Dewey, *The Public and its Problems* (New York: Holt, Rinehart and Winston, Inc., 1927), p. 98.

[14] *Ibid.,* p. 219.

The Contributions of Political Science to Urban Form

ROBERT C. WOOD *is Professor of Political Science at Massachusetts Institute of Technology, with particular interests in metropolitan government, federalism and public administration. His numerous writings in these areas are a major contribution to the urban problems field. They include "1400 Governments; the Political Economy of the New York Metropolitan Region"; "Suburbia: its People and their Politics"; and "Metropolis Against Itself." He is a member of the Committee on Urban Economics.*

An assignment to sketch the principal properties of urban politics in the United States today, to outline the ways scholars now observe that process, and to assess its influence on the form of the modern urban community is a challenging task. It is also an embarrassing one, on two grounds. First, what we know about urban politics suggests that its foundations are shaky and tenuous—so much so that the conflicts resolved, or avoided, and the bargains struck in the process have little to do with the character of urban life or with changes in urban form. Second, we do not know, in fact, very much about urban politics. Our generalizations are based on information drawn from a wide variety of sources, using postulates derived from quite different theories of what is relevant and irrelevant, and presuming to deal with phenomena which are assuredly widely different but which we treat in the same framework of analysis.

Within these limits, this paper will stress three themes. Substantively, it will characterize the urban political process as chronically beset with such tensions, conflicts, and diversity of participants as to be always in danger of disintegration and collapse. At least in recent history, but probably throughout our national life, it will be argued, the problem of amassing sufficient power to enable the development and execution of reasonable public policy has never been adequately solved. Hence, the conscious impact of political decisions on the development of urban form has been slight in comparison to other influences. Methodologically, it will immediately qualify that proposition by emphasizing the deficiencies and gaps in scholarly analysis which make students of urban politics constantly walk on eggshells, confront each other with apparently self-contradictory conclusions, and submit conflicting policy recommendations. Finally, it will suggest that the prospects for improving both the conduct of urban public affairs and the reliability of research hinge on a redefinition of the role of the academic community concerned with this problem and its internal organization. Contrary to present proclivities, the rearrangements would place the political scientist closer to the engineer in his profession than to the pure scientist embarked on "basic research."

Lest this point of departure seem unduly dour, let it be emphasized that the approach is relative. Years in a university "polarized around science and technology" sensitize even those of the most humanistic inclination to the exponential cumulation of data in the natural sciences, to the progress that the "hard side" of scholarship has achieved, and to their practical application. When the doubling time of scientific activities—production of Ph.D's, contributions to the literature, research funds, and personnel—occurs every twelve years, while the doubling time in nonscientific activities—the graduation of physicians, clerics, and other "soft-side" personnel, and their output when measurable—is every forty years, and that of the general population, sixty years, one tends toward professional self-

examination. Since an estimated 85–95 percent of all physicists who ever lived are still alive, one is entitled to some sense of anxiety about the onrushing herd.[1] Most important of all, when one reviews the organization, discipline, and process of systematic collaboration which goes on within the scientific and engineering communities, one becomes uneasy as to the performance of one's chosen discipline.

POLITICAL SCIENCE: DESCENT FROM THE PEAKS

It is against this background of the vast acceleration of scientific inquiry in general that the state of knowledge about urban politics in particular should be set. All of us who work in the field (or all in related disciplines who have to estimate the reliability of our findings) must begin with the recognition that the study of urban politics lags far behind the natural sciences in the treatment of the phenomena under observation. It also lags behind other social sciences in their studies of personality, of family behavior, economic behavior, and even of those parts of political science which deal with electoral analysis, the national government, and some parts of international relations.

Why this is so can be set down to three major conditions. First, as a subsection of political science inquiry into urban politics has been caught up in a debate over purposes and methods which has continued for at least a generation and which only now appears to be in part, on point of resolution. Second, within the realm of political science the study of urban politics has shown an unusual proclivity in the twentieth century to select the wrong properties of urban political behavior as relevant for investigation and has thus provided descriptions of manifest, rather than real, forces at work. Third, scholarship in this field has faced special complications and special subtleties. In the broadest sense of the word a comparative study, urban politics, in its original definition as "state and local," involves the comprehension of 212 metropolitan areas, 3047 counties, 34,381 cities and towns, and 54,459 special districts, or one government for each 2000 people and each 40 square miles in the United States. Thus a discipline unsure of its objectives has applied overly simple assumptions to an enormously complex field of investigation in the hope of producing, in some quick and dirty way, satisfactory generalizations for action.

It is true, of course, that the study of politics enjoys a long and distinguished tradition. While economics, sociology, psychology, and anthropology are comparatively recent arrivals on the academic scene, political science traces its heritage back to antiquity. In the past, in method and the substance of its concern, it has had much in common with history and philosophy, though unlike history and philosophy it has rarely been willing to set firm limits on the inferences and conclusions to be drawn from its work. But in an age of analysis, the rich legacy of political science has often seemed to operate as much as a handicap as a resource. To the last two generations of political scientists, at any rate, the question of what to do with their heritage has been a perplexing, recurrent question. Andrew Hacker has summed up the nature of the dilemma in this way:

> For better or for worse the term "political theory" has two quite distinct meanings for contemporary students of politics. It stands first of all for the history of political ideas . . . studied with due regard for historical circumstances which produced them and their influence on political practice. . . . this understanding of political theory is a more traditional of the two and an honorable tradition of scholarships supports it. The other conception of the theory is newer and, in consequence, less sure of its methods and purposes. Nevertheless it can be said that this approach calls for systematic study of political behavior in the modern world . . . sees as its subject the actual behavior of men and institutions in our own time. Systematic theory, then, is concerned to create generalizations which describe and explain contemporary political phenomena. By and large it places great importance on the methods of collecting data, for systematic knowledge must be founded on evidence rather than intuition. On the whole, this approach to theory tries to avoid making value judgments or entering into ethical controversies.[2]

It is not clear at all that these approaches are contradictory or mutually self-exclusive. Indeed, Hacker emphasizes both the empirical basis on which the great political thinkers from Plato to Mill have rested their arguments and the norms implicit in the newer approach as it undertakes to speak to the relevant issues of the day. And certainly methodologically elegant inquiries make little or no contribution if the knowledge they produce can simultaneously be acquired by casual observation, common sense, or cruder methods of inquiry.

But the fact remains, as Daniel Lerner has pointed out, that there is a basic difference between a perspective which emphasizes the dialectic and the systematic interjection of new information into the consideration of relevant propositions.[3] Recurrent themes in political thought there certainly are, each to be set in the circumstances of its own time. But what the circumstances are, how they modify the themes, what light they throw on the latter's viability are increasingly significant considerations and, in the complex world of urban political behavior, vital ones.

Moreover, a sizeable number of political scientists today are persuaded that the potential for identifying relevant circumstances of the environment, for specifying the relevant properties of political behavior, and for modifying that behavior deliberately is vastly greater than ever before. In particular, the increasing sophistication of the attitudinal study and the rapid development of the high-speed computer offer the prospect of testing empirically propositions on a scale and in depth that no other generation of scholars has possessed.

This emerging view of the character of political science suggests a narrowing of the range of concerns, a forswearing of undiluted normative speculation, and a descent from the peaks of political inquiry as the queen of philosophy to the substratum approximating that much maligned and misunderstood calling of "social engineering." There are sacrifices in this reordering, of course. Great names may appear less and less frequently within our ranks; fewer political scientists will sit immediately at the feet of policy makers. But the net result of cumulative knowledge may be something novel in urban politics: The capacity of political action actually to contribute decisively to urban form and to touch more fundamental aspects of urban life. In place of cities built by the Invisible Hand and the occasional esthetic whim of strategically located individuals, there may emerge purposeful public policy which has aspects of rationality and clearer satisfactions of public needs attached to it.

WHAT WE THINK WE KNOW ABOUT URBAN POLITICS

KEY COMPONENTS IN THE PRESENT SYSTEM

With this introduction as to the atmosphere of ferment and revisionism in which the urban political scientist works today, what generalizations can we make about the urban political process? What operating assumptions underlie the research now going on?

An answer to these questions turns, of course, on the definition chosen for "the urban political process." Perhaps the most popular conception of this process today focuses on decision making and decision makers, the choices exercised by political activists to settle, postpone, or bypass public issues in urban life. Here, the characterization is one of actors responding to a diverse set of social, economic, and political pressures, defining objectives, obtaining political influence of various types, striving to increase that influence through its strategic employment in coalition with or in opposition to other political actors in an assortment of arenas. In analyzing behavior in this process, the substance of the issue, and its effect outside the immediate arena, is less important than what happens to the objectives, resources, and relative positions of the participants and how they devise and utilize their strategies.

But we shall have to employ a larger conception of the urban political process if we are to discharge our assignment of linking politics to urban form and political science to its companion disciplines in the social sciences. We need a model that encompasses the decision makers and their activities but goes further to identify the generators of public matters and the consequences of public actions. There must be inputs and outputs related to the urban political process, transformers to channel "pressures" into "decisions," power exchanges coupling choices to programs so that one can fix the boundaries of urban politics in relation to the general process of urbanization and specify the particular variables with which it is concerned.

One way to approach this task is to conceive of the urban political process as a system of some seven identifiable and interlinked components, and then to fashion out of our present knowledge the best propositions we can about their properties. Ideally, any specific impulse ought to be capable of being traced from entrance to exit within the system and its mutations and modifications duly noted. We undertake such a characterization of the system and the propositions about its operations in the next few pages. Thereafter, we may be in the position to inquire what we still need to know and how to go about acquiring the new information.

1. *Urban Social Mobilization.* The designation of this first component is borrowed from our colleagues working with the politics of newly developing areas that are faced with comparative problems resembling our own. In these studies, the concept speaks to the transformation of rural, traditional societies into modern urban ones. So, the investigation focuses on the relationship between the more or less impersonal forces of urbanization and industrialization and resulting social and political attitudes toward change, including the willingness for the newly developing countries to engage in radically new processes of political recruitment and socialization.[4]

The concept has obvious relevance to our own domestic experience: the pressures that urban growth generates on government in terms of resources utilization, and the expectations and attitudes of urban populations toward government. As a starting point for understanding the urban political process at work, one identifies "real needs" that result simply from the interaction of people in a spatial area—the relevance of size, density, and income to the expansion of public services—and also those of a more elusive character where the cultural attributes of the population, their ideology and class structure come into play, and where expectations and values are superimposed on the simpler notion of need.

The distinction among the different categorizations of needs is a critical one, for it performs the functions of comparing characteristics of urban populations with the character of their politics. "Real needs" correspond to the language of economists when they inquire as to indivisible social capital required to support an industrial complex and as they distinguish these requirements from "private wants": streets per houses, water and sanitary facilities per families, hospital beds per 1000 persons. They are the public activities provided in various communities and correlated to various indices of urbanization, regardless of variations in local political patterns, and regardless of whether the activities are actually undertaken by government or not. However calculated, whether or not measurable, these tests are theoretically the prerequisites for organized urban existence. But "real needs" rapidly transform themselves if and as they enter the urban political process. They are capable of many interpretations and reinterpretations before they reemerge in the new wrappings of a "solution" to a public problem.

One proposition about urban social mobilization, close now to tautology, we borrow largely from the economists: *Real needs almost uniformly occasion an expansion in the resources devoted to the public sector, and their magnitude and rate of expansion is related to the environmental characteristics and stage of particular localities involved.* The first part of this proposition has been the acknowledged property of public finance for a century. The second has become clearer and more precise chiefly in the last decade, when the studies in St. Louis, Cleveland, and New York began to disentangle the snarl of correlated variables subsumed under the notion of urbanization. The a priori studies of Walter Isard and Richard Meier further clarify the proposition of "minimized needs" by calculating costs of developing a new urban settlement or maintaining a city above the starvation level.[5]

From the political scientists' point of view, however, a more relevant aspect of the mobilization process is the filter interjected by the perception of needs by political activists and influentials in the body politic. What generates the demand for "quality" in public services and the intercity differentials among apparently like communities, what accounts for the "unexplained" portions of the New York factor analysis, what role do personal or group pressures play when the production of goods and services is removed from the market place? An extreme position here is that of Edward Banfield who argues that the capacity of urban politics to ignore service and policy pressures approaches the infinite:

> The rapid growth of the metropolitan population will not necessarily have much political effect. To be sure, many new facilities, especially schools, highways and water supply and sewage disposal systems, will have to be built and much private activity will have to be regulated. But such things do not necessarily have anything to do with politics . . . Difficulties that are "political" arise (and they may arise in "private" as well as in "public" undertakings) only insofar as there is conflict . . . The general political situation is affected, therefore, not by changes in popula-

tion density or in the number and complexity of the needs that government serves ("persons," the human organisms whose noses are counted by census takers, are not necessarily "political actors") but rather by actions which increase conflicts in matters of public importance or make the management of it more difficult.[6]

One does not have to adopt Banfield's position (indeed one may suspect that the number of people and their density of interaction are importantly and directly associated with the character number and frequencies of conflicts) to recognize the capacity of politics to distort and shift the ordering of priorities of apparently objective needs or to invent new ones of psychic and class character. The stern face which the town fathers of the early American cities turned against the provision of relief, in an industrial age clearly caught up in the business cycle, maintained the ideology of the English poor laws for almost two centuries. Alternatively, the capacity of the latter-day nineteenth- and early twentieth-century boss to focus almost exclusively on welfare activities, although in a highly personalized and selective way led to gross negligence of a wide array of services. For example, Frank Hague's hospital center in Jersey City flourished while other public facilities fell into abandon; but for a time at least, this strategy enhanced Hague's role. Hence, a second proposition: *The urban political process is not directly concerned with the provision of goods and services, except when these "problem solving" activities can be translated into useful resources for the resolution of political conflict or its avoidance, or when, at infrequent intervals, in times of breakdown and emergency, an outright failure of law and order seems imminent* (for example, the Galveston flood and the invention of the Commission form of municipal government). The latter is a critical qualification. Regimes that escape from "objectivity" in the satisfaction of the desires of the actors ultimately collapse in the face of nature.

2. *The Expression of Needs.* An understanding of the subjective dimension in public need leads directly to an exploration of how the needs become articulated or reformulated in terms of goals or objectives. Civic textbooks make the connection almost in terms of a one-to-one correlation of felt needs and instant expression. Our third proposition runs to the contrary: *The great bulk of the urban population neither is conscious of its public needs nor anticipates*

that urban governments will fulfill them. Vast is the violence that has been done to the grass-roots mythology by such studies as Scott Greer's discovery of suburban isolates in St. Louis and Murray Levin's clinical examination of the alienated voter of Boston.[7] True, the axiom may not surprise the close student of local election turnouts, or lack of turnouts. But it substitutes measurable indices of withdrawal for impressionistic descriptions of the average citizen's view of the politician, Nast cartoons, and editorials against apathy.

The Levin formulation of a citizenry that feels powerless, normless, and estranged from the political process makes "need expression" a largely negative affair. Wanting nothing from the government except, perhaps, personal favors, believing themselves incapable of effecting political decisions or the kind of public service offered, the voters withdraw—or never participate in the first place. Popular action, therefore, becomes less and less meaningful in urban politics, and campaign activities less and less reasonable. And these studies are buttressed by the extraordinarily intriguing studies of political socialization in the American public school, which seek to establish at what age and into what groups the air of cynicism seems to set in and the relevant relationship to personality and to family situations.

To posit that a great number of people in an urban population expect nothing of their government, that a few expect everything in terms of personal livelihood, and that the majority become conscious of their expectations only in times of emergency or breakdown may be disillusioning. But it makes more understandable the popular failure to turn out for elections and school referenda, the critical role of communication strategy in the dissemination of information, and the difficulty of devising campaign strategy when voters believe nothing a candidate promises.

Parenthetically, the proposition also secures urban political science's links with psychology and sociology in much the same way as the first two propositions identify our relationship with economics. What it suggests is that the wide gap in the identification of the characteristics of an urban complex and the observable responses of governments as identified by financial indices of "output" is only occasionally explicable in terms of the behavior of the public at large. We need to turn elsewhere to understand the actual workings of urban politics, and to modify the notion of need from one of individual to group interest.

3. *The Effectuation of Responses to Need.* The vacuum of electoral response leads the urban political scientist to that will-o'-the-wisp of urban studies, the composition and characteristics of the urban elite. Here again, present doctrine conflicts with the stereotyped image of urban politics as boss-led or special interest dominated, for the fourth proposition runs: *Perceptions and decisions about public needs are made by highly diverse and segregated power centers, each operating with little relation to, or knowledge of, the other.* This characterization is put forth with considerable diffidence. We have only begun to assemble persuasive evidence on elite structures, and the most probable pattern is hardly a settled matter. Yet, the evidence we have points in this direction. Norton Long has the distinction of first formalizing the theorem in his *Ecology of Games.*[8] But Wallace Sayre, Herbert Kaufman, Robert Dahl, Edward C. Banfield and Frank Mungar have arrived at similar conclusions of many actors, in many arenas, pursuing separate goals in such a way that the total output of one urban political system is a laundry list of diverse items, coming to a total which is never added by a single hand.[9] At least in our larger metropolises, the urban ship of state breaks up into flotsam and jetsam, a highly fragmented series of conflicts, with groups forever assembling, disbanding, and reorganizing.

Quite different judgments as to the desirability of such a scattering of influentials are made by each observer, ranging from applause that from such diversity an open society is nourished at the local level to the conclusion that only nonsense results, since there is little correlation between elite goals and constituency needs, let alone "real needs." But, at present, the general consensus emerges that Lincoln Steffens' one man who "runs things" for better or for worse is replaced by cliques, coteries, and casual coalitions, operating with imperfect information, a high degree of uncertainty, and no fixed channels of either influence or power.

4. *Issue Resolution: The Ordering of "Needs."* If the requirements for maintaining law and order above the minimum for a great number of people engaged in highly specialized personal pursuits and living in relatively densely settled circumstances are obscure, the political outlook of the populace, passive, and their

representation, haphazard and often invisible, how do things happen in urban politics? Who decides what issues become debatable in urban politics, which ones receive priority, and how competing definitions of needs are resolved? Budget processes and formal grants of authority notwithstanding, a fifth proposition stands: *Conflicts are resolved and activities authorized usually on the basis of the lowest common denominator of voluntary assent of the active participants.* In one sense, this rule reestablishes the legal possessor of authority as the actual decision maker, since his is the strategic role of finally legitimizing an acceptable decision. But it makes him a most reluctant dragon. The convergent forces that play upon the official or officials who cannot avoid making decisions, dictate postures of vacillation and postponement as long as possible. Even after the action is taken, there is considerable doubt as to whether the decision will stick. One cluster of evidence here, of course, is the biographies of contemporary strong mayors and supposed shadow bosses, who ten years ago were heralded by the popular press as new urban "leaders." Now Wagner in New York, Daley in Chicago, even Dilworth in Philadelphia, and Lee in New Haven find their crowns tarnished and the manageability of their large enterprises become increasingly dubious. They have vast difficulty in fashioning a political strategy sufficient to maintain public acceptability. And DeSapio disappears, overthrown by a motley assembly of rank amateurs. So, too, the exhaustive comparative studies of George Duggar in the more restricted field of urban renewal reveal a mare's nest over which cautious administrators agonizingly preside.[10]

There are exceptions to the rule, though we are uncertain about their absolute magnitude. A sixth corollary proposition states: *A determined minority in command of its subfield may push its item of public business quickly to the top of the agenda.* So, the new sensitivity to the aspirations of the Negro community in central cities; to suburban organizations sponsoring mental health; or to opponents of what once appeared a routinized technical decision on fluoridation of public water supplies. Here perceived needs, usually in terms of seeking changes in governmental attitudes or ideology, can frequently, in Sayre's words, "energize" officialdom to action. These sudden thrusts may be widespread and it is difficult to predict the circumstances under which they appear. But when they occur, they produce, not generally balanced responses, but makeshift palliative intended to meet immediate demands, rather than provide long-run solutions. They tend to deflect conflict and to obscure problems—not to resolve them.

5. *Issue Validations: The Role of Institutions and Authority.* A "treading water" characterization of minimal response to conflict, arising from urbanization and the rapid ballooning of programs where consensus among the prime actors can most easily be achieved, raises the question of the relevance of structures and organization in urban government. A few years ago, many political scientists were on the verge of dismissing institutional analysis as irrelevant. Now, questions of institutional organization are dealt with increasingly in terms of the resources, strategy, and tactics they make available to the elite groups and the decision makers. Who is advantaged or disadvantaged by the strong-mayor form of government? What minorities have an opportunity to express their needs in a fragmented pattern of urban government and what minorities in a centralized one? What is the function of various kinds of elections in recruiting various kinds of people, and what do particular offices offer for the advancement of individual political careers? Charles Adrian's exploration of city manager governments suggests, for example, the interjection of strong institutional biases in favor of business, and middle-class definitions of needs and requirements; a contrary influence is often attributed to the mayoralty office in large cities.[11] Hence, the seventh proposition: *Governmental form is less related to the execution of tasks or provision of services than it is to the distribution of resources and means of access to decision making by elite groups.*

But organizational arrangements of a purely local nature do not exhaust the field, and political scientists have been increasingly dissatisfied with descriptions of the relevant institutions which operate in an urban area as those constitutionally defined as municipal in nature. The participation of state highway departments, the federal Bureau of Public Roads, the Housing and Home Finance agency, the Department of Defense in many urban fields—and the ever present "authority"—now parallels the customary local units of government. Their modes of behavior have to be described in terms largely unrelated to local constituency and local elites. So, an eighth proposition: *The urban political process is further interrupted and focused on separate substantive concerns by the interjection of higher levels of government chiefly through interbureaucratic negotiations.*

6. *Externalized Relations: The Metropolitan Dimension of Urban Politics.* The diffusion of jobs and households beyond the boundaries of the core city and the development of suburban political consciousness further complicate the process of the articulation, formulation, and expression of "need" in policy terms—and the task of analysis for the political scientist. Though our information about suburban political behavior remains impressionistic and at times contradictory, the following propositions are now current in the field.[12] Nine: *By reason of size and homogeneity, the suburban political process submits much more readily to the rule of an elite or a few elites.* Ten: *Participation or nonparticipation by the suburban public is more the result of satisfaction and civic consciousness than it is of alienation or frustration. The act of participation, however, may bear little relation to "needs," real or perceived.* Eleven: *The needs felt by suburbanites or recognized by their elite are for the most part capable of being resolved within their own political boundaries.* Therefore, proposition twelve: *The resolution of area-wide conflicts rarely takes place because the issues have no arenas in which to be raised.* Minimum "real need" requirements are met in ways (for example, authorities) which are structured to preclude conflict.[13] Attempts to articulate "metropolitan needs" are undertaken by self-appointed elites rarely possessing power resources of votes, money, or strategic positions.[14]

These characterizations of suburban behavior as essentially self-conscious isolation were probed in some depth recently by Bradbury Seasholes in the Boston area. His findings, based on leadership interviews in sixteen of that city's sixty-five suburbs, revealed the absence of a metropolitan outlook not so much as a matter of conscious, parochial separatism—ignorance of or unwillingness to deal with more general affairs—as it was a result of absence of opportunity and motivation for involvement and the high cost in time and effort of such a concern. The chief links with affairs of other communities appeared to be by joint use of scarce professional talents (planners) and an occasional seeking of abundant outside advice (professors). Those suburbs most disposed to consider the larger region had the highest incomes and were located the farthest distance from the central city—presumably attributes permitting some objectivity.[15]

7. *Consequences and Output.* Given the diffuse character of urban politics and the potential for irrational behavior, it has been fashionable in recent years for political scientists to deprecate attempts to build links between the urban political process and the social and economic repercussions which it occasions. Perhaps as an ultrasensitive reaction against a treatment of urban politics as the black box that receives problems and produces solutions and in an effort to emphasize the equilibrium function of political systems—the capacity to preserve a modicum of social stability and build consensus rather than to solve the problems—many political scientists prefer not to link political decisions to changes of economic and social systems. Nonetheless, the magnitude of the resources urban governments now command and the range of their clientele suggest some interconnection as inevitable. A thirteenth proposition, to end our list on an ominous note: *Program expansion of urban governments is initiated from without the system* (that is, federal or state sources) *or by highly mobilized elite groups successful in separating their activities from the process* (for example, schools). *Other outputs of regulatory or policy nature* (Miami Metro or New Haven renewal) *are random.*

The burden of the argument here is that federal and state assistance programs augment the resources of local participants active in these particular endeavors and relieve the budgetary and administrative ordeals of the presiding officials. Similarly, school programs and the activities of the authorities feature self-contained systems capable of defining needs and supplying their own resources. But, dramatic breakthroughs, like a major reorganization or a renewal program, are more likely to be the result of accident, not design. They are not the creature of a conscious effort by a powerful coalition; they are uncalculated occurrences of an improbable but possible convergence of forces in temporary agreement.

Taken together, these thirteen propositions about the properties of the main components of the urban political system suggest that the total system is characterized by (1) a substantial divorce from the process of social mobilization as it produces ''real needs'' occasioned by interaction of people in space—that is, it functions only minimally to ''solve problems'' except the most routine ones;

(2) on the part of the public, indifference to, at best, or frustration by, at worst, the operations of the system; (3) incapacity on the part of active participants to coalesce in meaningful power centers; (4) a disposition on the part of authority wielders to seek automatic or voluntary resolution of conflict rather than actively to secure settlement; (5) the use of institutions to raise issues rather than to settle them; (6) the creation of new power centers across the metropolitan terrain faster than the merger or regularizing of relations among old ones; (7) an increasing disposition of the system's output to be a function of stimuli from outside its own boundaries. In short, compared to criteria which suggests that government normally possesses qualities of purposefulness, rationality, regularized processes, and the power for the deliberate resolution of issues and conflicts, urban politics is devoid of most of the properties of a manageable enterprise.

Note that these observations carry no implications about what the urban political process ought to produce, or how it should go about transforming the inputs of social mobilization. Their criteria are the much simpler ones of a well-constructed system, whatever it turns out: What is its efficiency ratio, the results achieved for energy expended? How much power is effectively applied and how much wasted? How well-engineered are the parts for the functions they perform? It is the question of system design and operation which concerns us here, not disputations on ultimate purpose.

Yet, even with these limitations, the characterization remains only what we *think* we know about urban politics, a rash summary of the concepts and hypotheses a good number of political scientists might be ready to accept. What do we actually know about the system in the sense that if we undertook to apply the model to a given area there would be a high probability that we would find data conforming to our specifications? Here we are on shaky ground. Only two foundations seem secure: that older models are demonstrably unsatisfactory and that some versions of the new model, properly applied, make no impossible demands on methodology and data collection.

WHAT WE KNOW NOW

1. THE COLLAPSE OF THE CLASSIC MODEL

When we say that old ways of looking at urban politics no longer work, we are suggesting, again in an engineering analogy, that students selected the wrong "signals" for analysis out of the many discordant "noises" the system produces. Either they filtered out signals of obvious political power manifestations to the exclusion of those constraining or disrupting power, or they chose spurious signals that provided an apparent explanation of behavior but did not touch more fundamental variables—and therefore proved incapable of manipulation. Two recent research memoranda—that of Wallace Sayre and Nelson Polsby, undertaken for the Social Science Research Council, and that prepared by Delos D. Hughes, for the Urban Studies Program at Chapel Hill—summarize brilliantly the deficiencies of studies of Bryce, Steffens, and the successive waves of municipal reformers.[16] Their bibliographical and critical reviews will not be repeated here, though they are required reading for anyone wishing to trace the history of research in urban politics to its present state of development. But it is important to describe the two critical errors—the attribution of real power to the total system, and the essential superficiality of the properties examined on many occasions.

The Muckrakers were primarily guilty of the first error. Though they provide some of the most realistic literature in urban history, essentially their focus was narrow and their approach episodic.[17] Their attention was almost exclusively on the nomination, election, and reelection process and the circumstances necessary for effective boss rule. But the facts about the exercise of political power once amassed, the sharp limits to the kinds of activity local governments undertook and their generally weak response to the pressures of the day were scarcely touched on at all. Carl Bridenbaugh, Arthur Schlesinger, Sr., and Oscar Handlin put the role of urban politics in vivid perspective in their contrast of the mounting tide of immigration and the growing conditions of social and physical disorder with the puny responses of the political system.

But power, in the eyes of the Muckrakers, seems finally to have been defined as the capacity of the politicians of the day to depart in their personal behavior from middle-class norms, not in their capacity to resolve conflicts, make substantive decisions, or use governing powers in any systematic way. And, in careless interpretations, this definition of power as the management of the political organization was transformed into an all-inclusive image of a tightly controlled, closely directed, self-sustaining enterprise across the entire range of urban politics. So, our backward glances at urban political history now often posit a stable equilibrium of town fathers succeeded by immigrant bosses in league with shady business interests, which, in fact, was continually being undone by the pressures of growth and the intrusion of new participants and new interests. James Curley now appears in fiction as a boss, though his bases of support were shifting and unreliable, his relations within the Boston Democratic organization competitive and insecure, and his concerns with the conduct of his offices, negligible.

The error of reformist analysis was not that it failed to be broad, but that its methods of procedure in data assembly and its assumptions were heavily ideological in bias. The reformers were intent on making a case, and their approach resembled that of a lawyer. Thus, they rarely paused to test a priori beliefs by the noises the system was emitting. Their descriptions of each of our prime components bear testimony to their limitations.

So far as the definitions of needs or values are concerned, the reformers, from Bryce through the major metropolitan studies of the fifties, never conceived that there was any real question of the needs that a municipality existed to fulfill or of the values it chose to guard. In the classic phrase of Charles Taft there were "no Republican or Democratic ways to pave the street"; many a political scientist accepted this proposition of an urban government as a bundle of services derived from impersonal indices of urban mobilization as proposed by functional specialists.

With needs treated as a priori items incapable of being tampered with (at least in any legitimate fashion), no allowance was made for the filter process of either the constituency or the elites. From objective standards of service, one moved to a definition of the constituency as composed of active, interested citizens capable of rational behavior concerned about the affairs of the city, and willing to accept some generalized definition of the public interest.

Nor was the concept of an elite either formulated or looked for.

The influentials in the classic model were uniformly the publicly elected officials or the "best citizens." All others—bosses, immigrants, bookies—once discovered, were rejected as exogenous factors, introduced from some obscure source and required to be removed to prevent the malfunctioning of the system.

In such a framework, issues were related to simple honesty or dishonesty—indicators of the deviations from appropriate behavior. Institutions were accorded a majestic, almost magical role. Properly structured and properly developed, they were presumed to have a strange feedback effect of cleansing the system of the distorted influences of boss-led minorities and restoring the "real needs" as the generators of political activities. The emergence of the suburban and exurban clusters in the urban region with their characteristics of escape, of status, and psychological identity were summarily dealt with as so many units of government, so many duplicatory services and facilities, so many overlapping bureaucracies, so many separate tax levies and budgets which again prevented "efficient" functioning. The outputs of the system were simple: not the residue of bargains drawn up among groups with different values and different needs but the social capital required to allow the American economic system to perform its production and distribution functions.[18]

In the end, then, the observations which earlier urban political scientists chose to make were formalistic, categorical, and often norm-laden. The point is not that these noises did not exist, nor that in one way or another they have to be comprehended. The point is that they were essentially the ideological banners of one group of participants in the urban political process of the time, mistakenly paraded as systematic analysis.

One should not write off this analysis in terms of simple derogation. Faced with awesome choices and an abundance of material, few resources, and little time, the early students took what observations they could and fashioned them into an explanation of behavior of urban politics. That their observations are not now substantiated is largely a function of time, of more resources, of improved research aids. At a minimum, the history of the study of local politics provides us all now with a clearer understanding of where not to look and with the obligation to fit early observations into a more generalized and more accurate scheme. The performance raises, too, the question as to the relevance of the observer-actor role, a dual assignment treated with suspicion today, and to which we return later.

2. *RECONNAISSANCE FORAYS AND FLANK ATTACKS*

What reasons do we have to suppose that the signals that students of urban politics now select from noises are more reliable than those of their predecessors? Why accept our new formulations or suppose that political science is not still engaged in the process of endlessly raking coals of old fires?

The quick answer is that there is little basis for accepting the propositions as valid in their present form; much, for utilizing them as a basis now for calculated exploration. If the past ten years have seen the elaboration of new hypotheses, concepts, and perspectives, they have seen painfully little testing of the new approach on a basis that permits valid inferences. Somewhat maliciously, we have trod on the ruins of past scholarship, but our positive production remains scanty, and turned out at enormous expense. Thus, the reliability of our present knowledge turns on our capacity to solve some stubborn methodological problems and to expand considerably the scope of our empirical testing.

As to the methodological problems, quickly glided over in earlier sections, they run as follows:

1. *Urban Mobilization.* We have made substantial progress in the perfection of mathematical and statistical techniques suitable for display as the association among the dimensions of the community environment and governmental financial series, although problems in time-series and classification remain. But, existing procedures still pay too little attention to the roles that human perception and political manipulation play to distort and alter relationships. How to come to grips with the phenomenon of "raising expectations," how to deal with needs the census statistical series do not report, and how to anticipate new needs and new programs are most immediate problems.

Here, the work of William B. Storm and Wallace H. Best in Los Angeles dealing with measurement of public awareness of urban problems through carefully designed survey techniques, particularly in the development of an "apathy index," has opened up new lines of exploration.[19] The inverse relation between low visibility of services like fire and police and high satisfaction with them on the part of the public provides a provocative clue as to how to distinguish between settled needs and emerging ones that partake of conflict, and alternative means of resolution by different cities. This more systematic advance over the adventurous work of Thorndike and Simons in the thirties gives promise that we can interpret mathematical results with new perception and that we can broaden the array of indices that are measurable.

2. *Expression of Needs.* To know that the public has attitudes on some services is comforting, but to probe its willingness to express them actively and with some optimism requires survey work of a different nature. Greer, Levin, and others have, after all, made only isolated forays and one is entitled to wonder if the picture is so black, say, in Milwaukee, San Francisco, or Baltimore. In this area, the possibility of combining attitudinal studies with computer simulation, inquiring what the public would do and how different groups of voters might respond, shines brightest. Conditional formulation of questions and then computer calculations of the resulting attitudes of different alternatives offer, perhaps, the first major occasion for urban political scientists to use the machines to their fullest capacity. But we have scarcely begun research in this direction.

3. *Effectuation of Responses.* Studies of the elite bubble now with alarms and excursions, mostly between the sociologist and the new community specialist in urban politics. Sayre and Polsby have brilliantly traced the running controversy of the last decade whether a "general" elite rules in its own interests or a more fragmented pattern is more typical; there is little call to review their findings here. Suffice it to say, after five years of probing in widely separated areas, we have developed a highly refined theory of actors, resources, roles, strategies, and rules. Now the need is to relate the studies to some typology of communities so that our generalizations have a broader base of support than the cities in which the leading researchers happen to reside. Robert Salisbury, in an earlier critique of this paper, has suggested how the task might be tackled with more precision and more utility than we have managed up to now. He proposes that we compare variations in the power of governmental officials to reallocate resources with variations in (1) the

formal centralized authority of the officials, (2) their electoral security, (3) their technical skills, and (4) the configuration of group support of and opposition to the officials and the proposed resource reallocation. And Salisbury argues persuasively that the payoff will come with a more adequate understanding of the last category. Not until we can relate the kind and magnitude of group support necessary to effect a given amount of reallocation on a comparative basis, he believes, can we have meaningful answers to the implications of different patterns of power structures.

4. *Issue-resolution and Issue-validation Research.* Studies of elites, by extending observations through the process of examining actual decisions, have subsumed, for the most part, research on resolution and validation of issues. Theoretically, we encounter little difficulty in viewing officials and institutions as participants in the game, and some of our most important propositions are found in this area. But our method remains the episodic, expensive, and debatable case study, which continually raises issues of coverage and implementation. In competent literary hands, the case study can always refute an overly enthusiastic generalization. But, its capacity to advance positive knowledge and to build new generalizations on the present opportunistic basis by which cases are selected remains sharply limited.

We need here to begin to categorize types of decisions and develop a shorthand for identifying relevant participants and outcomes so that we can begin to catalogue the growing store of cases. ''Differentiation of pluralistic decision-making'' is the most common way of phrasing this objective.[20]

5. *Externalized Relations.* Methodological opportunities in suburbs are perhaps as great as in any subfield in political science. The possibility of skillful manipulation of public opinion polls and electoral behavior and financial statistics improve as our more precise classification of a typology of suburbs progresses. What the suburban mosaic offers to the political scientist is a chance to abandon the case study (almost inevitable in central city research), and to deal with suburban political behavior on a more probabilistic basis. By describing suburban units according to a few indices of both environmental and attitudinal dimensions and then going on to rank, categorize, sort, and re-sort their behavior, we should be able

to make proper samples of the largest universe afforded to the political scientist.[21]

6. *Outputs and Consequences.* Finally, we move now to join forces with our colleagues in planning. If more political scientists can be persuaded to abandon the view that their findings should have few consequences for social and economic systems, they acquire the opportunity to participate in pragmatic and policy-making concerns, to investigate the conflicts inherent in managing development, in guiding industrial location, in subdivision control, and in renewal of the core city. This is, in effect, the "politics of change," and here our understanding of the nature of urban renewal or the process by which the mass developer overruns the rural community is the least satisfactory of all. Why, for example, do the politics of highways produce "solutions," or at least action, while the politics of urban renewal tend to lag considerably behind; why are planners so far removed, usually, from sources of influence; what is the political implication of the new immigrants, Negro and southern white, to the central city and their pressures outward? These are questions which we have scarcely begun to tackle.

FILLING THE GAPS

1. *A MORATORIUM ON THEORY*

A review of research needs and problems promises excitement and progress in the years ahead, but it underscores the slender bases on which our present understanding of urban politics rests. What we do *not* want to study is fairly clear at the present time. How we proceed in the immediate future is also a subject of some consensus. But the gaps in our knowledge are awesome, and the catalogue of research needs grows every day. If the ten years which have just passed have seen the reformation of doctrine, they have also opened up a vast horizon of facts that we should, but do not, possess.

In these circumstances, where the elbow room for speculative thinking is still substantial and appealing and the methodology and data-gathering problems sticky and grubby, the temptation is strong to continue the research strategy of reconnaissance and selective inquiry. Our most recent literature displays a strong preference to search for refinements in theory that make propositions self-evident or capable of easy generalization. The emerging spectacle of multiple power centers, the continuing disintegration of governmental capacity to move towards solutions in important public policy areas, the day-to-day, busy-day, atmosphere in which urban politicians wallow, striving desperately to build some kind of popular reputation but avoiding the effort to solve problems, make it open season for impressionistic, intuitive, and derisive commentary. Such an appraisal of the urban political scene establishes the role of the observer as superior and comforting. So much variety, so many actors, so large a stage, so many touches of irony and comedy delight the clever and aggressive academic. They are grist for his mill; they provide selective analogies for new game theories; they offer a richness of comparisons of extremes never before available.

But the temptation of more theory should be resisted, at least until we work through the round of present hypotheses. The need now is to steel ourselves to more disciplined scholarship. Actors, resources, motivations, goals, arenas, strategies are perfectly acceptable points of departure for examining the internal workings of a city's politics. Suburban behavior viewed as a process of jostlings and maneuvers among domestic principalities provides an adequate framework for the assembly of available data. The whole can fit reasonably well in some ecology of games. But, if we continue to dabble at the edges, we will find ourselves with enough knowledge to know that old answers are not adequate, but with not enough information either to end a dialectic or to provide reasonable policy suggestions that might significantly change the current state of affairs. And that, it should be recalled, is precisely the basis for distinguishing between high-status and low-status sciences.

2. *URBAN OBSERVATORIES*

How do we test, in a way that allows us to move forward in resolving current methodological problems and provides a rapid, reliable feedback for the refinement and modification of theory? Obviously, not on a particularistic, individualistic basis that delights in the use of the old logical proposition that a single contrary fact destroys a carefully advanced theorem. Some notion of a collective enterprise has to be introduced into the ranks of urban political scientists.

One way to approach the problem is to reconsider the role of university centers of research in urban affairs, and the current practice of foundation grants to particular cities and for individual proposals of individual scholars in the hopes of immediate, "demonstration" payoffs. In this reconsideration, a useful analogy may be with the field stations, data centers, and observatories that natural scientists employ. With an agreed upon set of tools, an accepted field of observation, a common understanding of the phenomena to be observed, these institutions work together to build a cumulative record. It does not seem too far-fetched to suggest this procedure in our present research.

How would these observatories operate? Principally by making a common series of investigations under a single research plan which for the first time would provide us with professionally reliable findings simultaneously in a number of areas. Consider the possible benefits that might have been achieved if the same format for the study of New York City had been applied to Chicago, or that of St. Louis, undertaken in San Francisco. Think what might have happened if the same set of questionnaires (for all their limitations) administered to some 300 leaders in the Boston suburbs over the last two years had had their counterpart in the Cleveland, Kansas City, and Tulsa areas. Conceive of a set of reports periodically bringing together decisions in urban renewal on the same basis that integration conflicts are now analyzed throughout the South. Suppose the new Minnesota study of urbanization had been carried forth in the same framework as that of the New York Metropolitan Region. Suppose the Houston and Syracuse investigations had utilized a single research frame; or that a sample of different sized urban regions with different economic mixes now generated, not a single, but continuing reports over time.

THE POTENTIAL OF A NEW APPROACH

What would we gain by reorganizing our research efforts along the lines just suggested and by less reliance on piecemeal and sporadic data assembly? For one thing, there should be an increasing disposition to report negative results. One principal distinction between the social and natural sciences today is the latter's capacity to indicate what explorations have proven fruitless and what experiments should not be undertaken again. Steps like these contribute a focus and a commitment of energies to a single research objective, such as the massive coordinate effort which the International Geophysical Year represented. With the vastly expanded terrain that urban political scientists have to investigate, the more we can avoid dissipation and duplication of effort, the better off we are.

Second, a common agenda and a common system of reporting would allow us to tap resources not now available. The young instructor at the small college would provide observations, analysis, and findings which would add importantly to the extension of our knowledge. They would also allow him a constructive opportunity in scholarship not now available, and permit other research than the exercise of literary ingenuity. The few efforts political science in general has undertaken in this direction—the study of presidential nominating politics and the compilation of national election statistics—have paid dividends in the finding of talent as well as the ordering of data.

Third, more coordinate efforts might bring the resources necessary to pay for the tools we need to use now. A simulation of urban traffic flow that demonstrates the effect of different strategies for moving traffic on the transportation system capacity, and which also indicates the attitudes of elites and voters alike respecting each strategy—before any one is executed—seems now a feasible undertaking. Its potential for demonstrating to cautious elites how they may be leaders without political danger appears sizeable. The funds required to develop and perfect such a simulation, however, are available only in the largest of foundations or in government agencies. Yet, given a place as an item on a national research agenda, this simulation could be completed in one year.

Fourth, and perhaps most important, the research regrouping of urban political science might help to end the disturbing controversy about the appropriate behavior of the professions in their research and policy roles. Sayre, Polsby, and Hughes are not alone in their severe criticism of the earlier generation of municipal reformers for posing as ''social engineers.'' The last two Syracuse seminars on metropolitan research reported a continuing debate on whether scholars can advise as well as observe policymakers, and still maintain their integrity.

The question was posed as if there were a choice. Again, the contrast with the ''hard side'' of scientific endeavor is instructive. Natural scientists defend strenuously their right to engage in basic research, unfettered by the issue of relevance. But few seem to doubt for the moment that there *will* be a practical effect; that what Robert Oppenheimer has called the ''ennobling'' and the ''utilitarian'' purposes of scientific inquiry are ultimately joined; and that calculated manipulation of the natural universe will result. When we have enough to say in urban politics about actual behavior, then the possibilities of manipulation and development will become clearer. It is only when advice proceeds from ignorance, half truths, ill-understood diagnoses that the charge of charlatanism arises. One does not avoid involvement in the real affairs of the world by honest inquiry. One becomes inevitably caught up in the enterprises men care about.

To reinstate the role of policy advice and cool the controversy over professional integrity does not mean that the urban political scientist emerges as the bearer of panaceas and all-purpose plans for reforms. If the last decade has made any contribution in this respect it has not been to indicate the clear policy alternatives which lie before us but to emphasize the difficulty in finding any realistic alternatives at all. The postresearch experiences in St. Louis and Cleveland reflect the fate of major proposals for reordering urban government and politics. The ways we proceed will more likely be by discovering the possibilities for incremental advances in assembling political power at the urban level and for bringing together greater—but not great—coalescences of authority, and improvements in communication. It is the exploration of these far more limited choices which promises real comfort to ourselves and the policy makers.

But the end purpose remains the production of knowledge and then reflection as to how it may bear on the issues of the day. If we are right in our present supposition that the foundations of urban politics have always been weak and are in the process of further dissolution, that most Americans are likely to live out their everyday lives under circumstances of disorder, confusion, temporizing, and indecision, then the need to know enough to act increases in direct proportion. With the present urban political process requiring management, we should not view our prospects for gaining more information in monistic terms nor confuse conscious policy making with manipulation and manufactured consent. The world of learning and reason has always been the source of providing notions about "a better way out" since the process of building urban civilization began. It ought to continue to serve the same function, all the more so as our capacity to know, to establish, to demonstrate, and to prove increases rapidly over time.

Notes

[1] Walter A. Rosenblith, "On Some Social Consequences of Scientific and Technological Change," *Daedalus* 90:3 (Summer 1961), pp. 510–517.

[2] Andrew Hacker, *Political Theory: Philosophy, Ideology, Science* (New York: The Macmillan Company, 1961), p. vii.

[3] Daniel Lerner, *The Human Meaning of the Social Sciences* (New York: Meridian Books, Inc., 1959), Preface.

[4] James S. Coleman, Gabriel A. Almond, Lucian Pye, and Carl Deutsch are among those who have pioneered in this field. See, for example, Almond and Coleman, eds., *The Politics of Developing Areas* (Princeton, N.J.: Princeton University Press, 1960).

[5] Of the many sources in the literature of local public finance, the most relevant summarizing pieces can be found in Werner Hirsch's contribution in John Bollens, ed., *Exploring the Metropolitan Community* (Berkeley: University of California Press, 1961); Seymour Sacks and William F. Hellmuth, Jr., *Financing Government in a Metropolitan Area* (New York: The Free Press of Glencoe, 1961); Walter Isard, *Methods of Regional Analysis* (New York: John Wiley & Sons, Inc., jointly with Technology Press, M.I.T., 1960); Jesse Burkhead, "Metropolitan Area Budget Structures and Their Significance for Expenditures," *Proceedings of the National Tax Association*, 1959, pp. 279–295; and Dick Netzer's "Financial Needs and Resources Over the Next Decade: State and Local Governments," *Public Finance: Needs, Sources and Utilization* (Princeton, N.J.: Princeton University Press, 1961).

[6] Edward C. Banfield, "The Political Implications of Metropolitan Growth," *Daedalus* 90:1 (Winter 1961), p. 67.

[7] See Greer's paper on the Metropolitan Community prepared for the 1961 Syracuse Seminar on Metropolitan Research, and Murray B. Levin, *The Alienated Voter: Politics in Boston* (New York: Holt, Rinehart and Winston, 1960).

[8] Norton E. Long, "The Local Community as an Ecology of Games," *American Journal of Sociology,* LXIV (November 1958), pp. 251–261.

[9] Wallace S. Sayre and Herbert Kaufman, *Governing New York City: Politics in the Metropolis* (New York: Russell Sage Foundation, 1960); Robert Dahl, *Who Governs?* (New Haven: Yale University Press, 1961); Edward C. Banfield, *Political Influence* (New York: The Free Press of Glencoe, 1961). For an extensive bibliography of periodical literature, see Wallace Sayre and Nelson Polsby memorandum on research in urban politics, undertaken for the Social Science Research Council (Summer 1961), footnotes 21 and 22. See also, David B. Truman, "Theory and Research on Metropolitan Political Leadership: Report on a Conference," S.S.C.C., *Items,* 15 (March 1961).

[10] George A. Duggar, "A Framework for the Analysis of Urban Redevelopment Policies: Some Financial Factors in Local Programs and Some Implications," *Papers and Proceedings of the Regional Science Association,* 2 (1952).

[11] Charles Adrian, "A Typology of Non-Partisan Elections," *Western Political Quarterly* (June 1959), pp. 449–458, as well as an unpublished paper by Duane Lockard, "On Non-Partisan Elections," (1960); C. A. Harrell and D. G. Weidford, "The City Manager and the Policy Process," *Public Administration Review* (Spring 1959), pp. 101–107; and Adrian *et al.*, "Leadership and Decision-Making in Manager Cities: A Study of Three Communities," *Public Administration Review* 3 (Summer 1958), pp. 208–213.

[12] Fred I. Greenstein and Raymond E. Wolfinger, "Suburbs and Shifting Party Loyalties," *Public Opinion Quarterly,* XXII (Winter 1958), pp. 473–482 vs Jerome C. Manis and Leo C. Stine, "Suburban Residence and Political Behavior," *Public Opinion Quarterly,* XXII (Winter 1958), pp. 483–489.

[13] Robert C. Wood, *1400 Governments,* (Cambridge: Harvard University Press, 1961), Chap. 5.

[14] Greer, *op. cit.*

[15] Bradbury Seasholes, *Boston Political Atlas,* Falk research memorandum, mimeo., M.I.T., 1961.

[16] Sayre and Polsby, *op. cit.*, and Delos D. Hughes, "Research in Urban Politics," (Chapel Hill: May, 1961).

[17] Sayre and Polsby, *ibid.*, pp. 1–12; Hughes, *loc. cit.*, pp. 1–4.

[18] J. R. Herson, "The Lost World of Municipal Government," *American Political Science Review,* 51 (June 1957), pp. 330–345.

[19] William B. Storm and Wallace H. Best, "Public Awareness of Metropolitan Problems: Some Survey Research Estimates," *Metropolitan California: Papers Prepared for the Governor's Commission on Metropolitan Area Problems,* (Sacramento: 1961).

[20] Sayre and Polsby, *op. cit.*, pp. 26–27.

[21] Cf., Charles S. Liebman, "Functional Differentiation and Political Characteristics of Suburbs," *American Journal of Sociology,* 67 (March 1961), or Wood, *op. cit.*

Urban Government Services and Their Financing

WERNER Z. HIRSCH *is Professor of Economics at Washington University, St. Louis, Missouri, and Director of its Institute for Urban and Regional Studies, which is engaged in research on a variety of phases of urban life and form. He is chairman of the Committee on Regional Accounts and member of the Committee on Urban Economics of Resources For The Future; has been a consultant on national and regional economic affairs for numerous private and governmental agencies. His frequent books and articles are directed to both the professional and layman with national, regional, and urban economic interests.*

The cities and metropolitan areas have only very recently commanded the economist's attention but the challenge and interest of their complex affairs have rapidly increased concern with urban economics. In response to the urgent need for analyses as instruments for progress, Resources For The Future, with the financial assistance of the Ford Foundation, established the Committee on Urban Economics. This committee has subsequently identified five major areas of interest.[1]

The first area is referred to as Structure and Growth: National-Regional Structural Relations and Metropolitan Economic Growth. It is concerned with the total array of those producing and consuming activities carried on in our urban communities that determine their character and growth. Its further interest extends to the economic relationships among cities and between them and the rest of the world.

A second area, Intrametropolitan Organization and Change, centers on the distribution and organization of population and economic activities in the various parts of the urban region. At one extreme, it is concerned with the factors that influence the location decisions of firms and individuals or households within the region. At the other, it encompasses the problems of servicing these great spatial concentrations of people, buildings, and activities through transportation and utility systems, etc., and the influence of public and private decisions on the form of the metropolis.

The Economics of Urban Human Resources is the third area. The urban population is considered in its dual role of producer and consumer, and much interest focuses on the way in which urbanites carry out these functions within urban institutions. Of particular interest are the processes, institutions, and structure of urban labor markets, the migration to, from, within, and between urban areas, and the urban aspects of the patterns of group discrimination in the urban economy.

The fourth area is Regional Accounts. It is concerned with the development of an analytical framework and data-flow systems that can facilitate private and public decisions on the urban scene.

Finally, the Committee on Urban Economics has identified a fifth area, Urban Government Finance and Welfare. Urban governments perform a variety of services and are responsible for maintaining an environment within which a viable and efficient urban economy can function. It is this area with which we will be concerned here.

The economist is basically concerned with the allocation of scarce resources among competing ends. Whether the ends should be met by the private or public sector depends largely on the philosophy of the people and the nature of the goods to be produced. While it is not easy to gauge public sentiment precisely, it appears that in the United States, where we have a mixed economy, the government sector should perform only those functions that cannot be provided effectively by the private sector.

In many respects, this essay might be considered a sequel to Robert

C. Wood's in this book. It will concentrate on only four major issues of urban government finance; all are closely related and urban observatories can play a key role in each of the four.

One important issue centers around the nature of public goods and their pricing. Another relevant issue in a mixed economy is government's main function, namely, to create an environment conducive to efficient and desirable private economic activity. Thus, it might be said that urban government activities are not ends in themselves. Instead, they are the means toward the creation of an appropriate environment for private decisions. In line with this view of urban government, we shall contruct a generalized decision-making model.

A society that relies on a federated political and fiscal system cannot avoid a large number of governmental units. While it is the political scientist who is mainly concerned with this problem, the economist also has a substantial interest. Intergovernmental relations in urban areas can lead to efficiency or waste, equal or unequal treatment of citizens, lack of funds and thus inadequate services, or high service levels. Because of these considerations, a section will be devoted to a discussion of intergovernmental relations in urban areas, with particular emphasis on their fiscal aspects.

Finally, a person-parcel framework will be developed particularly appropriate for decision making relative to urban areas and for the efficient operation of governments. There are many other issues that loom large in the financing of urban governments, for example, types of taxes that are being used or that might be used, the demand and supply of urban government services, the problems of measuring urban government service levels. We shall not be able to explore these questions here, although they are important.

Before examining certain aspects of urban government finance, the magnitude of the task governments face in rendering services to urban America should be indicated. But we have very few relevant statistics that pertain to urban government services. For example, we have no way of knowing how much governments spend in serving urban America. For this reason, we shall try to present certain recent information that indirectly sheds light on the financing task and tax resources of governments servicing the urban population in general and metropolitan areas in particular.

The 1960 Census of Population found nearly two thirds of the entire population of the United States residing within metropolitan areas—112.9 million persons of the nationwide total of 179.3 millions.[2] Metropolitan areas account for more than two thirds of the population in seventeen out of the fifty states; for one half to two thirds, in another nine states. The entire District of Columbia is part of the Standard Metropolitan Statistical Areas; more than 85 percent of the people in the states of California, Rhode Island, New York, and Massachusetts live in SMSA's. The metropolitan areas are growing more rapidly than any other sector of the United States. The 212 areas recognized in 1960 as "metropolitan" accounted for 84 percent of the increase in the nation's population during the last decade and in the one previous, for 80 percent.

Recent trends and current developments suggest that within another two decades, by 1980, the United States will have a population of 260 million persons, with approximately three fourths of this number residing in metropolitan areas—that is, more than 190 million persons.

Metropolitan areas of the United States account for a major portion of the country's economic activity. In June 1960, more than three fourths of all bank deposits in the United States were attributed to metropolitan areas.[3] In 1958, metropolitan areas accounted for about three fourths of the value added by manufacture, total number of industrial employees, and all manufacturing payrolls.[4] More than two thirds of all "housing starts" occurred in these areas in 1959 and again in 1960.[5] These figures indicate the magnitude of the tasks faced by governments in metropolitan areas and are suggestive of their possible tax sources.

At the time of the 1957 Census of Governments, there were only 174 SMSA's as compared with the 212 designated in the 1960 Census of Population. At that time, local governments in the 174 SMSA's spent about $20 billion, a total which excludes direct outlays by state agencies in and for metropolitan areas. They collected over 70 percent of all local tax revenue, including 84 percent of local nonproperty taxes. They made 66 percent of all local government expenditures and accounted for 74 percent of all local government debts. They were responsible for 61 percent of all local expenditures for education, although their share of public school enrollment was only 52 percent. The proportion of their local expenditures for other governmental functions was even higher, averaging 70 percent and exceeding 80 percent of the nationwide total for such functions as parks and recreation, fire protection and sanitation.[6] Tentative computations suggest that, in 1960, local government expenditures in the 212 SMSA's amounted to about $24 billion. The amount spent by all governments to serve the urban population is clearly much larger.

THE NATURE OF URBAN GOVERNMENT SERVICES AND THEIR PRICING

CHARACTERISTICS

Public goods supposedly have inherent qualities which require public production. Their main purpose is to satisfy wants which, according to Musgrave, are of two types—social wants and merit wants.[7] Social wants are those satisfied by services available to all, although individuals utilize different amounts and derive different benefits. People who do not pay the taxes that support the services are not excluded from the benefits that result.

Merit wants arise where society feels that a private market solution provides too much or too little of a good. Once merit wants are recognized, government can take steps to interfere with the market mechanism. These interferences represent a spectrum of attitudes by governments on certain goods.[8] At one end of the spectrum we find a complete sumptuary tax on heroin. At the other end of the scale, schools are subsidized and all children are forced to attend. In between are such goods as cigarettes, with a tax to discourage their consumption, and public libraries, designed to encourage the use of books.

The following statement by the Rockefeller panel is illustrative of merit wants:

> The skills that we need most critically today are not necessarily those that we reward most highly. Today we look especially to the scientist, the diplomat, the government administrator, the educator for critically important contributions to our society. Our scale of material and social rewards and incentives, however, still reflects an age when the attraction of talent into these fields was not accorded a very high priority. If teachers are not adequately paid today, it is at least in part because society has not

yet come to esteem the teaching function sufficiently or to evaluate its social contribution adequately.[9]

The servicing of certain merit wants, presently in the hands of local governments, might have to be transferred to higher levels to provide the necessary financing.

The difficulty of pricing public goods results because consumer-voter-taxpayers do not reveal their preferences. If they were to make known their true demand for public goods, the proper quantity and quality could be produced and the appropriate benefit tax levied. In the absence of preference information, the rational consumer of public goods will tend to understate his demand, hoping to benefit without paying or by paying as little as possible.

Keeping in mind the crucial characteristics of a public good, it can be seen that many urban government services do not qualify as pure public goods. Relatively few involve major social wants, although some of the more important involve substantial merit wants. We should develop methods for charging the consumer for these urban government services, which only to a minor extent fulfill social and merit wants.

Thus, we have both private and public schools and private and public collection of refuse. Industry often maintains its own fire and police departments. In Denmark, a large number of local governments have contracts with a private concern that has established fire brigades over the whole country. Private companies operate waterworks and sewage lines; they collect taxes, operate transit systems, generate electricity. Preferences are also revealed for many urban government services and, although individuals' tastes and demands for them differ, a social optimum may be approached because of the wide selection of service levels in various jurisdictions.

Persons who move into an urban area can consider a host of variables that bear on the location decision. If the individual has children, the quality of public education is important. The availability, quality, and cost of such services as are derived from beaches, parks, police and fire protection, roads, parking facilities, golf courses, etc., also enter into location decisions. By and large, the consumer-voter-taxpayer has to make his location decision based on prevailing urban government services and taxes. Future changes might be taken into considerataion, but they are hard to forecast.

Thus, it appears that while the federal government, which furnishes such services as national defense, cannot hope to arrive at a market type solution to determine the level of expenditures on public goods, urban governments might be able to do so in a number of cases. It depends on the extent to which urban governments rely on charges and fees as against taxes, the amount of information available to consumer-voter-taxpayers, and the flexibility of the system.

Citizens can always vote for changes in services and taxes but the method is slow and produces incomplete results. As a further alternative, residents can move into another community but generally such extreme action is only taken if large scale incentives are offered by a rival area.

USER CHARGES

For those goods and services provided by urban governments that fall short of being pure public goods, a strong argument can be made in favor of permitting market forces to operate freely in determining the kinds and quantities of services to be supplied. The market system can operate both when the individual or firm purchases services or goods from a government enterprise and when one governmental jurisdiction purchases goods or services from another.

According to Lyle C. Fitch, user charges can best be levied if the following conditions are met:

> 1. The charge must be administratively feasible. Among the other requirements, the service must be divisible into units whose use by the beneficiary can be measured, like kilowatts, gallons of water, trips across a bridge, or miles travelled on a turnpike.
>
> 2. The immediate benefits of the service should go mainly to the person paying for it. This condition, not always easy to apply, means that if a person refrains from using this service because of the charge, the rest of the community suffers relatively little loss . . .
>
> 3. The charge should encourage economical use of resources. Metered charges, for instance, encourage consumers to conserve water and electricity by turning off faucets and lights.[10]

Charges help balance demand and supply, particularly important where excess demand produces undesirable results, as in public parking. During much of the day, the number of would-be parkers exceeds the available curb parking spaces. Lacking a better system, spaces are allocated on the first-come, first-served basis. A charge may be the most efficient way of rationing space, so that it is available to those who need it most.

The price-market test of resource allocation greatly simplifies the problem of citizen participation in the governmental process. Where services and goods are bought by individuals, each consumer takes part in the decision-making process by determining how much of the service he will buy.

The budgetary problem can be simplified by reliance on user charges and the demand-supply rule, but it must be remembered that public enterprise operations are affected by the political process. Political participation in many decisions is essential, particularly when framing organizational form and investment policies and in integrating the particular function with other community services.

As Fitch points out, ''Some of the most urgent area-wide needs are appropriately financed partly or wholly by charges. They include the services which are frequently provided by private regulated utilities such as gas and electricity, water, and mass transportation and other transportation facilities, port development, waste disposal, many recreational services, and hospital services.'' [11]

In summary, public goods fulfill either social or merit wants. Relatively few urban government services fall into the first category and many of these services can be furnished by the private market. This is not always a satisfactory solution because it frequently results in a smaller quantity of services than society feels is desirable. While the federal government will continuously be forced to employ taxation to meet such pure public goods as national defense, it can be argued that urban governments should increasingly rely on user charges, which can greatly improve resource allocation and facilitate financing.

A GENERALIZED DECISION-MAKING MODEL FOR URBAN GOVERNMENTS

It is important that decision makers realize the potential impact of their decision on the community once they have determined which goods should be offered by urban governments. With this in mind, an effort will be made to present an urban area interaction model that can be used to simulate alternative urban government activities and assess their relative desirability. It will be followed by a brief presentation of a model associated with the theories of Professor Richard Musgrave, often referred to as the three budget function model.

URBAN AREA INTERACTION MODEL

A useful model should relate urban government activities to the area's health and well-being and, in turn, a variety of external and internal forces to certain net social benefits that can accrue to area people because of urban government activities. Such a generalized decision-making model can take the form of an urban area interaction approach. It can be visualized with the help of a flow chart. (See Figure 1.) The model is composed of four major elements, which are portrayed as boxes. Box 1 represents External Forces and is wired directly to boxes 2 and 3, Internal Urban Government Sector Environment and Internal Private Sector Environment, respectively. Boxes 2 and 3 are also wired to one another. All three boxes, in turn, are wired to box 4, denoting major dimensions of Urban Area's Health and Well-being. Boxes 1, 2, and 3 are the inputs and jointly affect box 4, the output. Clearly there are numerous feedbacks. One of the important inputs is the public sector environment of urban areas, that is, the many public policies that can be adopted by urban governments. Table 1 presents some of the major policies that are open to these governments and that affect urban government sector environment.

Activities of urban government in box 2 interact with activities represented in boxes 1 and 3, with a resultant flow to box 4 where the impact on the major dimensions of the Urban Area's Health and Well-being is registered. There often is a feedback from box 4.

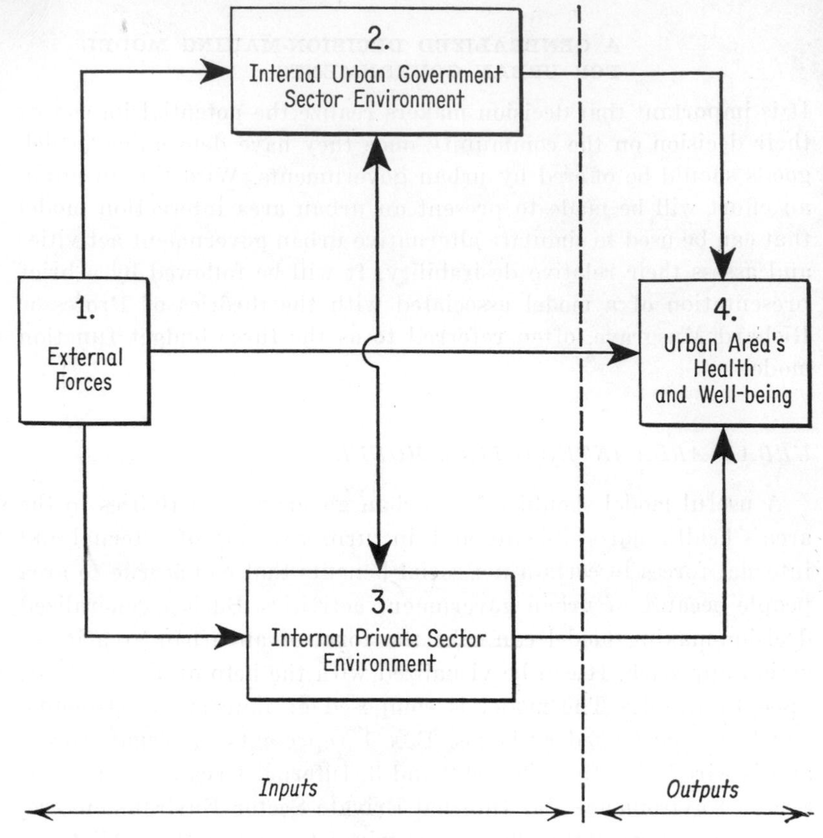

Figure 1. An Urban Area Interaction Model.

It is useful to identify five major dimensions of an Urban Area's Health and Well-being:

1. Per capita personal real income
2. Basic employment stability
3. Net social benefits
4. Economic growth
5. Amenities of life [12]

Let us take another look at the circuit. If we are concerned mainly with urban area, government-initiated steps, in a sense we manipulate switches in box 2. While there is a constant flow over all circuits, the circuit flowing out of box 2 has been modified and will lead to interactions with all the other flows. The results will register in box 4.

This model will lend itself to the simulation of alternative actions taken by urban governments and their effects on the status of the area.

Not all actions are independently taken by urban government. Many are in response to external or internal private sector forces. Similarly, there is much interest in understanding the impact of certain external and internal private sector policies on that dimension of the area's health and well-being which comes under the heading of net social benefits. Net social benefits (or costs) of government services can be defined as the difference between the amounts consumers would be willing to pay for public goods and services (consistent with benefits received) and what they actually pay. Measuring merely per capita income neglects this important welfare element.

Table 1

URBAN GOVERNMENT POLICIES AFFECTING THE URBAN GOVERNMENT SECTOR ENVIRONMENT

Public services and expenditures (other than traffic and transit)

Capital investments, current expenditures, and service levels

administration of justice	public health
correction and probation	public welfare
education and culture	public works
general government	recreation
hospitals	regulation and licensing
protection and policing	sanitation

Taxation (including fees and bonds)

tax types	borrowing and its costs
tax rates	

Traffic and transit by transportation system (ease of circulation in region)

highways and roads	operating mass transportation system
planning and building highway system	routing
operating highway system	scheduling
regulation of access	rate making
regulation of speed	maintaining mass transportation system
regulation of traffic flow	

maintaining highway system
planning mass transportation system
  type
  location
building mass transportation system
parking facilities
planning location and size of facilities
building facilities
  rate making
maintaining facilities

General government climate
  efficient and honest administration
  imaginative leadership
  closeness and responsiveness to people

Land use planning and regulation
  planning
  zoning
  condemnation
  urban renewal
  neighborhood conservation

Planning and regulation of resources other than land
  water
    regulation of supply
    rate making
    antipollution measures
    flood control measures
    watershed protection
    recreation
  air
    smoke control
  waste
    waste disposal
  forests and parks
    recreation
  beaches, etc.

A simplified example may be used to illustrate this model. The urban government rezones a large piece of land from residential to industrial purposes, that is, a dial in box 2 has been turned and the flow from box 2 to box 3 is modified. Private decision-making units throughout the country may then reaxamine, in the light of their specific needs, the desirability of locating in the particular region. Let us assume that one such unit, an automobile manufacturer, decides to build a large assembly plant on this rezoned land. Building and operating this assembly plant is the direct outcome of the new local environment. Dials in box 3 will be turned and the flow from it to box 4 will be modified. The direct effects on the region's economy take the form of local inputs to the plant. The automobile manufacturer purchases labor, raw material, and public services from the local economy. How much of his input the manufacturer can purchase inside the region depends on the local economy's responsiveness. In any case, local decision units, as a result of the action of the plant, can visualize certain new business opportunities that, if materialized, can greatly change the region's health and well-being, recorded in box 4.

This generalized decision-making model is obviously a simplified version of the complexities of life, but it has a number of virtues. Criteria by which urban government policies are to be evaluated are clearly defined. Use is made of a multiple set of criteria by which the status of an urban area in two different time periods can be compared. Admittedly, we appear to be a long way from quantifying these complex interrelationships.

Urban government policies are assets (or liabilities) to the area in varying degrees. Changes in local government policy can affect the local asset picture and may influence private units to alter their decisions. Table 1 lists some of the major policies open to urban government.

In part, urban government policies modifying the local public sector environment are mainly means to an end. In the short run, some are mainly ends in themselves and are included among the dimensions of an Urban Area's Health and Well-being. Thus, public services, expenditures, and taxes are the backbone of net social benefit analysis. Similarly, the general government climate, public services as they bear on educational, recreational, and cultural facilities, and traffic and transit, affect the amenities of life offered by the region.

MUSGRAVE'S THREE BUDGET FUNCTION MODEL

Musgrave's model can be modified to become applicable to urban governments and is akin to the generalized decision-making model presented in the previous section.[13] However, it emphasizes budgetary decisions, and thus is more limited in its scope of inputs. It is also concerned with only three outputs—goods and services, income redistribution, and stabilization, making it more limited from the output standpoint. The Musgrave model was developed in relation to the federal budget, conceived of as the composite of an allocation budget, an income redistribution budget, and a stabilization budget.

The allocation budget must provide public goods and in so doing, it allocates resources. The preferences of citizens are evaluated and the goods provided within the framework of a balanced budget.

The benefit principle should guide taxation. Since urban governments are mainly concerned with providing public goods and services, their emphasis is on the goods and services budget. They face two major tasks—to induce citizens to reveal their preferences and to raise funds to finance services. These two aspects could lead to a demand and supply analysis of urban government services.

In connection with the income redistribution budget, the federal government uses the "pure" redistribution tools of taxes and transfers to reach the "proper" size distribution of income. This budget, too, is balanced. Although the income redistribution aspect of the budget is less important for urban than for federal government, it cannot be neglected. It should play an important role when tax and service decisions are being made and when adoption of private services by urban governments is under consideration. For example, before a decision is reached to take over a private water, sewer, or transit company, the redistributive effect should be carefully examined. A publicly owned water, sewer, or transit system will not pay local, state, and federal taxes. Tax losses will have to be made up by increased taxes, which, to the extent that they are progressive, will tend to reduce the inequality of income that existed before.

The redistribution budget can also be used to satisfy merit wants. How far-flung the income redistribution effects of urban government activities can be is well illustrated by public education. In the United States, a redistribution of income takes place from adults to school-age children, that is, from one generation to the next. Furthermore, other things being equal, there are redistributions from high- to low-income groups, from wealthy regions to poor ones. To the extent that parents, who are affiliated with certain religious groups, choose other than public educational facilities for their children, income is transferred from members of these groups to the remainder of the community. Income is also transferred from childless adults to parents and their children, and from small to large families.

The redistribution budget is especially important whenever the urban government unit is large, since people pay taxes under the same rules and receive the same services, whether the governmental units are large or small. Usually, the larger the unit, the greater the income differentials, the more common the expenditures on welfare type services with redistributing characteristics, and the stronger the political power of low income groups.

The stabilization budget of the federal government uses the tools of monetary and fiscal policy to provide for stabilization and, if desired, also for growth. This budget does not need to be in balance. In the past, the stabilization aspect of urban government budgets has been minor. However, with the increase in the capital budget of urban governments and our improved understanding of the business cycle, the stabilization budget is gaining in importance.

For example, in 1961, Senator Joseph S. Clark introduced into the Senate an emergency employment bill.[14] Its purpose was to provide an incentive, through federal grants, for state and local government bodies in areas with much unemployment to accelerate their capital expenditure programs. He proposed to achieve this goal through the initiation of projects that could be promptly started and completed. The assistance would automatically terminate when the rate of unemployment fell below 4 percent of the civilian labor force. The bill was endorsed by President Kennedy in principle but was temporarily deferred because of the large increases in the defense budget.

Urban governments have increasingly expedited the spending of funds for capital improvements in times of recession. In addition, there is some inherent stabilizing quality in the urban government capital budget. Usually the funds are voted one, two, or even more years before they are spent. Thus, in part, they are voted into existence during periods of prosperity and principally spent when economic activity has slowed down.

INTERGOVERNMENTAL RELATIONS IN URBAN AREAS

Urban government services can be defined as public goods rendered to persons living in urban areas; they are supplied by a variety of governments. These governments have intricate relationships. Basically, urban government services are offered and financed by governments operating in part on the same level, and in part on different levels, and yet joining forces in various ways.

BASIC GOVERNMENT DUTIES

It is common to separate government into executive, legislative, and judiciary branches. In order to understand changes in intergovernmental relations with respect to urban government services, we will subdivide the legislative (and regulatory) duties into two phases—legislation designed to raise funds, and legislation where funds are not requisite. In brief, government has the following duties:

1. To administer
2. To legislate and regulate without raising funds
3. To provide funds to translate legislation into action
4. To provide the judiciary

What is the history of governments' fulfillment of these duties? In countries with a federated political and fiscal system, higher levels of the judiciary have long reviewed many verdicts of lower courts. Local courts necessarily have less power and prestige than higher ones.

Where the provision of funds to translate legislation into action is concerned, changes in philosophy and practice have taken place. Until the end of the eighteenth century in England, for instance, governments responsible for expenditures were also called upon to procure the income. The responsibility principle required those who determined the expenditures to pay for them, assuring their constant awareness of the expenses connected with these activities. Rarely were any funds transferred between governments.

This was the period of a barter economy in which taxes were paid in part in the form of labor, and transportation was poor. These facts, together with the responsibility principle, favored small government units and local taxation.

Five administrative considerations served to reenforce this tendency:

1. Accessibility of local offices and institutions
2. Technical considerations favoring small units
3. Desire to deal with officials personally known to the constituent

4. Availability of expert knowledge in the local area
5. Highly local character of most public services

With the years, many of these forces have gradually disappeared and new forces, pulling in the opposite direction, have come to the fore. This trend will be discussed after an examination of the main factors that have persuaded different governments to accept various duties and functions.

MOTIVATION

Intergovernmental relations, especially fiscal relations, have been guided by a variety of motivating forces. The following four are perhaps the most important:[15]

1. Intervention and encouragement
2. Equalization
3. Technical taxation conditions
4. Responsibility

1. The Intervention and Encouragement Motive. Higher levels of government can intervene to encourage urban governments to offer more of a merit good, to stimulate them to greater efficiency, to adopt new programs, etc. Resistance can stem from people's reluctance to have Washington make decisions for them and from their preference, rather, to bungle things themselves. The main struggle centers around legislative and administrative power. While higher levels of governments are not anxious to capture the financing responsibility, they often use funds as a carrot by which they ultimately assume administrative powers.

Local bodies want no interference but have difficulty in refusing aid. The central body wants to regulate, however, and well realizes that offering funds is a first step towards acquiring this right. For this reason, urban governments will usually strive to obtain unconditional grants, while state and federal governments will try to make them as conditional as possible. Yet, with the passage of time even unconditional grants tend to become conditional.

The encouragement principle works in the face of the public's resistance to increases in local taxes. Thus, if a state or federal tax is collected in an urban area and returned to the local government, the latter will usually consider itself richer and spend more than before, even if the additional state and federal taxes exceed the local government grant. Local governments appear to be heavily influenced by the status of their cash balances. Regardless of whether the citizen's after-tax income has declined, the urban government is unlikely to reduce its activities unless its cash balances have declined.

2. The Equalization Motive. Inequities arise in a federated type of political and fiscal system because governments differ in their tax sources, needs, and cost and benefit spillovers. Until quite recently, the absence of good communication and the subsequent unfamiliarity with conditions elsewhere made comparisons difficult and prevented dissatisfaction with conditions at home. Specialization, urbanization, and improved communications have increased the stature of the equalization motive.

Greater differences between the trade structure of cities, higher absolute taxes, greater mobility, greater familiarity with conditions in other areas, and the transition from real property taxes to income taxes, have all helped to make the problem of equalization far more important than ever before.

It is useful to distinguish between tax equalization and net fiscal resources equalization. Net fiscal resources are equalized when tax and government service differences are the same throughout the country. Such equalization is more difficult to attain than that of taxes. It also leaves the question of which taxes to equalize—wealth or income taxes. Since a choice must be made, income is likely to be the more appropriate guide. In any case, our main concern is to reduce and not to eliminate inequalities.

There are four main sources of inequality: differences in tax base, in the need for public services, in the quality of the public services, and in technical conditions. The latter may result from the fact that some local governments are too small and perhaps have too few children to use their schools and teachers efficiently. They can be too small to make effective use of the official machinery and yet too large to dispense with it entirely.

Some of these forces will pull in the same direction. Small incomes tend to go hand in hand with high percentages of unemployed and sick, who must be treated at public expense. Demands are usually greatest on impoverished local governments. The unemployed are often in favor of large unemployment benefits; the sick are interested in good hospitals. At the same time, poor local governments have the greatest difficulties in meeting these demands and, as a result, the poorest local governments tend to have the worst services.

Spatial spillover of the costs and benefits associated with urban government services also play an important role in intergovernmental fiscal relations. For example, public education creates benefits to the person who is being educated, his family, his neighbor, his community, and society at large. Some of the benefits accrue immediately, while others only begin to be realized after ten or twenty years. During this period, the person is likely to change his residence. Is it therefore equitable to ask a local school district to finance the education of people who will benefit the nation at large and, more specifically, other communities? In a dynamic America, those communities that educate people today cannot necessarily expect the later influx of educated people to be commensurate with the out-migration of those it originally educated. This spatial spillover has greater than passing interest. If more of the well-educated leave the school district than enter it, its tax base is likely to erode and the local financing of schools will tend to become more difficult.

The fact that we should be primarily interested in the equalization of net fiscal resources, and not merely of taxes, makes calculations very difficult. Actually, matters are further complicated since the full tax burden seldom falls on those who actually pay the tax. Thus, equalization efforts should relate to tax burdens and service levels.

Equalization can lead to waste.[16] However, more economic use of funds is likely if percentage grants are employed in an attempt to reduce inequalities and are not made towards the actual but towards some calculated standard expenses. For these reasons, Sweden, for example, in cases in which varied percentage grants have been used, has chosen to make such grants not towards the actual but towards the calculated expenses.

3. *Technical Taxation Conditions*. A shift of the financing function to higher levels of government is also encouraged by certain technical problems. Income taxes, for example, are not well suited for local application. In addition, they have virtually been preempted by the central government. Yet these taxes are dominant at the

present time. There may, therefore, be a temptation on purely technical taxation grounds to let the central government take over the financing. The fact that income taxes are the most easily imposed, and that they are most efficiently collected at the national level, has helped to bring about a nationalization of financing. This ascendancy of the income tax has in certain instances led to further administration and regulation by the central government.

4. *The Responsibility Motive.* It is important that the recipient of funds carries out their administration as responsibly as possible. Responsibility is thus not an independent motive, but rather leads, for instance, to hesitation in giving a grant and perhaps also in the choice of its special forms. The higher the marginal grant, the less responsibility local governments tend to feel.

Those systems for which grants are made according to objective criteria, as are the English road grants, have the great advantage of preserving intact the local government's sense of responsibility. The same advantage is obtained through the system of tax division. Here also an extra income can be given to the local government with negligible effects on the authority's sense of responsibility. Every economy benefits the local government and it must bear the whole cost of every extra expense. Even where local governments receive grants that are not destined for any particular purpose, but that are paid in the form of block grants, they affect the sense of responsibility since these grants reduce the cost of all government services when compared to costs of private goods and services. Block grants, however, do not disturb the marginal relationship between categories of public expenditures.

CHANGING RELATIONS

There is a trend toward centralization of government. Contributing factors are probably the high degree of industrialization, improvement in transportation and communication, the replacement of a barter economy by a money economy, rapid urbanization and increase in population density, and considerations of efficiency and equity. They set the framework within which the four main motives affecting intergovernmental relations operate.

How has the centralization of urban government functions taken place? One important vehicle has been the transfer of duties to higher levels of government. Centralization of all four government duties does not necessarily take place simultaneously. In the general movement toward centralization, in most cases financing has proved to become centralized more thoroughly than the other duties. It is much easier politically to obtain the local authority's agreement to transfer financing to the state or federal government than to transfer legislative and administrative powers. To resist another's offer to pay a part of one's expenses is difficult. In addition, however, there are taxation-technical, equalization-political, and power-political considerations, all pulling in the same direction. Urban governments have become accustomed to spend more and more time in negotiating for funds with state and federal governments.

Another vehicle of centralization has been the transfer of specific services or functions. For instance in England, work in relation to roads and highways has been transferred from the parishes to the districts to the counties and now finally to the central government.

While the transfer of local urban government duties and functions to higher levels of government can take place gradually, consolidation constitutes a more complex transition. Consolidation or merger of local urban governments is usually difficult. It has succeeded in part in the United States with regard to school districts. To some extent it has also been accomplished in Sweden.

While merger has certain advantages, it has substantial disadvantages. For example, it is by no means clear that all the functions connected with the public school system will be best discharged, technically speaking, within areas of the same size. It is quite possible that one unit is best equipped to make the decisions on the location of a school, a somewhat larger unit best prepared to decide on the nature of the instruction and type of teachers, and a third unit best qualified to obtain the necessary money.

Proponents of metropolitan consolidation have mainly argued in terms of efficiency, equity, and a chance to offer better and more varied services. It has been contended that urban governments could benefit from major economies of scale, as do private firms, once they grow and consolidate. Work carried out during the last few years at Washington University has revealed that this may be a fallacious argument.[17] Many of the forces that lead to economies of scale in the private sector do not exist in the public sector. On the contrary, certain inherent qualities of urban government services will not permit growth of the operating unit. Thus, for instance, primary schools must remain quite small as long as parents are unwilling to allow their children to walk long distances to school. Likewise, the size of a firehouse in the city is determined to no small extent by the area that it must protect. Its size is basically dependent on the maximum distance that a fire truck can cover to reach the scene of a fire within an acceptable time span. Furthermore, consolidation will tend to lead to further unionization of municipal workers and most likely to higher wage rates.

The equity argument is mainly based on intercommunity benefit and cost spillovers. For example, the cost of mosquito protection in one community depends partly on the level of services provided in another. The extreme case is the service that cannot be provided by one community alone. In Los Angeles, for instance, no single community could successfully fight smog.

The American people have shown a great reluctance to give up their veto power on urban government actions. A good example is the virtually universal defeat of moves to consolidate metropolitan area governments. Such consolidation would mean shifting urban control from local governments to larger consolidated governments further removed from the people. In an age of affluence, where many urbanites have moved into suburbia in order to benefit from the amenities of suburban life, consolidation would remove the veto power that suburbanites presently hold with respect to their small municipal and school governments. While such consolidation might possibly improve the efficiency of urban government and change the type and quality of services rendered, apparently these benefits have appeared subordinate to the losses foreseen in maintaining the suburban amenities of life.

Another argument entails the need for close relationship between government and the people. Traditionally, local government has been sentimentalized as the last bastion of "town meeting" government. Urban government must be kept small, some have argued, in order for the people to control it at the grass-roots level. It has also been contended that local government is the only level at which people and government can effectively meet and engage in democratic give and take.

Perhaps the strongest force against consolidation in the past has been fear of change. A change involves uncertainty. Most urbanites do not feel that the urban problem is sufficiently acute and severe to warrant major changes, particularly if the implications cannot be clearly foreseen. Finally, business firms, so far as their local economic activities are concerned, have often little to gain and much to lose by the strengthening of local government to the point where it can employ the tactics of a countervailing power. Firms are in a stronger position dealing with many small urban government units than with a single large one.

For all these reasons, it appears that until the plight of urbanites and suburbanites greatly increases, they will be reluctant to agree to large-scale metropolitan consolidation. The urban crisis will have to become much more severe before consolidation can become an important vehicle for improvement.

MAJOR FORMS OF INTERGOVERNMENTAL FISCAL RELATIONS

In the United States, civil government is largely a state and local responsibility. In 1960, for example, when civil government cost about $63 billion, 54 percent of these expenditures occurred at the local, 28 percent at the state, and only 18 percent at the federal level. State and federal aid to local governments amounted in 1960 to $10 billion, about 30 percent of local general revenue. We do not know what percentage of urban government revenues took the form of state aid. However, since state legislators seem to favor rural areas, we would surmise that the figure for urban governments would be less than 30 percent. Federal payments made directly to local governments are small even though they have increased over recent years. In 1961, direct federal grants and payments to local governments in lieu of taxes totaled $676 million and provided less than 2 percent of local general revenue.[18] This aid was for housing and community development, airport construction, waste treatment facilities, and to support education in federally affected areas. These unqualified grants, while small at present, have increased sharply from $9 million in 1927, to $56 million in 1942, to $237 million in 1952, to $676 million in 1961.[19] Further major increases especially for area redevelopment, mass transportation and community health services can be expected.

In addition to these direct grants to urban governments, the federal government also aids by providing grants to states which in turn use them to subsidize local governments. Local governments also benefit from loans, loan guarantees, technical assistance, personnel training, and research support.

The major instruments available for the distribution of funds between governments are grants-in-aid, tax sharing, and intermunicipal grant arrangements. In theory, grants-in-aid can originate at any level of government but, in practice, they generally emanate from the higher level.

It is convenient to classify grants-in-aid to urban governments in accordance with their specificity and distribution formula. Insofar as specificity is concerned, the following categories are useful:

1. General, unallocated grants to multifunction government
2. General grants allocated to a particular group of service functions of a multifunction government
3. General grants allocated to a particular service function
4. General grants for specific measures
5. Specified grants for specific measures

General, unallocated grants are block grants given for urban government activities with no restrictions on their application. As we go down the list, grants become increasingly specific. Thus, for example, a specified grant for a specific measure could be given to a school district to increase the number of its science teachers.

There are at least four different types of formulas by which funds can be allocated to urban governments:

1. Fixed percentage
2. Varying percentage
3. Amount is determined by specified criterion
4. Payments made if local government's expenditures exceed a specified amount

Perhaps the most commonly used distribution formula employs fixed percentages. Matching funds are a special case in this general category. Usually the higher the percentage distribution of the higher level of government, the stronger the encouragement and the weaker the responsibility.

In the absence of specified criteria the percentage can vary. Thus, for example, the contribution of higher levels of government can increase or decrease over time.

A variety of criteria can be used to distribute grants and other aid. The amount can be fixed per subsidy unit, with the unit's size varying from the total government unit to any part thereof. For example, many state school subsidies are based on the number of pupils in average daily attendance; other criteria could be the number of the district's inhabitants, number of unemployed, or road mileage. The subsidy need not be fixed. Instead, it can vary inversely to the jurisdiction's financial ability. Furthermore, a ceiling might be placed on the maximum grant per subsidy unit. Subsidies inversely related to the jurisdiction's financial ability are consistent with the equality motive.

Finally, grants above a minimum expenditure level are mainly designed to encourage urban governments to carry out new programs. In the extreme, the entire amount above a specified level could be subsidized and this indeed would tend to weaken the responsibility motive. A more appropriate distribution formula would tend to pay a fixed percentage at the specified minimum level; or a varying percentage formula could be applied. In the latter case, the percentage contribution of the higher level of government could vary directly with income and thus be consistent with the equality motive.

Grants-in-aid have a tendency to perpetuate themselves. Two general reasons were noted in a recent report of the Advisory Commission on Intergovernmental Relations. In the first place, vested interests in their continuation come into being with the initiation of a new grant. Once a particular grant continues for a few years, it becomes an integral part of a state and local budget and constitutes one of the assumed sources of revenue in the processes of budgetary planning. Secondly, efforts to redirect grant programs toward newer and more urgent problems within a given program area usually result in an additive rather than a substantive creation.[20] The Commission recommended that congressional acts provide for careful review procedure and granting of funds for a period not to exceed five years. Extension of a grant would require a new act and thus would facilitate review.

State governments can play a major role in coordinating and facilitating urban government taxation. Many urban governments tend to rely increasingly on nonproperty taxes. These taxes are best imposed cooperatively by a group of economically interdependent jurisdictions. The Advisory Commission on Intergovernmental Relations has recommended that cities and other jurisdictions comprising an economic area be provided with uniform taxing powers and authority for cooperative tax enforcement.[21]

In situations where a particular nonproperty tax is widely used locally, but the state does not itself use the same tax, the state can nonetheless help urban governments by facilitating the pooled administration of the separate local taxes through a state-administered agency. It can also authorize local jurisdictions to join together in creating an administrative agency for themselves.

It is usually desirable to minimize needless variety among local nonproperty taxes. The state can write generally applicable specifications into authorization acts, which are permissible with regard to the structure and administrative features. At the same time, states should help limit urban governments to the more productive taxes. Leveling many different types of taxes increases costs and enforcement difficulties.

Another method of handling intergovernmental fiscal relations is tax-sharing. In many respects, its effects resemble state grants to local governments. Taxes are shared in some specified proportion among several public bodies. However, there is an important difference between grants and sharing. With grants, the size of the sum transferred depends upon the amount of the expenditure, while in tax-sharing it depends on the size of the tax shared.

In tax-sharing, that proportion that goes to the local government will normally be the same for all local governments. This need not be the case, however, as a distribution formula could be used to give the largest share to poor local governments.

There are situations when both state and local governments use the same type of tax. An example is the income tax, levied both by some states and cities. A promising coordinating device is the local tax supplement to the state tax. It gives local jurisdictions access to the superior enforcement resources of the state and eases taxpayer compliance, yet leaves the decision to impose the tax to local initiative.

Tax-sharing may take place not only between the federal or state and local governments but also between local urban governments themselves. Under intermunicipal tax-sharing, a part of the tax collected in one local government area goes to another. The system is used in a highly diversified metropolitan area where some local governments serve residents, while others are principally occupied with industry and commerce. On the other hand, intermunicipal grant arrangements are not common in the United States, being mainly used in Denmark.

INTERGOVERNMENTAL COOPERATION IN TAX ADMINISTRATION

Tax administrations at all three levels of government have the responsibility of enforcing the laws required for financing governmental services. The governmental system of the United States is predicated on a division of jurisdictional responsibilities among governmental levels. These levels exist only to complement one another in reaching the common goal of serving the people's needs. The existence of three levels of government results in overlapping of taxes and necessitates that various governments function in unison wherever the public interest so dictates.

It is important that all three levels of government enjoy a good tax administration. Taxpayers' respect for federal tax administration has complementary benefits for state and local administrations, and vice versa.

Congressional recognition of the need for intergovernmental administrative cooperation in tax administration goes back to the Revenue Act of 1926, which sets forth explicit provision for giving the states access to federal tax return information. The interest of local governments came to the fore in 1935. The Costigan Amendment appears to have been offered on the floor of the Senate in response to the collective petition of the National Association of Tax Assessing Officials, the United States Conference of Mayors, and the American Municipal Association. It requested access to federal returns to assist in the administration of local personal property taxes.[22] However, federal tax returns have not been opened directly to local officials, only to state; it appears useful to accord local officials the same access to this information.

A PERSON-PARCEL FRAMEWORK

Activities in urban areas are basically person- and place-oriented. This statement is also true of urban government activities, which can best be analyzed in relation to persons, parcels, and street sections. Urban government services are provided to people and for people; to parcels; to street sections. Thus, on the output side, urban government services must be linked to people and land, that is, to those who demand services. The public pays for them either in the form of taxes or charges. Some taxes are income related. Thus, it is evident that an analysis of urban government operations and finances fits neatly into a person-parcel framework.

DECISIONS WITH REGARD TO PUBLIC SCHOOLS

Let us use public education as an example. Insofar as the demand aspect is concerned, public education has a specific client population. To forecast the demand for public education in a given school district necessitates substantial information on key characteristics of this client population.

It is useful to visualize the amount of education that will be demanded, as a function of:

1. Price tag placed on education
2. Size of school population
3. Income of school district population
4. Quality of education
5. Tastes and mores of school district population [23]

The demand for public education is people-related; location information, possibly by parcel, is of interest in identifying pupils who are eligible to attend a district's schools and in determining the general population of the school district. Parcel information is even more important in relation to specific schools. The number of pupils who can be expected to attend a given school depends on the density of school-age population within a given radius from the school. The need for school facilities at a given point in space depends on the expected school-age population within a specific radius.

From the supply point of view, the client population is no longer the school-age group but the entire district population. All adults are voters and taxpayers.[24] The supply of local funds to school districts is closely related to real property values in the district. Parcel information is therefore essential. In the United States, state funds for local school districts are raised mainly in the form of sales and income taxes. Parcel information helps to identify the location of the sales and income tax client population.

A similar argument applies to other urban government services, including fire protection, police protection, and refuse collection. Additional factors must be considered in the provision, regulation and pricing of urban transportation.

PLANNING, TRANSPORTATION, AND LAND USE

It is important to remember that a person works at a given site (parcel) and there produces either public or private goods. When these outputs are consumed, they become inputs of persons who work, reside, travel, or engage in recreation at this or another site. Street sections make the movement of people and goods possible.

Persons who make spatial decisions must understand spatial arrangements within regions, as well as their planning and projection, in order to select acceptable guiding principles.[25] In accordance with economic theory, each economic unit (person, firm, government) selects its own best alternative from an infinitely large number of choices. The spatial pattern of an urban economy can thus be conceived of as resulting from optimum-seeking activities of persons, each one in pursuit of the best combination of quantity of space and its location vis-à-vis all other units. Allocation takes place through the market mechanism. An equilibrium is reached when space is so allotted among users that no two can gain by exchanging combinations. Urban government decisions not only constitute the rules of the game, but can also inject forces that lead to a revision of existing or evolving spatial patterns.

The amount of space a household will use depends on its consumption preferences in relation to a host of variables, including the breadwinner's place of work. The space a firm will use depends on the nature of the enterprise and its internal economy, that is, technology and scale of operation. People and goods must be moved through space; movements are costly both in terms of time and money.

In theory, then, the spatial behavior of a unit reflects the most profitable adjustment of its internal economy to the economic environment. It seeks to purchase space and location to maximize its net returns or satisfactions. In line with this theory, persons, both as consumers and producers, constitute one cornerstone, and space constitutes a second. With a good deal of information about pertinent characteristics of persons and small spatial units, we could begin to consider alternative arrangements between persons and parcels. Any such step, however, should take the existing pattern of relationships as a point of departure. It is useless to assume that all these relationships can be changed in the short run. Instead we are concerned with persons' marginal changes, to move their abodes and places of work.

In the long-run planning stage, people can make decisions with regard to the location of their residences, places of work, etc. In the short run, they make trips between locations to engage in transactions of one sort or another, and the transportation system facilitates assembly of persons engaged in those transactions. Circulation and traveling results from the exchange of labor for wages (as in the journey to work), shipment of goods and services, and the participation in social and recreational experiences. All these elements often come under the heading of "Movement Demand" or "Circulation." They stem from the communication requirements of urban society and its activities.[26]

"Traffic demand" is the demand for movement viewed in the light of the geography of origins and destinations of its trips. The traffic demand of work trips, for example, constitutes the desire lines of travel for all workers between their homes and their employment sites. Its concern is the distribution in space of places of work and dwellings.

Trip purpose data testify to some regularities in urban transportation emerging from the institutional aspects of society. Data for fifty cities indicate that about 56 percent of all person-trips are between pairs of purposes, at least one of which is work and business.[27] The trips between home and work constituted about one third of the total trips tabulated. Thus, the journey to work is the overwhelming trip purpose and the most important single element in circulation.

According to a study of origin-destination data from thirty-eight cities by the Bureau of Public Roads, the average household originated approximately one work trip each day, one business trip every seven days, one social recreation trip every other working day, one shopping trip every fourth working day, one school trip every tenth working day, and a miscellaneous trip every fourth working day.[28] Here again the dominance of the journey to work is obvious. Social and recreational trips form the next most important class.

While it is true that families generate traffic, actual movement is in terms of a specific person with specific characteristics. Thus, many of those family data could be translated into person data and possibly become more meaningful for our purposes.

The journey to work, the technological link between the labor force and the production process, is the most significant class of person movement in any urban region in terms of order and relative volume. In addition, it probably has the lowest price elasticity of demand of all of the classes. The rigid constraint of the journey to work is responsible for the massive peaking of demand for transportation services in urban areas and, hence, the low load factors.

If we concentrate on the home-work relationship and construe all other transportation classes to play an intermediate role in household location and transportation behavior, demand for movement is the product of the employed labor force and the frequency of the work periods—the total number of work trips during a period of time necessary to support the process of production. To characterize traffic demand requires identification of the distribution of employment and households in urban space.

These, then, are some of person-, parcel-, and street section-associated issues and relationships which need to be considered by urban governments in offering services; in developing, regulating, and operating urban transportation systems; and in planning and controlling land use.

DATA

What, then, are the chances of finding data to implement such a framework? There can be no doubt that the rapidity of research on urban problems in general, and on urban government finance in particular, will depend in large part on the availability of data and a powerful system to analyze and present them.

Urban governments perform at least eleven major functions whose direct beneficiaries can differ. This information is presented in Table 2.

With this breakdown in mind, it might be useful to collect information for urban government decisions based on the smallest possible unit. First steps have been taken to identify needed and available person-, parcel-, and street section-centered data. The next step will be to design a unified information system for metropolitan areas, and possibly for states, which incorporates two basic data files—one relating to person, the other to real property. The latter could include two subfiles—one for parcels and one for street sections. Firms could possibly be treated as dummy persons, cross-referred to parcels.

Information on persons might be divided into seven main categories, according to the nature of phenomena described by them:

Identification and linkage data
Demographic data
Economic data
Education data
Health data
Welfare data
Law enforcement data

At the outset, the collection of merely local, state, and federal government data in the master file would be sufficient. Ultimately, information from private sources, especially utilities, banks, credit bureaus, etc., might be added.

In a similar manner, parcel and street section data could be categorized. A brief review of available data sources has shown a wealth of information presently in the hands of local, state, and federal governments. With the aid of a high-speed data-processing system, it should be possible to implement the person-parcel framework and greatly improve urban government decision making.

Particularly promising is a system of state processing centers, all integrated by the federal government. Major metropolitan areas and cities could constitute subcenters that would draw on the state-

Table 2

FUNCTIONS AND BENEFICIARIES OF URBAN GOVERNMENTS

MAJOR FUNCTION	PRIMARY BENEFICIARY (AND INFORMATION OBJECT CATEGORY)
1. Administration of justice	Persons and property
2. Correction and probation	Persons
3. Education and culture	Persons
4. General government	Persons and property
5. Hospitals	Persons
6. Protection and policing	Persons and property
7. Public health	Persons and real property
8. Public welfare	Persons
9. Public works	Property
10. Recreation	Persons
11. Regulation and licensing	Persons and property
12. Sanitation	Property

wide network of collection and processing of key data. In this way, we could gradually move from a manual and inefficient local and state government record system to one that is unified and mechanized.

SOME ISSUES AND POSSIBLE SOLUTIONS

What then are the prospects for urban governments and their finances? The answer clearly depends in part on the objectives on which influential groups in our society agree and the methods they will choose to attain those ends.

It appears that most urban government services are underfinanced. Thus Lyle C. Fitch, president of the Public Administration Institute, stated in 1957, "the root of the metropolitan financial problem [is] how to divert a larger share of resources to government use, or more simply, how to get more funds than existing revenue systems will produce, without unduly impinging on private production."[20]

In addition to agreement on more and better urban government services, I propose that greater emphasis be placed on efficient resource allocation. An earlier part of this essay indicated that many urban government services fulfill social and merit wants to a relatively small degree. To improve resource allocation by local urban governments, more user charges should be employed together with taxes that rely on the benefit principle. The responsibility to redistribute income and assure stability and growth should rest with the federal government.

While there now appear to be few forces that lead to an immediate increase of reliance on user charges, major changes in intergovernmental fiscal relations will continue to occur. State governments, and particularly the federal government, will be asked to shoulder an increasing burden of local urban government finance. Existing fragmentation of urban governments has led to great inequalities. These, in turn, are generating forces calling for equalization through intervention by higher levels of government. There are many signs that urban renewal, transportation facilities in urban areas, flood and pollution control, education, airport construction, etc., will be increasingly supported by the federal government. States are also likely to increase their support to local urban governments, although to a lesser degree since they are handicapped by lack of funds and rural overrepresentation. Much imaginative research remains to be done to provide federal and state funds to local urban governments without major increases in inefficiencies and waste.

In order to improve urban government planning and bring it further into line with national objectives, federal and state governments are likely to spend increasingly large funds to subsidize planning for community facilities and programs. If such a system were properly designed and administered, it could prove a most important carrot leading not only to more intelligent investment decisions but also to greater efficiency of programs.

Subsidies to local urban governments change the existing benefit-cost relationship. In highly fragmented metropolitan areas, a major portion of urban government benefits and costs can spill over from one jurisdiction to the next. Those that lose more than they gain tend to object to local tax increases unless the leakage is closed or compensated. An understanding of the spatial intercommunity spillover of benefits and costs can guide the grant-in-aid program so that it can more adequately fulfill its purpose.

There are also major benefit and cost spillovers between a metropolitan area and other parts of the nation. To a major extent, such benefit spillovers result from migration. Population movements out of the South result in increases in education cost in St. Louis, welfare costs in Cleveland, or public hospital charges in Los Angeles. The migration of the underprivileged and undereducated into core cities constitutes a major drain on their tax resources and should provide a basis for grants-in-aid.

A more flexible federal and state grant-in-aid program may be needed. Jesse Burkhead deplored the absence of "a regional social diseconomies board with authority to parcel out spillover gains and losses." [30] Perhaps states as well as the federal government should set up boards whose function is to neutralize spillovers or adjust them in order to facilitate the attainment of over-all objectives.

Much additional work is needed to measure benefits and costs of urban government services and their spillovers. Benefit-cost information will not assure the acceptance of urban proposals by officials and voters but will help to identify and project policies that promise distinctly larger benefits than costs.

It will become increasingly important to guard against the enactment of federal programs that can have a major adverse effect on the rendering of urban government services. We should learn from past mistakes. For example, the Federal Highway Act has virtually ruled out an efficient solution to traffic and transit problems in metropolitan areas. By subsidizing highway construction, this legislation has placed the private car, which from society's viewpoint is the most inefficient means of transportation, in a very advantageous position. As a result of this law, highways will continue to be built and more and more people induced to use private cars, thereby again ultimately increasing congestion. Incentives are lacking to seek such efficient solutions as subways or other means of high-speed transportation. Thus, the very efficient Paris Métro, which is both convenient and inexpensive, appears beyond reach in this country unless new major federal legislation is enacted.

The Federal Housing Act has inadvertently complicated the problems of urban governments. It has greatly favored the financing of suburban homes in the past and as a result has attracted huge numbers of young families into suburbia, complicating the already difficult tasks of suburban governments. Effective urban renewal programs, and more favorable financing of old homes in urbia, could go a long way in reducing the fiscal crises of suburban governments.

It seems unlikely that large-scale metropolitan consolidation will occur unless conditions in metropolitan areas become much worse. Some partial consolidation might take place for services benefiting from substantial economies of scale, such as water and sewage. Federal funds could attract metropolitan areas to coordinate certain functions and carry them out in a unified manner.

One attractive possibility is the creation of a federal corporation for metropolitan areas. Such a corporation has been proposed in a document issued by the Joint Committee of Congress on Washington Metropolitan Problems. It would develop a transit system for the District of Columbia.[31] A congressional act could establish such a corporation, devoid of taxing powers but endowed with federal funds and dependent on revenues from user charges. A federal corporation would naturally have most significance in the District of Columbia where it would directly serve the national public interest. Once successfully established there, it might prove to be a new institutional setting that could serve as the basis for carrying out a unified program for metropolitan areas throughout the country.

In the meantime, congressional legislation would be desirable to give advance consent to compacts between states for setting up agencies charged with interstate metropolitan area planning on a comprehensive basis, including mass transportation. If accompanied by grants-in-aid to state and local governments for developing such comprehensive plans, this step could go far toward improving the difficult situation of urban governments in multistate metropolitan areas.

Another key potential is state legislation. In accordance with statutory requirements, states could authorize local units of government within metropolitan areas to establish service corporations or authorities for the management of area-wide activities, especially transportation facilities. With the initial provision that such corporations are subject to voter approval on the basis of an area-wide majority, they should be empowered to borrow, and to impose user charges. States could also provide financial help and, perhaps of more importance, establish a state agency that would integrate and assist urban governments.

Finally, urban governments themselves should strive for greater efficiency. Introduction of cost accounting methods would be a significant contribution and more research is also essential to quantify the output associated with urban government services and people's preferences for them.

Notes

[1] Committee members are: Harold J. Barnett, Joseph L. Fisher, Lyle C. Fitch, Alvin H. Hansen, Walter W. Heller, Werner Z. Hirsch, Edgar M. Hoover, Harvey S. Perloff (chairman), Richard Ruggles, Howard G. Schaller, Leo F. Schnore, Arthur M. Weimer, Robert C. Wood.

[2] U.S. Bureau of Census, *Population of Standard Metropolitan Statistical Areas: 1960 and 1950,* 1960 Census of Population, Supplementary Report, PC (S1)–1, p. 7, April 10, 1961.

[3] Federal Reserve System, *Distribution of Bank Deposits by Counties and Standard Metropolitan Areas,* (December 1960).

[4] U.S. Bureau of the Census, *1958 Census of Manufactures.*

[5] *Construction Review* (March 1961), p. 15.

[6] U.S. Bureau of the Census, *Local Government Finances in Metropolitan Areas* 3:6, 1957 Census of Governments.

[7] Richard A. Musgrave, *The Theory of Public Finance,* (New York, McGraw-Hill Book Company, Inc., 1959), pp. 42–46.

[8] Some of the following examples were given by Charles M. Tiebout in his paper, "Normative Aspects of Metropolitan Finance," at the 1959 meetings of the Southern Economics Association.

[9] The Rockefeller Panel Reports, *Prospect for America* (New York: Doubleday & Company, Inc., 1961) p. 352.

[10] Lyle C. Fitch, "Metropolitan Financial Problems," *The Annals,* 314 (November 1957), p. 70.

[11] *Ibid.,* p. 72.

[12] For a detailed discussion of these dimensions, see Werner Z. Hirsch, "A General Structure for Regional Economic Analysis," *Design of Regional Accounts* (Baltimore: The Johns Hopkins Press, 1961), pp. 1–32.

[13] Musgrave, *op. cit.,* p. 628.

[14] "Emergency Employment Acceleration Act of 1961," S. 986 in the Senate of the United States, February 20, 1961, *Congressional Record,* 107, Pt. 2, pp. 2372–2375.

[15] See Kjeld Philip, *Inter-Governmental Fiscal Relations* (Copenhagen: Institute of Economics and History, 1954), pp. 92–103.

[16] For a detailed discussion of equalization policy, see Kjeld Philip, *op. cit.*, pp. 124–40.

[17] Werner Z. Hirsch, "Expenditure Implications of Metropolitan Growth and Consolidation," *Review of Economics and Statistics,* 41 (August 1959), pp. 232–41.

[18] Advisory Commission on Intergovernmental Relations, *Local Non-Property Taxes and the Coordinating Role of the State* (Washington, D.C.: Government Printing Office, September 1961), pp. 18, 51.

[19] U.S. Bureau of the Census, *Historical Summary of Governmental Finances in the United States,* 4:3, 1957 Census of Governments, pp. 22–23, and *Governmental Finances in 1960.*

[20] Advisory Commission on Intergovernmental Relations, *Periodic Congressional Reassessment of Federal Grants-in-Aid to State and Local Governments* (Washington, D.C.: Government Printing Office, June 1961), pp. 21–22.

[21] Advisory Commission on Intergovernmental Relations, *Local Non-Property Taxes and the Coordinating Role of the State* (Washington, D.C.: Government Printing Office, September 1961), p. 6.

[22] Advisory Commission on Intergovernmental Relations, *Intergovernmental Cooperation in Tax Administration* (Washington, D.C.: Government Printing Office, June 1961), pp. 3–4.

[23] For a partial illustration, see Werner Z. Hirsch, "Determinants of Public Education Expenditures," *National Tax Journal,* 13:1 (March 1960), pp. 29–40.

[24] They are taxpayers in the ultimate sense, even if they do not make out annual checks to the school district. As long as they live and/or buy in the district, some school tax burden is likely to fall on them.

[25] Lowdon Wingo, Jr., *Transportation and Urban Land* (Washington, D.C.: Resources For The Future, 1961), p. 132.

[26] Demand for movement is often measured in terms of the number of purposeful trips required per day. In large metropolitan areas it seems to vary somewhere between 1.75 and 2.0. For example, the 1957 figure for St. Louis is 1.76. (St. Louis Metropolitan Area Highway Planning Study [St. Louis, 1959], I, *Highway and Travel Facts,* Summary, 4th page; and II, *Tables and Reference Data,* p. 19, Table B-2.)

[27] Frank B. Curran and Joseph T. Stegmeier, "Traffic Patterns in Fifty Cities," *Public Roads–A Journal of Highway Research,* 30:5 (Washington, D.C.: U.S. Department of Commerce, Bureau of Public Roads, December 1958).

[28] Robert E. Schmidt and M. Earl Campbell, *Highway Traffic Estimation* (Saugatuck, Conn.: Eno Foundation, 1956), p. 20.

[29] *Loc. cit.,* p. 66.

[30] Jesse Burkhead, "Comment," *Design of Regional Accounts,* p. 68.

[31] *Preliminary Financial and Organizational Report regarding Metropolitan Transportation,* (Washington, D.C.: Joint Committee on Washington Metropolitan Problems, Congress of the United States, 1959), pp. 16–22.

Urban Form: The Case of the Metropolitan Community

LEO F. SCHNORE *is Professor of Sociology at the University of Wisconsin. His many writings, particularly on his special interests in population, human ecology, and methodology are important contributions to the urban problems field. He is a member of the Committee on Urban Economics and of its subcommittee on Census Monographs and is Secretary of the Committee on Urbanization of the Social Science Research Council.*

Does urban sociology offer any distinctive contributions to the study of urban life and form? It was one of a number of specialized approaches to the city and its problems that appeared almost simultaneously in the twenties as new subfields within the traditional academic disciplines. Urban life and form soon became the focus of the whole Chicago School of sociologists led by Robert E. Park. As Albert J. Reiss, Jr., has observed, these men "saw three principal areas of sociological inquiry into urban life: the study of the ecology of the city, of its social organization, and of the psychology of its inhabitants."[1]

These three areas have not received equal attention over the years. In his "The Growth of the City" of 1923, Ernest W. Burgess, Park's colleague, sketched the outlines of "the ecology of the city," asserting that land uses, population, and urban institutions were distributed in a series of concentric zones focusing upon the urban core, the central business district. Fifteen years later, Louis Wirth, in "Urbanism as a Way of Life," provided a virtual catalog of hypotheses concerning the distinctive features of urban social organization and psychology. In the years that have followed, the themes set out in these two expositions have been restated a number of times, and some of them have come under sharp attack, but far more attention has been given to the topics treated by Wirth.[2] Students of the urban scene, whether sociologists or not, have been less interested in the morphology of the city than in interpersonal relations in the city milieu and the role of the larger urban environment in shaping personality development. The result is that we have a substantial literature devoted to sociological treatments of *urban life*. The subject of *urban form* poses another problem altogether.

What is urban form? One can quickly become lost in a semantic bog if he is unwilling to accept arbitrary limitations on the uses of such a term, but the subject of urban form has not been a popular sociological specialty, no matter what meaning may be read into the phrase. *For present purposes, we shall simply take "form" as the rough equivalent of "spatial structure," and hold that one of the largest contributions to general urban studies on the part of sociology lies in the work that has been done on the spatial structure of the metropolitan community.* This subject represents a logical extension of the earlier interests of Chicago sociologists in the ecology of the city, and constitutes a continuing interest on the part of some sociologists in the morphology of urbanism. Economists and geographers share these concerns, but we will limit ourselves to the efforts of sociologists working in the ecological tradition.

THEORY AND RESEARCH ON THE METROPOLITAN COMMUNITY

The seminal theoretical work on "metropolitanism," *An Introduction to Economic History*, published in 1922 by N. S. B. Gras, was actually an interpretive historical inquiry, not a sociological treatise. Rejecting earlier theories that posited a series of evolutionary stages of economic organization culminating in the national economy, Gras argued for recognition of the "metropolitan economy" as the successor to the "town economy," with London after the mid–sixteenth century regarded as the prototype.[3] His views exerted a profound influence upon the thinking of many sociologists—most notably, R. D. McKenzie, a student of Park and Burgess, who subsequently taught at the University of Michigan. McKenzie published a full-scale monograph on *The Metropolitan Community* in 1933, the first statistical treatment of the subject. He turned away from Gras's historical concerns and identified "the metropolitan community" as the product of revolutionary changes in local transportation and communication occurring in the twentieth century:

> By reducing the scale of local distance, the motor vehicle extended the horizon of the community and introduced a territorial division of labor among local institutions and neighboring centers which is unique in the history of settlement. The large center has been able to extend the radius of its influence; its population and many of its institutions, freed from the dominance of rail transportation, have become widely dispersed throughout surrounding territory. Moreover, formerly independent towns and villages and also rural territory have become part of this enlarged city complex . . . The metropolitan community, therefore, comprises a cluster or constellation of centers. Smaller cities and towns tend to group themselves around larger ones somewhat as planets group themselves around a sun.[4]

The study of "the city" as a continuous area of dense settlement was thus supplemented by the recognition of clusters of cities forming a "supercommunity." This larger entity gained its unity through a territorial division of labor between more or less speccialized parts, including the metropolis itself and the nearby hinterland, urban and rural, and McKenzie brought together a variety of materials mainly from census sources in order to document "the rise of the metropolitan community."

Research on this broader area of interdependent relations was greatly facilitated by the recognition of "metropolitan" units on the part of data-collecting agencies of the federal government. Beginning in 1910, population statistics were made available for "metropolitan districts" consisting of large cities and the immediately adjacent territory beyond their borders. With minor revisions in criteria, these units continued to be delineated by the Bureau of the Census up through the census of 1940, and they were used exclusively for the reporting of population data. In advance of the 1950 census, responsibility for this activity shifted to an interdepartmental committee consisting of representatives of a large number of federal agencies, and many additional series of social and economic data have been regularly reported for Standard Metropolitan Areas (1950) and Standard Metropolitan Statistical Areas (1960). It is only recently, then, that "metropolitan" data have come to be available on matters other than those covered in the decennial census of population. These matters deserve mention here because the character of the available data seems to have had a large part in shaping the research that has been carried out. Norman B. Ryder's observation concerning fertility research bears repeating here:

> It does not seem unfair to assert that the existence of vast stores of official data . . . has made the development of the subject excessively dependent on these stores, so that the forms in which data are presented in these sources have become the frames of reference for analysis. To put the point in the form of a question: Have demographers chosen their methods and concepts because they are theoretically relevant or because the data already exist in these forms? [5]

Whatever the answer to this question, it does appear that empirical research on "metropolitan" topics has been rather one-sided. McKenzie described the rise of the metropolitan community as an emerging system characterized by two principal trends:

> (1) The increase in the aggregate population of the community and the expansion of the area within which local activities are carried on in common; (2) the increased mobility of products and people, resulting in a wider range of individual choice, more specialization of local services and a more closely-knit community structure.[6]

Studies of these latter processes—increased mobility, specialization—are rather hard to find. Granted, migration, residential mobility, and commuting have been studied in a metropolitan context from time to time, but the mobility of products—commodities and services—has received less attention than the mobility of people.

Intrametropolitan "specialization of local services" has been largely ignored, at least as it may represent an unfolding process observable over time, and no one has seriously tried to grapple with the question of whether or not the metropolitan area is tending toward "a more closely knit community structure." These are not trends that can be easily inferred from inspecting a series of census reports.

At the same time, it must be said that the other processes identified by McKenzie—population growth and territorial expansion—have been thoroughly documented by subsequent research. In particular, we have three excellent historical-demographic analyses of twentieth-century developments by Warren S. Thompson, Donald J. Bogue, and Amos H. Hawley.[7] Not only do we have data for metropolitan areas in the aggregate, but we can also trace the experience of individual areas in some detail. If one is interested in the decentralization of residential population, for example, it is possible to assemble historical statistics in a simple way that permits the approximate dating of relative outward shifts in particular places. (See Table 1.) Our study has suggested that at least one city, New York, was decentralizing as early as the 1850's, and that it was joined by nine others before the turn of the century. At the same time, this inquiry has demonstrated that it was not until the 1920's, when automobile ownership became widespread, that a majority of large American cities began to exhibit growth rates lower than those of their surrounding rings.[8]

Census materials, then, have been employed to establish the main trends of metropolitan growth and expansion over the years. But what of the evolving spatial structure of the metropolitan community? McKenzie spoke of it as a "new type of supercommunity organized around a dominant focal point and comprising a multiple of differentiated centers of activity."[9] What do we know of the evolution of this urban form? Unfortunately, we must depend upon cross-sectional "snapshots" if we wish to learn anything more than the gross facts of population redistribution.

PREWAR METROPOLITAN PATTERNS: THREE STUDIES

As we shall see, ecological studies of the spatial structure of the metropolitan community also tend to be based on census materials.

Five investigations deserve close attention, particularly from the standpoint of research design. The first three portray the ecology of the metropolitan community as it existed on the eve of World War II.

The Structure of the Metropolitan Community. The first of these studies was the extremely ambitious doctoral dissertation written at the University of Michigan by Donald J. Bogue. Using materials from the 1939 "economic censuses" (business and manufacturing) in combination with 1940 population census data, Bogue assigned every square foot of the continental United States to one or another of 67 preselected "metropolitan communities," and examined patterns of population density, wholesale and retail trade, services, and manufacturing according to broad distance zones and directional

Table 1

POPULATION OF CENTRAL CITY AS A PERCENTAGE OF TOTAL METROPOLITAN AREA POPULATION, SELECTED CITIES, 1850–1960 [a]

Census Year	New York	Cincinnati	Boston	St. Louis	Buffalo	Cleveland	Detroit	Syracuse	Phoenix	Austin
1850	*50*	—	26	50	30	27	24	26	—	—
1860	48	67	26	58	42	46	33	31	—	—
1870	43	*70*	30	67 [b]	51	63	42	41	—	—
1880	43	67	*35*	68	57	75	49	42	—	—
1890	41	66	26	*72*	66	79	62	61	—	—
1900	68 [b]	63	43 [b]	71	*69*	85	68	64	27	47
1910	67	54	42	68	68	*86*	76	69	32	53
1920	66	50	41	68	67	83	*77*	71	32	61
1930	64	47	36	60	63	73	72	*72*	32	68
1940	64	43	35	57	60	69	68	70	*35*	79
1950	61	35	34	51	53	62	61	65	32	*82*
1960	53	47 [b]	28	38	41	49	44	51	66 [b]	88 [b]

[a] Standard Metropolitan Areas as defined in 1950, with definitions retrojected to earlier census years. The italicized entries designate the census dates at which the central cities contained maximum proportions. In four cases (New York, Boston, Phoenix, and Austin) this maximum is not the largest percentage shown in the column because city areas were considerably extended by annexation of territory after decentralization was under way on the older areal basis.

[b] A major annexation to the central city occurred in the preceding decade.

sectors.[10] Presented as "a study in dominance and subdominance," it demonstrated the existence of a complex but orderly geographic division of labor between spatial units spread over a wide landscape extending far beyond the city itself. Understandably enough, this study has not been replicated for other years. Confined as it is to 1939–1940 materials, it yields a richly detailed cross-sectional view of the level of territorial differentiation achieved in a highly industrialized society favored by an advanced system of transportation and communication, and it fully deserves recognition as a classic contribution to metropolitan research.

Other studies, much smaller in scope, have adopted major elements of Bogue's design, assigning outlying areas to one or another metropolis and proceeding to search for spatial patterns in demographic, social, or economic characteristics.[11] In actual fact, however, there are reasons for doubting the utility of a full-scale replication of the Bogue study, given one of its major characteristics—the assumption of a set of "closed" metropolitan communities, wherein the experience of a particular area is implicitly regarded as independent of the experience of other areas occupying positions in the total spatial structure of the national economy. Nevertheless, this research must be regarded as a major accomplishment—a breakthrough both substantively and methodologically—for it pointed the way to a structural interpretation of census materials.

Differentiation in Metropolitan Areas. Still another study—also a doctoral dissertation from the University of Michigan—has taken up the question of the territorial division of labor, but in a more restricted area.[12] This study, by Leslie Kish, demonstrated the existence of an orderly pattern of differentiation among subcommunities found within the immediate orbit of the metropolis, that is, within the metropolitan community itself rather than in the broader metropolitan region studied by Bogue. Some nine demographic, economic, and political characteristics of incorporated places as of 1940 were examined in a probability sample of twenty-four areas. Again, distance was of central concern, and it was found that subcenters near the central city were much more variegated than those at greater distances; within an "inner metropolitan belt," in fact, high levels of differentiation were clearly observable, while substantially lower levels were found in areas beyond the immediate sphere of metropolitan influence.

With the use of an ingenious measure of intraclass correlation, Kish was able to show bands of "metropolitan influence" varying in width according to the size of the metropolis. Other than the size factor, however, this study stressed variation *within* metropolitan areas, ignoring area-to-area variation, and it implicitly took the metropolitan community as a "closed" system. Again, one must be struck by the cross-sectional nature of the inquiry, and a whole series of questions is likely to occur to the reader concerning trends over time in levels of differentiation. For example, when did the patterns observed in 1940 emerge? Have the bands of influence been expanding at a measurable rate? Are suburbs becoming more differentiated or more like each other? Despite his inability to answer such questions, Kish produced important bench mark data, and provided significant details on another facet of metropolitan spatial structure.

Metropolitan Site Selection. A third study of prewar patterns was more directly concerned with the economic aspect of metropolitan spatial structure. In addition, it involved an attempt to derive longitudinally oriented propositions from cross-sectional data. We refer to "Metropolitan Site Selection," by Walter Isard (an economist) and Vincent H. Whitney (a sociologist), a study of the territorial differentiation of retail trade in subcenters of 10,000 or more inhabitants, found in a series of seven distance zones ranging up to seventy miles from the metropolitan center.[13] The spatial structuring of retail activities was clearly manifested in the data. As of 1939 (the data of the Census of Business used in the study), total per capita sales were substantially higher in the central city than in the nearby suburban zones; beyond about twenty miles, however, per capita sales rose in a roughly regular gradient with distance. This pattern was interpreted by the authors as a reflection of the drawing power of the metropolis, which tends to attract shoppers from the immediately contiguous zones. At a greater distance, the "friction of space" presumably operated to discourage longer trips to the metropolitan center, and functioned as a protective barrier against the competition of the metropolis, guaranteeing higher sales for smaller outlying cities that served as trade centers for their own immediate hinterlands. More important, Isard and Whitney were able to show orderly variations by distance in specific trade categories: the center was heavily specialized in general merchandising and exhibited "dominance" over the nearby suburbs in such lines as apparel and jewelry, but not in food sales and in the automotive group, where sales were more evenly distributed.

Despite the clarity of the major findings, certain characteristics of the Isard-Whitney research design make for difficulties in interpretation. Like the studies by Bogue and Kish, it took the metropolitan area as a kind of "closed system," though this seems justifiable in a study of retail trade patterns. In addition, however, the study was highly aggregative, combining data for ten metropolitan centers and their surrounding cities; the results were thus presented in the form of weighted averages—averages that are heavily influenced by the patterns exhibited in the largest places, and that may conceal a great amount of variation from area to area. Moreover, the authors excluded a number of outlying places near cities of intermediate size, and they further eliminated all cities that had fewer than 5000 inhabitants in 1890, "in order to diminish as far as possible the special effect of suburban cities whose growth has been primarily associated with the centrifugal flow of population from the central cities."[14]

These limitations were imposed in an effort to develop an historical argument; Isard and Whitney assumed that the outlying cities had been very similar to each other in terms of retail structure in 1890, and they then interpreted the "site selection" patterns observable in 1939 as the product of trends over time in the direction of greater trade specialization that followed upon major improvements in local transportation and communication. Yet their data are intrinsically cross-sectional in form, and a longitudinal argument is necessarily strained. Technically speaking, the effects of aggregating the data over ten metropolitan regions and the consequences of arbitrarily eliminating outlying cities are also extremely difficult to assess. Replications of this study would be improved if they were confined to individual areas and if they allowed the full range of city types to be represented. Moreover, historical inferences would be more soundly based if a series of observations at different points in time were employed.

METROPOLITAN PATTERNS: TWO RECENT STUDIES

The studies by Bogue, Kish, and Isard and Whitney provide a wealth of cross-sectional evidence on the internal spatial structure of the metropolitan community just prior to World War II. Two more recent investigations that have focused on postwar patterns were carried out at the University of Chicago by Donnell Pappenfort and by Otis Dudley Duncan and his colleagues.

The Ecological Field and the Metropolitan Community. The Pappenfort study demonstrated the utility of postulating a more inclusive "field" within which individual metropolitan communities are found.[15] Using data for production units (factories) located in Illinois, and their spatially separate administrative centers (home offices) located throughout the United States, Pappenfort was able to show that production units in Illinois are dissimilarly distributed according to the location of their administrative centers. Illinois factories with Illinois home offices are distributed with primary reference to Chicago, the dominant metropolis in the state. At the same time, Illinois factories with administrative offices outside the Chicago Standard Metropolitan Area are located with reference to the influence of adjacent and even more distant metropolitan areas. According to Pappenfort, "the consistency of the relationships suggests that they may reflect general principles of ecological organization on the national level that the contemporary interpretation of the metropolitan community [as a closed system] does not include." [16]

Metropolis and Region. Further confirmation for this more inclusive structural conception is found in *Metropolis and Region,* by Otis Dudley Duncan and his colleagues. Like the other works discussed above, this study was cross-sectional in orientation, designed to yield "a mid-century bench mark." Frankly ecological in outlook, it assumed that "to understand metropolitan communities we must examine them in the context of a more inclusive system." [17] The "more inclusive system" turns out to be more than the "region" as it is ordinarily conceived in the literature of metropolitanism, for it often embraces the whole of the national economy and society. In the case of manufacturing, for example, it was shown that the "urban hierarchy" is a national system, while broad regions appear to have relatively self-contained hierarchies for the provision of certain services. As the authors showed, each kind of metropolitan function may entail a distinctive type of regional relationship.

The notable advance achieved by this study was the incorporation of an "open system" conception of the metropolis in the very design of the research. Much of the novelty of the study stems from this fact, together with the related use of actual data on interarea exchanges—tabulations of the flow of commercial and financial payments and receipts between each of thirty-six zones making up the Federal Reserve System. These interregional data were complemented by materials on the spatial patterning of bank loans. Similarly, new light was cast on the concept of "metropolitan dominance." Unlike Bogue's classic study (and others influenced by it), the approach taken by Duncan and his colleagues "does not rest on a prior classification of nonmetropolitan parts of the country into metropolitan regions [and] metropolitan influence or 'dominance' is not conceived as flowing to each hinterland areal unit from a single metropolitan center."[18] Instead, the nonmetropolitan territory of the United States was examined in terms of Pappenfort's concept of a generalized "ecological field."

TWO ISSUES IN RESEARCH DESIGN

Cross-sectional versus Longitudinal Studies. One could easily make a case for a research program essentially based on straightforward replications of the five ecological studies reviewed above. Certainly our understanding of metropolitan structure would be considerably enhanced by the assemblage of many more "snapshots" for additional dates, so that gross trends could be detected. These studies capture certain static aspects of an evolving structure at certain points in time, but they tell us very little indeed about the nature of that evolution. Drawing longitudinal inferences from cross-sectional data involves hazards that are too familiar to require discussion here. But the difficulties involved in actually conducting longitudinal studies when one is working with data assembled on an areal basis are less widely recognized. To take only one example, consider the implications of the simple fact that most census data are reported for political units—cities, counties, states—as of a particular point in time.

Political boundaries change, and even if one is content to confine himself to research on demographic matters, ignoring questions of spatial structure, there is a serious practical difficulty that faces anyone conducting research on population growth or other changes within metropolitan areas, namely, the possibility of *changes in the territorial units under study.* Thus, only one serious effort has been devoted to a careful assessment of annexation as a "component" of population growth in metropolitan centers and rings; Bogue examined this factor, along with the contributions of natural increase and net migration, for the 1940–1950 decade. This problem turns out to be much more severe for the 1950–1960 intercensal period, when three out of four metropolitan centers extended their legal limits.[19] Thus, the best intentions in the world may be frustrated by the form in which mass data are made available. Anyone who has had experience in working with these materials quickly comes to appreciate why cross-sectional research designs are so frequently used in the investigation of problems that seem to cry out for longitudinal study.

Open versus Closed Systems. We have also observed that most of the work that has been done on this subject exhibits a kind of "intra-metropolitan" bias, for it takes the metropolitan community as a relatively self-contained or quasi-independent system. We have seen that efforts to identify the place of the metropolitan community in some larger field are recent and rare. Like everyone else, sociologists acknowledge the fact of interdependence when they observe that metropolitan agglomerations inevitably depend upon other areas for food and fiber, but they seem to ignore the implications of this fact in carrying out their studies. Again, however, there are practical reasons that influence the design of metropolitan research. The "simple" problem of determining the spatial limits of the metropolitan community makes it clear that there are many difficulties in attempting to bound what is literally an "open system."

This matter can be best understood if one contrasts the problems facing an investigator who prefers to undertake a comparative analysis of a number of places rather than an intensive study of a particular area. As an example, consider Gottmann's monumental work on *Megalopolis,* the densely settled northeastern seaboard of the United States.[20] This remarkable study provides a noteworthy example of an open-system conception, analyzing a sprawling series of "supercommunities" that could hardly be understood without reference to its place in the nation and the world. The extent to which this unique cluster of contiguous metropolitan areas exhibits internal unity is still an open question, but it is quite clear that the study of any particular area is more likely to sensitize the investigator to the relations between it and the outside world than a study that attempts simultaneously to deal with a number of areas, all of which are interrelated in some degree. Just as we found pressing practical reasons for cross-sectional rather than longitudinal designs, we come to appreciate the difficulties involved in working with an open-system conception in comparative analyses of the metropolitan community. To say that something is difficult, however, is not to say that it is impossible, and we shall see that there are at least a few points at which the metropolitan system can be "opened" in a way that permits its study as part of a still larger system.

TWO SUBJECTS FOR FUTURE RESEARCH

Let us consider the future directions that ecological analysis might take, building upon the work that has already been accomplished, and taking account of the issues discussed above. Two broad topics seem particularly amenable to an approach that takes the spatial structure of the metropolitan community as a point of departure: "population shifts" on the one hand, and "movement systems" on the other. In both cases, questions of research design are crucial, but work is somewhat farther advanced in the first instance.

Population Shifts. As we have noted, the growth and territorial expansion of the metropolitan aggregate over time has been charted in detail, but these population movements have yet to be linked to historical shifts in social and economic organization. Thus, Reiss has asked "what is the relationship between *types* of economic organization, or functional specialization, and metropolitan growth? Historical research is particularly needed on the relationship between urban aggregation and changes in economic organization." [21] Changes in industrial and occupational composition of individual metropolitan areas provide one means of accounting for differentials in population growth. Certain sectors of the national economy are growing rapidly, while others are lagging. Are these changes reflected in the growth of individual metropolitan areas? The larger ecological field should be kept in the forefront of such an analysis, and an open-system conception appears to be necessary, for the growth of any particular metropolitan area is achieved only at the expense of other parts of the nation.

Within the metropolitan community itself, however, the redistribution of residential population may be regarded as incidental to the internal reorganization of spatial relations. As a consequence, a closed-system approach still has some utility. Nevertheless, the unresolved problems are many and vexing. To take only one example, consider the sheer description of the phenomenon variously labelled decentralization, deconcentration, or suburbanization. Despite the considerable attention devoted to this subject, much remains to be learned. As Duncan has observed:

> Extensive attempts to measure the [suburban] trend and efforts to isolate its determinants are prominent in the literature . . . This is a field of research with more than ordinary difficulties of conceptualization and measurement. All too often researchers . . . have somewhat naively accepted findings of differential growth rates between central and peripheral portions of urban communities as evidence of a specific process of "suburbanization" or "decentralization," without attempting an operational distinction between these alleged processes and the normal tendency for expansion to occur on the periphery of the community area . . . One may hazard a guess as to the approach needed to clarify this problem. *Comparative studies in considerable longitudinal depth* should match a city of a given size at a recent date with one of the same size at a remote date and note whether the recent pattern of growth is a more dispersed or "suburban" one than that occurring at the earlier period. An adequate comparison would require detailed examination of patterns and changes of population density.[22]

Assuming that the existing problems of terminology and measurement can be solved, shifts in residential population must still be linked to *other* processes occurring within the metropolitan community. One of the logical next steps consists of treating the growth of subareas as responsive to changes in the local housing inventory. The recent attention to the changing spatial structure of "housing opportunities" in two case studies by Beverly Duncan and her colleagues points the way toward resolving many of the difficulties that attend research focusing exclusively upon the movements of residential population.[23] Thus, longitudinal studies of closed metropolitan systems continue to offer considerable promise, especially as questions of timing are brought to the fore.

In this connection, a whole family of research questions is related to the problem of "history." Efforts at urban renewal and the troubles facing central business districts have made us all conscious of the obsolescence of the metropolitan core. But we are even more conscious of the differences between metropolitan areas than we are of the similarities among them. One factor that produces differences is the constant turnover visible in the metropolitan community—families being formed and dissolving, firms entering business and failing, etc. Each of these units begins its life and is obliged to take its place in an existing structure. Moreover, each cohort—or set of units "born" in a given year—emerges in an era marked by a somewhat different technological repertoire, and its activities are likely to be affected by the character of the tools and techniques of the age. But elements of technology are readily diffused, and may make for similarities that outweigh the differences.

One can conceive a model of "incremental growth and residues," wherein *the timing of major periods of growth* may be the crucial factor in accounting for the differences and similarities among metropolitan communities and their areal parts. The growth rings observable in a tree's trunk tell us not only its age, but also something of its year-to-year experience, whether favorable or unfavorable. It is commonplace to remark on the differences between pre- and post-auto cities, at least with respect to general form and physical structure. If one adds some attention to the historical variations in the style and architectural design of homes, shops, and factories, much of the physical appearance of contemporary metropolitan communities can be understood by reference to their periods of florescence. Internally, one can detect cross-sectional differences between whole residential neighborhoods, shopping areas, and industrial districts that are the products of history.[24]

Still another line of analysis involves the study of short-term growth differentials within metropolitan areas in terms of the roles played by various subareas—whether "neighborhoods" within the great city or "suburbs" in the ring. Here again, cross-sectional research designs appear to be appropriate. The results of one such study are shown in Table 2. These data represent an effort to portray

Table 2

GROWTH RATES, 1940–1950, IN METROPOLITAN SUBURBS AND SATELLITES OF 10,000 OR MORE INHABITANTS, BY FUNCTIONAL TYPE AND OTHER CHARACTERISTICS

	Percent Increase in Population, 1940–50			Number of Suburbs		
Selected Characteristics of Metropolitan Suburbs	*Residential*	*Employing*	*All*	*Residential*	*Employing*	*All*
A. *Regional location*						
Northeast	13.3	6.1	8.1	65	110	175
North Central	30.0	17.1	22.8	65	57	122
West	63.6	47.1	53.1	37	43	80
South	77.4	47.4	60.4	20	19	39
B. *Central city size*						
500,000 or more	27.8	12.4	18.2	136	142	278
100,000–500,000	36.1	13.8	21.6	32	40	72
less than 100,000	79.5	36.9	42.9	19	47	66
C. *Suburban size,* 1940						
50,000 or more	15.1	10.0	11.5	17	31	48
25,000–50,000	18.8	14.9	15.8	18	55	73
10,000–25,000	30.9	19.1	24.4	90	102	192
less than 10,000	104.1	92.6	99.3	62	41	103
D. *Distance from central city*						
0–10 miles	27.2	16.4	20.8	112	92	204
10–20 miles	40.8	18.2	25.3	61	84	145
over 20 miles	29.4	15.9	18.1	14	53	67
E. *Metropolitan area economic base*						
Manufacturing	23.6	12.2	16.1	79	105	184
Diversified	33.0	19.3	23.9	89	98	187
Retail	68.9	23.4	29.2	17	23	40
Other	412.7	64.8	103.4	2	3	5
F. *Suburban rent level*						
Low	31.7	12.8	15.9	7	26	33
Average	29.0	15.1	18.8	91	173	264
High	36.3	44.1	38.4	89	30	119
G. *Age of suburb*						
more than 50 years	21.8	12.2	15.0	102	178	280
40–50 years	33.1	36.2	34.6	35	31	66
30–40 years	51.8	66.2	57.5	25	12	37
less than 30 years	116.6	168.5	126.6	25	8	33
All suburbs	31.9	17.0	22.1	187	229	316

SOURCE: Leo F. Schnore, "The Growth of Metropolitan Suburbs," *American Sociological Review,* 22 (April 1957), pp. 165–173.

recent growth differentials between two types of metropolitan subcenter: (1) "residential suburbs," having more employed residents than jobs, and (2) "employing satellites," having more jobs than employed residents. The guiding assumption is that variations in growth are associated with these typological differences.

Table 3

COMPONENTS OF POPULATION CHANGE IN THE CONSTITUENT PARTS OF THE DETROIT STANDARD METROPOLITAN AREA, 1940–1950

	Percent Change, 1940–1950, Due to:		
Area	Natural Increase	Net Migration	Total Change
Total Standard Metropolitan Area	15.9	10.9	26.8
A. Central city	14.1	−0.2	13.9
B. Total ring	19.8	34.3	54.1
1. Small subcenters and fringe	20.0	67.3	87.3
2. Large subcenters (10,000 or more)	19.6	5.6	25.2
a. Employing satellites	17.8	−3.8	14.0
b. Residential suburbs	23.6	25.7	49.3
Employing satellites			
Pontiac	16.4	−5.5	10.3
Dearborn	26.6	22.8	49.4
Ecorse	24.5	11.4	35.9
Hamtramck	12.9	−25.9	−13.0
Highland Park	7.5	−16.2	−8.7
Wyandotte	24.7	−4.3	20.3
Residential suburbs			
Mount Clemens	23.8	−5.5	18.3
Saint Clair Shores	26.7	63.8	90.5
Birmingham	23.6	14.5	38.1
Ferndale	24.4	7.4	31.8
Royal Oak	30.5	56.4	86.9
Grosse Pointe Park	2.3	1.1	3.4
River Rouge	20.1	0.7	20.8
Lincoln Park	30.3	62.1	92.4

SOURCE: Original computations derived from vital statistics and census reports, 1940–1950. Satellites and suburbs are operationally defined in Leo F. Schnore, "The Functions of Metropolitan Suburbs," *American Journal of Sociology,* 61 (March 1956), pp. 453–458.

In this kind of demographic-ecological research, it is desirable to distinguish the components of population change—natural increase versus net migration. As Table 3 demonstrates, satellites and suburbs within a single metropolitan area may experience highly dissimilar forms of growth and decline, ranging from the rapid growth of such residential suburbs as Lincoln Park, Royal Oak, and St. Clair Shores—growth stemming from both natural increase and net in-migration—to the actual losses registered in the employing areas of Hamtramck and Highland Park, both of which are politically independent enclaves within the city of Detroit that are losing large numbers of people as land uses change and as population groups replace each other.

With respect to the areal sources of in-migration—the more variable of the two components of population change—some further effort should be devoted to distinguishing "streams" of migration (for example, city to ring, intracity, ring to city), and to considering distance as well as direction of movements; survey-based studies have elucidated different "reasons" for moves of varying distance and direction, and migrant selectivity also appears to vary according to type of stream. For example, the city-to-ring stream appears to select families in the expanding phase of the family cycle, while the countercurrent is often said to be made up of older persons whose children have moved out of their parental homes to establish their own households.[25]

Still another phase of metropolitan population redistribution that is deserving of further analysis is the changing color composition of the larger urban agglomeration and its various parts. A recent study has thrown some light upon the relative decentralization of whites and nonwhites in the twelve largest metropolitan areas between 1930 and 1960. Table 4 shows the expected patterns—mounting proportions in the rings—for the total populations and for the whites in each area. In six areas, however, the 1960 proportion of nonwhites found in the ring is actually *lower* than that found there in 1930. In another five areas, there is practically no change in this proportion, and the San Francisco-Oakland SMSA provides the only real exception to the common pattern.[26] While this study makes use of the gross distinction between the central city and the ring, the use of finer areal units (for example, census tracts) permits a more detailed examination of changes in the color composition of

Table 4

PERCENTAGE OF POPULATION IN THE RINGS OF THE TWELVE LARGEST STANDARD METROPOLITAN STATISTICAL AREAS (1960), BY RACE: 1930–1960

STANDARD METROPOLITAN STATISTICAL AREAS (1960)	PERCENTAGE OF POPULATION IN RINGS, BY RACE: 1930–1960											
	Total Population				*White*				*Nonwhite*			
	1960	*1950*	*1940*	*1930*	*1960*	*1950*	*1940*	*1930*	*1960*	*1950*	*1940*	*1930*
Twelve largest SMSA's: all	50.0	38.5	33.0	31.2	54.9	40.9	34.2	32.1	17.0	16.7	17.8	19.3
New York	27.2	17.4	14.4	13.1	29.5	18.3	14.6	13.2	10.9	8.8	10.8	10.5
Los Angeles–Long Beach	58.1	49.1	42.8	40.7	61.1	51.0	43.7	41.3	27.3	21.0	22.3	27.1
Chicago	42.9	30.1	25.7	24.1	48.8	32.7	26.9	25.1	9.0	8.1	8.2	8.2
Philadelphia	53.9	43.6	39.6	37.8	59.9	46.9	41.4	39.0	21.6	21.7	25.0	26.4
Detroit	55.6	38.7	31.7	28.0	63.0	41.8	33.2	29.0	14.1	16.1	12.7	12.8
San Francisco–Oakland	60.2	48.2	35.9	31.9	64.1	49.6	36.2	32.0	33.0	34.8	28.8	28.4
Boston	73.1	66.8	65.1	64.0	74.9	67.8	65.7	64.4	22.4	24.2	33.3	37.5
Pittsburgh	74.9	69.4	67.7	66.9	77.6	71.4	69.1	67.9	37.9	39.5	47.7	48.4
St. Louis	63.6	50.2	44.3	40.7	69.7	53.2	46.1	42.2	27.7	28.9	28.3	26.6
Washington	61.8	45.2	31.7	27.8	77.0	53.8	35.9	30.0	16.0	16.9	18.3	21.1
Cleveland	51.2	37.6	30.7	27.6	59.5	41.6	32.7	29.1	2.8	3.0	3.8	4.8
Baltimore	45.6	32.4	24.6	22.4	54.6	36.1	26.3	23.2	14.3	17.1	16.7	18.3

SOURCE: Harry Sharp and Leo F. Schnore, "The Changing Color Composition of Metropolitan Areas," *Land Economics*, 38 (May 1962), Table III, p. 179.

metropolitan communities. No matter how fine the observational grain, however, descriptions of trends in the redistribution of such subgroups should be linked to changes in land use, and particularly to shifts in the spatial structure of the housing market.

In summary, more imaginative uses of the very rich materials from the Census of Population and Housing and other similar sources of mass data will certainly yield greater returns than have been heretofore realized. We know the main trends. What seems to be required is the *systematic interpretation of major population shifts as responses to other changes in the spatial structure of the metropolitan community.* Despite the fact that much basic descriptive work has been accomplished, much remains to be learned about the causes of population growth and territorial expansion of the metropolitan system. The needed work includes conceptual clarification, the development of appropriate research designs, and the resolution of some basic problems of measurement. We need more demographic "facts," and we need them assembled in more useful ways, for the data should also serve for testing hypotheses concerning changes in ecological structure and their role in bringing about major population shifts.

Movement Systems. McKenzie referred to the increased mobility of products and people as a typically metropolitan trait, and some attention has been devoted to the recurrent circulation of various elements within the metropolitan community. Traffic studies, in particular, have yielded a wealth of information on commuting and other types of trip, and they tell us a great deal about the spatio-temporal structure of the urban complex. The relevance of these flows and exchanges has been ably identified by Donald L. Foley in a statement concerning the internal functioning of the city:

> In the contemporary large American city a mosaic of functional areas has evolved seemingly as an inevitable counterpart of the broader fact of economic specialization. Ecologists term this process segregation. So long as a city is characterized by specialization and, specifically, by segregation, we can expect that communication and movement among these divergent functional areas will be necessary if that city is to function as an integrated community . . . The development of efficient communication devices, particularly the telephone and postal service, has made it possible for much daily activity to be handled without movement of persons.

Nevertheless . . . a vast amount of daily travel is necessary . . . Movement of persons in the course of carrying out day-to-day activities provides a dynamic mechanism by which the city's various functional areas are linked.[27]

But more than the city per se is involved in the circulation process. The entire metropolitan complex manifests patterned movements in space. After all, one of the key features distinguishing the modern metropolis from large cities of the past is the ease and rapidity of exchange or movement, whether of persons, commodities, or information. Moreover, smaller cities, which also enjoy the advanced transportation and communication facilities of the metropolis, share this relative ease of movement. The unique features distinguishing internal movement in the metropolitan community appear merely to reflect the enhanced complexity associated with a far-flung system of interdependent nuclei.

Compared to small cities, where the regular ebb and flow of traffic is so readily visible, it appears that physical movement in the metropolitan community is much less simple with respect to direction and over-all orientation. In contrast with the simple in-and-out movement between center and periphery of the small city, the metropolitan community appears to have a very high proportion of *lateral movements,* in complicated crosscurrents and eddies. Commuting, in particular, is not merely a matter of centripetal and centrifugal flows morning and evening, but a confusing and asymmetrical compound of variously oriented threads of traffic, overlaying the older (and perhaps rudimentary) center-oriented pattern.

This greater complexity of movement, of course, is related to the feature that we have identified as typologically essential to metropolitanism—functional interdependence reflected in an extreme territorial division of labor. This interdependence between the constituent segments of the whole metropolitan community is only achieved via specialization of land use, and areal specialization requires complex movement systems. Certainly the existence of 1960 census data on workplace, together with comparative use of more than 150 "origin-and-destination" traffic studies in American cities, should yield a more realistic cross-sectional image of this aspect of metropolitan circulation.[28] (In fact, the *recurrent intracommunity* movement of people manifested in "commuting flows" might soon be more adequately understood than the *nonrecurrent intercommunity* movement known as migration.)

The internal circulation of commodities and services, and the flows of waste, fuel, and power, remain virtually unexplored in the ecological literature, despite their presumed importance. These are truly "functional prerequisites" for the maintenance of modern metropolitan communities. Moreover, the internal flow of information has not been charted in detail. The rapid circulation of intelligence may be regarded as one of the crucial permissive factors allowing a sprawling metropolitan population to act in concert. Widely dispersed activities are only integrated, coordinated and synchronized by easy means of communication. The frequently noted separation of production phases of manufacturing from central office functions is a case in point. Physical processes requiring large amounts of land have shifted toward the periphery, while managerial and clerical functions have remained in the metropolitan center, where they enjoy the advantages of numerous "external economies." Such a separation would be unthinkable without the assurance of a rapid and continuous flow of information between the spatially discrete parts making up the metropolitan system.

But more than *internal* circulation is at issue. We possess only a limited understanding of the *external* flows and linkages that give coherence to the whole national system of cities. Granted, intercity traffic in people (via common carriers and automobile) and in certain commodities can be measured with some precision, and the exchange of messages between communities can be similarly assessed, but we have an imperfect understanding of the routes and volumes of such flows as streams of capital.

The work of Duncan and his colleagues in *Metropolis and Region* points the way to studies of intercity and interregional flows, conducted from a spatial-structural point of view. Another question that should be answered in the near future has to do with the "megalopolis" or "strip city." The new 1960 census data on workplace (coded in terms of counties and large cities) should permit an assessment of the extent to which neighboring metropolitan areas are actually linked into some larger unity via exchanges of commuters. All in all, the place of "movement systems" in the functional integration of the metropolitan community would seem sufficiently important to warrant more concerted research effort, whether conducted from the standpoint of an open or closed system.

THE EXPORTABILITY OF THE METROPOLITAN CONCEPT

It might appear from the foregoing discussion that metropolitan theory and research is characterized by an ethnocentric preoccupation with the United States, and some writers have asserted that this is the case for urban sociology in general and metropolitan studies in particular.[29] This is not the place in which to debate questions concerning urban sociology's "proper" objectives, for example, whether or not truly "global" propositions should be the goal. Actually, it is rather remarkable to find that the drumfire of criticism directed against the ethnocentrism of urban sociology has reached a crescendo at the very time that advances are being made in a comparative direction. Although the criticisms would have had some real point and force in earlier years, when "comparative urban research" consisted largely of scattered case studies of individual cities in other cultures, recent work on metropolitan topics has been conducted on a scale that promises at least the possibility of discovering cross-cultural regularities. Let us consider some concrete examples.

Perhaps the most impressive undertaking of all is the literally global research being conducted by a group of scholars at International Urban Research, University of California (Berkeley). This center, under the direction of Kingsley Davis, is the successor to the office established at Columbia University in 1951 as the World Urban Resources Index. Its major product to date is a volume delineating metropolitan areas on a worldwide scale. Though it has some technical limitations, this compilation of basic data provides enormously useful information on some 720 agglomerations in every part of the world.[30] These demographic materials have been employed in a number of recent comparative studies, and others are under way.

Some of these investigations have been worldwide in scope, examining the correlates of metropolitanization around the world as of the early fifties, and studying the recent growth of large metropolitan agglomerations in some eighty countries and territories in the various major world regions.[31] Table 5 provides a regional summary,

Table 5

METROPOLITAN GROWTH IN WORLD REGIONS, ca. 1940–ca. 1952
BY 1937 LEVEL OF PER CAPITA ENERGY CONSUMPTION

			INDICES OF METROPOLITAN GROWTH ‡			
REGIONS	*Per Capita Energy Consumption (Kilowatt Hours), 1937* †	*Degree of Metropolitanization, ca. 1940*	*Average Annual Percentage Growth of Metropolitan Population*	*Ratio of Metropolitan Growth to Total Growth*	*Percentage of Total Growth Claimed by Metropolitan Areas*	*Excess Growth of the Metropolitan Population*
North America	10,074	51.6	2.1	1.40	77.2	1.50
Oceania	3,543	53.3	2.4	1.00	55.0	1.03
Europe	3,117	33.7	1.1	1.57	55.1	1.64
U.S.S.R.	1,873	17.7	1.9	3.80	84.7	4.79
South America	758	17.7	3.7	1.68	37.7	2.13
Middle America	702	16.0	4.3	1.79	32.1	2.01
Africa	686	9.0	3.9	2.44	23.2	2.58
Asia	286	10.5	3.8	2.53	24.2	2.30
All regions	1,676	21.4	2.0	1.67	39.1	1.83

SOURCE: Jack P. Gibbs and Leo F. Schnore, "Metropolitan Growth: An International Study," *American Journal of Sociology,* 66 (September 1960), p. 164.

† SOURCE: Nathaniel B. Guyol, *Energy Resources of the World* (Washington, D.C.: U.S. Department of State, 1949), Table 43.

‡ SOURCE: International Urban Research, University of California (Berkeley).

and illustrates one of the uses of these new materials, based on metropolitan units possessing a high degree of comparability. The table shows clearly that higher rates of metropolitan growth are found in the under-developed areas, while lower rates are exhibited in the industrialized regions of the world. At the same time, metropolitan areas are capturing a very high proportion of the total increase accruing to the industrialized nations. These facts are surely not surprising, but they do document the existence of patterns that had been discussed only impressionistically prior to this study. These same materials have also been employed in case studies of particular countries. Wilkinson, for example, has used them to launch an investigation of metropolitanization in Japan, and other recent inquiries have focused upon metropolitan development in Italy and the United Kingdom, where explicit contrasts with U.S. patterns can be drawn.[32]

All of the foregoing studies deal primarily with population aggregation, with special emphasis upon *levels* of metropolitanization and *rates* of metropolitan growth. As in the literature on American metropolitan communities, it must be said that there are fewer examples of frontal assaults upon problems of spatial structure. For many years, "comparative" ecological work consisted of case studies of the spatial structure of individual towns and cities in other parts of the world. The cumulative impression yielded by these scattered accounts led many students in the field to believe that cross-cultural regularities were not to be found. Reviewing these works, Noel P. Gist concluded that they

> . . . present ample evidence that ecological theory based on the study of American cities is not necessarily applicable to cities in other parts of the world. The few Latin American studies, for example, clearly indicate that the prevailing ecological configurations in American cities of the United States are not characteristic of cities below the Rio Grande, although technological and other factors are tending to produce ecological patterns more nearly like those of the North.[33]

In actual fact, however, there is some evidence suggesting that large urban agglomerations throughout the world *do* manifest patterned regularities in spatial structure, at least if one confines attention to a specific feature for which data are available from many times and places. Whereas other aspects of urban life and form may very well exhibit profound variations from culture to culture, one formal feature displays a striking similarity in many cultures. More specifically, the residential redistribution of urban dwellers according to social class exhibits a fairly high degree of predictability with reference to the center of the urban complex. Given growth and expansion of the entire aggregate, and given appropriate improvements in transportation and communication technology—in short, given metropolitan development—the upper strata tend to shift from central to peripheral residence, while the lower classes increasingly take over the central area abandoned by the elite.[34]

Although this generalization is necessarily modest in scope, a reading of the available evidence suggests that other and more significant cross-cultural regularities might be found if they were made the objects of diligent search. (These regularities, of course, need not be in the form of universals.) In any event, a serious effort to extend the geographic scope of metropolitan research is well under way.

CONCLUSIONS

We have here assumed that the sheer growth of *metropolitanism* might cause us to focus on this particular mode of "urban form." With Duncan and his colleagues, we are persuaded that the continuing study of the metropolitan community is no mere intellectual exercise. In their words:

> At a time when journalists are making the "exploding metropolis" virtually a household word there is no need to plead the timeliness of an essay on metropolitanism. But though our topic is timely we are not primarily concerned to diagnose a social problem or to suggest remedies for the manifold ills of metropolitan areas. The maladies on this familiar roster—traffic congestion, housing obsolescence, frictions among shifting population groups, financial quandaries, governmental fragmentation, and the like—are most likely not fundamental problems in themselves. Rather, they symptomatically reflect an accumulation of lags in the mutual adjustment of units and functions of the metropolitan community—lags which are perhaps inevitable in a period of sporadic and unco-ordinated, though not unrelated, changes in community structure.[35]

Whether we have been successful in persuading others of the importance of the matters discussed here must be left to the judgment of the reader. We have said that urban form has received scant attention by sociologists, except for those who employ an ecological approach and focus on spatial structure. The virtues of the body of work reviewed here seem to lie in its treatment of the metropolitan community as a functioning whole—an interaction system—and in the data it provides on some of the more gross morphological features of the metropolitan community as they are reflected in space and time. Some progress has been made in developing an understanding of the constituent areal parts of this supercommunity, and in identifying the internal linkages between them. More recent ecological research has provided an account of the place of the metropolitan community in a larger field or system external to it, and to which it is inevitably responsive. Finally, metropolitan research is becoming less confined to the United States.

Nevertheless, all of the existing problems would not be solved by simple appreciation of the facts of internal and external interdependence provided by an ecological perspective. Whether longitudinal or cross-sectional in orientation, a full-fledged theory of urban form requires much more attention to the units or building blocks with which we intend to work, and far more effort must be directed toward the development of empirically oriented taxonomies. Despite the efforts of sociologists, economists, political scientists, and geographers, we are still obliged to work with rather crude typologies—central cities, rings, classifications of the economic base, community specialization. Similarly, we make do with such oversimplified polarities as "residential suburbs" versus "employing satellites." Finally, we have not even started to develop the full implications of the concept of "megalopolis," an elusive but challenging concept which has yet to be subjected to searching critical scrutiny. Studies of morphology require attention to taxonomic questions, and these are the tasks for the future.

Notes

[1] Albert J. Reiss, Jr., "Urban Sociology, 1945–55," in Hans L. Zetterberg, ed., *Sociology in the United States of America: A Trend Report* (Paris: United Nations Educational, Scientific, and Cultural Organization, 1956), p. 108. In addition to urban sociology and urban geography, the University of Chicago also served as the birthplace of the scientific study of city politics.

[2] Ernest W. Burgess, "The Growth of the City: An Introduction to a Research Project," *Publications of the American Sociological Society,* 18 (1924), pp. 85–97; Louis Wirth, "Urbanism as a Way of Life," *American Journal of Sociology,* 44 (1938), pp. 1–26. Two recent treatments of Wirth's central themes may be found in William L. Kolb, "The Social Structure and Functions of Cities," *Economic Development and Cultural Change,* 3 (1954), pp. 30–46; Philip M. Hauser, "On the Impact of Urbanism on Social Organization, Human Nature and the Political Order," *Confluence,* 7 (1958), pp. 57–69. The available textbooks in urban sociology all depend heavily upon Wirth's formulation. The ecology of the city is treated in James A. Quinn, *Human Ecology* (Englewood Cliffs, N.J.: Prentice-Hall, Inc., 1950), and in Amos H. Hawley, *Human Ecology: A Theory of Community Structure* (New York: The Ronald Press Company, 1950).

[3] N. S. B. Gras, *An Introduction to Economic History* (New York: Harper & Row, Publishers, 1922). See also N. S. B. Gras; "The Rise of the Metropolitan Community," in E. W. Burgess ed., *The Urban Community* (Chicago: University of Chicago Press, 1926), pp. 183–191.

[4] R. D. McKenzie, *The Metropolitan Community* (New York: McGraw-Hill Book Company, Inc., 1933), pp. 6 and 71.

[5] Norman B. Ryder, "Fertility," in Philip M. Hauser and Otis Dudley Duncan, eds., *The Study of Population: An Inventory and Appraisal* (Chicago: University of Chicago Press, 1959), p. 413. For background on the emergence of official metropolitan units, see Henry Shryock, Jr., "Tne Natural History of Standard Metropolitan Areas," *American Journal of Sociology,* 63 (1957), pp. 163–170.

[6] R. D. McKenzie, "The Rise of Metropolitan Communities," in Research Committee on Social Trends, *Recent Social Trends* (New York: McGraw-Hill Book Company, Inc., 1933), reprinted in Paul K. Hatt and Albert J. Reiss, Jr., eds., *Cities and Society* (New York: The Free Press of Glencoe, 1957), p. 202.

[7] Warren S. Thompson, *The Growth of Metropolitan Districts in the United States, 1900–1940* (Washington, D.C.: Government Printing Office, 1947); Donald J. Bogue, *Population Growth in Standard Metropolitan Areas, 1900–1950* (Washington, D.C.: Housing and Home Finance Agency, 1953); Amos H.

Hawley, *The Changing Shape of Metropolitan America: Deconcentration Since 1920* (New York: The Free Press of Glencoe, 1956). The main trends are summarized in Leo F. Schnore, "Metropolitan Growth and Decentralization," *American Journal of Sociology,* 63 (1957), pp. 171–180.

[8] See Leo F. Schnore, "The Timing of Metropolitan Decentralization: A Contribution to the Debate," *Journal of the American Institute of Planners,* 25 (1959), pp. 200–206. The subtitle refers to a previously published exchange: Robert Schmitt, "Suburbanization: Statistical Fallacy?" *Land Economics,* 32 (1956), pp. 85–87, and Amos H. Hawley, "A Further Note on Suburbanization," *ibid.,* pp. 87–89.

[9] *Op. cit.,* pp. 6–7.

[10] Donald J. Bogue, *The Structure of the Metropolitan Community: A Study in Dominance and Subdominance* (Ann Arbor: University of Michigan Press, 1950). The large size of the units under study suggests that they might better be regarded as extensive "metropolitan regions" rather than "metropolitan communities," for the latter term has come to be used to designate the localized area whose population is integrated with reference to daily activities; as such, it is roughly coterminous with the commuting area or the local labor market. Bogue's units are mapped in F. Stuart Chapin, Jr., *Urban Land Use Planning* (New York: Harper & Row, Publishers, 1957), p. 98.

[11] For example, see Theodore R. Anderson and Jane Collier, "Metropolitan Dominance and the Rural Hinterland," *Rural Sociology,* 21 (1956), pp. 152–157. This is a study of the hinterlands of four metropolitan centers in Missouri.

[12] Leslie Kish, "Differentiation in Metropolitan Areas," *American Sociological Review,* 19 (1954), pp. 388–398.

[13] Walter Isard and Vincent H. Whitney, "Metropolitan Site Selection," *Social Forces,* 27 (1949), pp. 263–269.

[14] *Ibid.,* p. 264.

[15] Donnell M. Pappenfort, "The Ecological Field and the Metropolitan Community: Manufacturing and Management," *American Journal of Sociology,* 64 (1959), p. 380.

[16] *Ibid.,* p. 385.

[17] Otis Dudley Duncan *et al., Metropolis and Region* (Baltimore: The Johns Hopkins Press, 1960), p. 4.

[18] *Ibid.,* p. 8.

[19] Donald J. Bogue, *Components of Population Change, 1940–1950: Estimates of Net Migration and Natural Increase for Each Standard Metropolitan Area and State Economic Area* (Oxford, Ohio, and Chicago: Scripps Foundation for Research in Population Problems, Miami University, and Population Research and Training Center, University of Chicago, 1957); Leo F. Schnore, "Municipal Annexations and the Growth of Metropolitan Suburbs, 1950–1960," *American Journal of Sociology,* 67 (1962), pp. 406–417.

[20] Jean Gottmann, *Megalopolis: The Urbanized Northeastern Seaboard of the United States* (New York: The Twentieth Century Fund, Inc., 1961).

[21] Albert J. Reiss, Jr., "Research Problems in Metropolitan Population Redistribution," *American Sociological Review,* 21 (1956), p. 572.

[22] Otis Dudley Duncan, "Human Ecology and Population Studies," in Hauser and Duncan, eds., *The Study of Population,* p. 697. Italics added.

[23] Beverly Duncan and Philip M. Hauser, *Housing a Metropolis—Chicago* (New York: The Free Press of Glencoe, 1960); and Beverly Duncan, Georges

Sabagh, and Maurice D. Van Arsdol, Jr., "Patterns of City Growth," *American Journal of Sociology,* 67 (1962), pp. 418–429.

24 An enlightening informal discussion of the evolution of housing areas is contained in a work by Hoover and Vernon, who observe that "each successive residential development can be thought of as responding to the conditions of its period and depositing a record of the past." Edgar M. Hoover and Raymond Vernon, *Anatomy of a Metropolis* (Cambridge: Harvard University Press, 1959), p. 208.

25 Philip M. Hauser, *Population Perspectives* (New Brunswick, N.J.: Rutgers University Press, 1960), pp. 115–117.

26 Harry Sharp and Leo F. Schnore, "The Changing Color Composition of Metropolitan Areas," *Land Economics,* 38 (1962), Table III, p. 179.

27 Donald L. Foley, "Urban Daytime Population: A Field for Demographic-Ecological Analysis," *Social Forces,* 32 (1954), pp. 323–324.

28 See Leo F. Schnore, "Three Sources of Data on Commuting: Problems and Possibilities," *Journal of the American Statistical Association,* 55 (1960), pp. 8–22.

29 The most vigorous expression of this view is to be found in Gideon Sjoberg, "Comparative Urban Sociology," in Robert K. Merton, Leonard Broom, and Leonard S. Cottrell, Jr., eds., *Sociology Today: Problems and Prospects* (New York: Basic Books, Inc., 1959). An explicit criticism of the ethnocentrism of "metropolitan" research and theory is contained in Thomas O. Wilkinson, "Urban Structure and Industrialization," *American Sociological Review,* 25 (1960), pp. 356–363.

30 Suzanne R. Angelucci *et al., The World's Metropolitan Areas* (Berkeley: University of California Press, 1959). See also, Jack P. Gibbs and Kingsley Davis, "Conventional versus Metropolitan Data in the International Study of Urbanization," *American Sociological Review,* 23 (1958), pp. 504–514. Because "Standard Metropolitan Areas" in the U.S. were accepted at face value, 147 of the 720 metropolitan areas were delineated by the use of criteria other than those described in the publication, and there is no evidence that the IUR criteria were tested for metropolitan areas in this country. Boundary changes for cities around the world are not reported, so that the population data (shown for two dates) must be used with caution in attempting to assess the significance of any changes in city versus ring population, but total metropolitan growth can be studied.

31 Leo F. Schnore, "The Statistical Measurement of Urbanization and Economic Development," *Land Economics,* 37 (1961), pp. 229–245; Jack P. Gibbs and Leo F. Schnore, "Metropolitan Growth: An International Study," *American Journal of Sociology,* 66 (1960), pp. 160–170; Jack P. Gibbs, "The Growth of Individual Metropolitan Areas: A Global View," *Annals of the Association of American Geographers,* 51 (1961), pp. 380–391.

32 See Thomas O. Wilkinson, *op. cit.,* and his "Agricultural Activities in the City of Tokyo," *Rural Sociology,* 26 (1961), pp. 49–56. See also Leo F. Schnore, "Le aree metropolitane in Italia," *Mercurio,* 3 (1960), pp. 19–24; and, *idem,* "Metropolitan Development in the United Kingdom," *Economic Geography* 38 (1962), pp. 215–233.

[33] Noel P. Gist, "The Urban Community," in Joseph B. Gittler ed., *Review of Sociology: Analysis of a Decade* (New York: John Wiley & Sons, 1957), p. 170.

[34] See Gideon Sjoberg, *The Preindustrial City: Past and Present* (New York: The Free Press of Glencoe, 1960), pp. 97–99. A detailed review of the available evidence for the United States and Latin America may be found in Leo F. Schnore, "On the Spatial Structure of Cities in the Two Americas: Some Problems in Comparative Urban Research," mimeographed paper prepared for the Committee on Urbanization, Social Science Research Council, n.d.

[35] Duncan *et al., op. cit.*, p. 1.

Social Problems Associated with Urban Minorities

LEE NELKEN ROBINS *is Research Associate Professor of Sociology in the Department of Psychiatry and Neurology at Washington University, St. Louis, Missouri. She has written extensively on the social problems of children and adults and is presently engaged in research projects for the U.S. Public Health Service and the National Science Foundation.*

The sociologist feels somewhat uneasy about the study of social problems because when he labels a pattern of behavior a problem he appears to be stating both that the behavior is disapproved by solid citizens and that he concurs in their judgment. This role as judge of the moral worth of behavior is not one he fancies. He feels, rather, that his proper interest in human behavior is in understanding its range of variation, the social factors determining its occurrence, and its social consequences.

Nevertheless, because a central interest of his discipline is the study of norms and of conformity and nonconformity with those norms, he inevitably becomes interested in rates and distribution of nonconformity, and, hence, in social problems. The analytic concepts with which the sociologist has worked are those of age, sex, and racial, cultural, rural-urban, and class groups. When the occurrence of nonconformity with norms has been analyzed in terms of these concepts, it has been apparent that nonconformity is by no means randomly distributed throughout society, but has much higher rates of occurrence in the disadvantaged or minority groups than in the dominant majority. The sociologist, reflecting his traditional liberal political leanings, has responded to this undeniable association between social problems and minority groups by offering plausible explanations for this association that tend to exempt the minority groups from blame. He has offered explanations in terms of readjustments consequent to industrialization; differences in cultural traditions; social disorganization resulting from the impingement of a fully developed urban civilization on the simpler, tightly organized small community; the inevitable adjustment process involved in the assimilation of Europeans and rural Americans to urban American life; traditions of slavery and servility, which poorly prepare for independence and strong achievement goals; effects of uprooting individuals from their native communities with consequent loss of strong community control over their behavior; psychological damage resulting from prejudice and identification with the persecutor; and the frustrations suffered by individuals of low socioeconomic status who accept the achievement goals fostered by the majority without having the character traits, education, and financial assets required to achieve such goals. These explanations have in common not only the fact that they tend to defend the minority group against accusations of bad character or inherent inferiority, but also the fact that they are largely untested propositions, whose correctness and relative importance are yet to be assessed. In addition, they largely fail to consider a striking aspect of the association between social problems and minoritiy groups: minority groups that have shared many of these social situations proposed as conducive to the development of social problems have, in fact, very different rates of social problems.

One constantly recurring question in attempts to explain the distribution of social problems among minority groups is the question of whether the behavior observed, which does not conform with the majority's norms, represents a genuine violation of norms shared by the minority and majority groups or indicates, rather, that the minority group has a different set of norms of its own. This question has been raised in particular in studying organized crime, which can be viewed both as a violation of the majority's norms and as conformity to the norms of a delinquent subculture. Answers to these questions: who commits acts that are defined as social problems, why do they do so, should "social problems" be defined in terms of the values of the offender or of the total society, are vital if the social scientist is to act as an expert called in to advise on ways of reducing the rate of social problems. But his role as adviser disturbs him. If following his advice leads to a reduction in the rate of deviant behavior in minority groups, is he not using his knowledge to reduce the diversity among American subcultures and to defend the values of the dominant majority against those of minority groups?

At the present time, we can offer a definition of social problems, some insight into observed relationships between minority groups and social problems, some tentatively supported hypotheses about why these relationships occur, and an outline of possible approaches to reducing their rate, reminding ourselves that our interest in doing so is always suspect. We can hope that we are attacking problems which cause as much distress to the nonconformer as to the outraged conformist, thereby justifying our right to meddle. But, as will become evident in the course of this paper, the knowledge we have to go on at the present time is scanty and much research still needs to be done before we understand the causes of social problems or the best means of attacking them, assuming we have settled our ethical questions.

FOUR COMPONENTS OF SOCIAL PROBLEMS

Social problems may be defined as recurrent events that involve sizable groups of people, that cause distress either to the people directly involved or to the members of the larger society, and that are believed to be subject to amelioration or prevention through a change in the organization of the society as a whole or in some part of that society. Social problems appear to exist if one or a combination of the following four situations occur:

1. There are relatively widespread violations of the majority's norms. Crime, divorce, public drunkenness, and wife desertion are examples of behavior that fit this category.

2. There is a significant deviation from what is generally accepted

as an attainable level of health. Physical and mental health problems that are considered either to result from man-controlled causes (for example, venereal disease and occupational diseases) or to be receiving less than the optimal treatment or prevention considering the current level of medical knowledge are included here.

3. Solvent segments of society are called upon to meet costs of care for other parts of society that are preferably met by the persons receiving the care. Payment, through taxes or gifts to private agencies, of unemployment benefits, welfare subsidies, or hospitalization would be included here.

4. Society is failing to provide for the fulfillment of the vocational, intellectual, and social potential of its members. We would classify here failure to complete education commensurate with natural endowment and widespread subjective feelings of worthlessness, boredom, or isolation.

Obviously, many social problems involve several of these categories simultaneously: the sexual deviant may be mentally ill, feel worthless, violate the sexual norms of the society, and cost the majority money when he is placed in a hospital for the criminally insane. Yet, illustrations may also be found for the existence of problems that occur only within a single category. For (1), divorce; for (2), silicosis; for (3), public care of mental defectives; for (4), lack of satisfaction with leisure time activities.

These four classifications of social problems obviously differ with respect to whether the chief suffering is sustained by the proportion of society who personally make up the problem population or by the remainder, or nonproblem segments, of society. In categories (1) and (3), nonproblem segments are the chief sufferers either through offense to their standards of behavior or to their pocketbooks. In categories (2) and (4), the problem populations are the chief sufferers. But, with respect to many problems both groups suffer, as was pointed out some twenty years ago by E. W. Bakke.[1] He defended the unemployed against accusations that they were taking relief funds to avoid working by pointing out that a successful occupational role is essential to the American male's self-satisfaction, and that the recipients of relief funds were usually no better pleased to be receiving them than the reluctant majority to dole them out.

THE URBAN-RURAL QUESTION

Under the list of explanations offered for the occurrence of social problems, we included readjustments necessitated by the advent of industrialization. The most popular current image of society among sociologists grows out of a theory called functionalism that sees society as a set of interlocking social subsystems (the family, religion, the economy, the power structure), which intermesh more or less perfectly, so that one can predict the nature of one subsystem if one knows the nature of the others. For instance, Protestantism, a power system based on merit rather than inheritance, and a small nuclear family relatively cut off from secondary kin are supposed to be compatible with a highly rationalized money economy. In the long run, according to this theory, one subsystem tends to accomodate to the others until all function smoothly together. When there is a major change in one of these subsystems, a whole chain of readjustments is required, and the temporary poorness of fit between subsystems results in what we have chosen to call social problems. Since the most striking change in our society over the last century has been in the direction of industrialization and resultant urbanization, it is not surprising that the occurrence of social problems has been frequently laid at the doors of urban society and industrialization. This relationship between social problems and urbanization, which fits the theory so well, has been easy to support with statistical evidence that social problems tend to occur more frequently in cities than in rural areas. Divorce rates, mental hospital admissions, suicide rates, crime rates, percentage of the population on relief rolls, have all been found to be higher in cities. Interpretation of these statistics has, to be sure, been confounded by the known effect of two phenomena: (1) that cities usually keep better records than do rural areas, so that some of the difference may be a difference only in recorded rather than in real rates; and (2) that cities provide more facilities for coping with social problems, which in turn makes them more readily perceived. The official crime rate, for instance, increases when more policemen are added to the staff because they are then able to handle more minor infractions. Similarly, the number of people known to desire psychiatric treatment increases with each new hospital or clinic facility opened. Yet, despite these artifacts in our measurements of the frequency of the occurrence of social problems, it is probable that social problems are more frequent in cities, partly because the greater density of population and goods creates more opportunities for aggression and more temptation to theft, and partly because city workers are more susceptible to unemployment than farmers, since fewer city workers are self-employed. These factors would operate to produce a higher rate of social problems in the city than in rural areas even if the functionalist theory of the accommodation of social institutions were in error. But our tendency to romanticize the American rural past as an era in which everyone was productive, devoted to the family, and happy has probably made us exaggerate the extent to which the city is the center of social ills. Death rates of infants, for instance, are higher in rural areas, and recent studies of family patterns indicate that urban families see as much of relatives outside the immediate family as do rural families, challenging the popular image of the isolation of the nuclear family in the city, an isolation that was supposed to have devastating effects on mental health.[2] Certainly with respect to our fourth category of social problems, failing to provide for the fulfillment of vocational, intellectual, and social potential, rural areas can be more readily indicted than cities. It is the essence of the city's attraction that it provides for maximum variation in the expression of vocational and avocational interests and permits the greatest exploitation of the human potential.

Several kinds of social problems then exist which may cause suffering either to the offended majority or the problem minority. Social problems occur both in cities and outside them, but are more conspicious in cities because of better record-keeping, more facilities to detect and treat the problems, and the inherently greater potentialities for conflict, overcrowding, and competition as density increases. The area in which the city has the most to offer—fulfillment of human potential—also becomes more conspicuous as a social problem in urban settings because of the striking disparities between the extent to which various subgroups reap these benefits. When achievements are so high for some, the deprivation of others becomes even more obvious.

THE NEGRO IN THE CITY

Cities have been disproportionately settled by minority groups in America. Only the Negroes and Scandinavians have been predominantly rural. And with some exceptions (the Jews and Japanese, for instance), minority groups have been disproportionately afflicted with what we have called social problems. The Negroes constitute the minority group which has suffered the highest rate of social problems over the longest period of time. In addition, since Negroes are the largest minority group in America, the high rate of their social problems is more disturbing to society as a whole than the rate of any other group. Because the Negro has had so long a history of social problems, our explanation of their occurrence as part of the temporary strains of readjustment and assimilation to the melting pot of American society fits less comfortably here than with European minorities, whose rates of social problems have sharply declined as the interval since immigration increases. But Negroes have now been assigned the bottom of the economic barrel since the end of the Civil War. Other immigrant groups entering America since have already risen out of the lower strata, leaving their social problems behind them. Not that the whole idea of readjustment is irrelevant to the association of Negroes with urban problems. The Negro was, until World War I, primarily a rural southern dweller. The pattern of migration of the Negro both into cities and out of the South, beginning about 1915 and occurring with increasing speed since World War II, has been so marked that between 1900 and 1950 the percentage of the Negro population in cities has risen from 17 percent to 48 percent and the percentage outside the South has risen from 10 percent to 32 percent.[3] The Negro is becoming urban both in the South and in the rest of the country. Almost without exception, the movement of the Negro out of the South has been to a city, but even those who remain in the South have been migrating into southern cities.

The urban Negro has shared some of the advantages of urban life as indicated by his longer life span and his higher level of education as compared with rural Negroes.[4] But compared with urban whites, he suffers disproportionately from social problems under all four of our categories. He violates the majority norms through a high rate of crime (even making a reasonable discount for the greater likelihood that he will be accused of crime because of police prejudice), family desertion, illegitimacy, physical violence, and divorce. His state of health, as indicated by a life span shorter than the urban white's and a high rate of chronic illness, falls well below that attainable at our best level of medical care. His cost to society in welfare services and public hospitalization is high because his position at the bottom of the socioeconomic hierarchy makes him the most vulnerable to economic fluctuations and the least able to provide for major illness. His unstable family patterns result in high demands for aid to dependent children. The Negro's low rate of self-fulfillment, as measured by low educational achievement, low rate of entry into the skilled occupations and professions, and low rate of participation in cultural activities, is particularly striking. The issue has, of course, been raised as to whether there is an underlying difference in human potential between Negroes and whites. But arguments about what the upper limits of that human potential may be seem irrelevant to the current situation, when the gap between potential and achievement is so conspicuously gross both for Negroes and for many whites.

The higher rate of so many social problems among Negroes makes of particular interest the areas usually designated as social problems in which their rates are *not* high. Negroes apparently do not have a higher rate of the major psychoses,[5] with the exception of paresis, which is a complication of venereal disease, and they have a particularly low suicide rate.[6] Their failure to show high rates of psychosis and suicide raises the issue of whether these phenomena that are widely believed to reflect life stress, are in fact so determined.

SOCIOECONOMIC STATUS

All urban minority groups, with the exception of the Jews and Japanese, tend to have lower socioeconomic status than native-born, white Protestants of Anglo-Saxon ancestry. Low economic status in turn is associated with all these variables which we have identified as social problems. The question then arises as to what extent the high rate of social problems in minority groups, including the Negroes, can be explained in terms of low socioeconomic status. Answering this question is inordinately difficult. Manifestly, socioeconomic status is not the *whole* answer, since some minority groups (the Chinese, Japanese, Jews) had a markedly low rate of crime, public dependency, and divorce even *before* they rose in socioeconomic status. And it is precisely those groups with fewer social problems originally than others of their socioeconomic level who have made the most striking gains in status. Comparisons of juvenile delinquency rates between Negroes and whites where attempts have been made to control socioeconomic status indicate that rates are higher for Negroes than for whites of equally low social status.[7] Similarly, a study of premarital sexual behavior indicates less conformity with norms of premarital chastity by Negroes than whites when subjects are matched both for parents' occupation and their own educational level.[8] One can certainly raise a question whether it is possible to match socioeconomic status for whites and Negroes adequately, since simply being Negro in America contributes to lower ranking on a prestige scale than if one were white with equal income, education, and housing. But at least rough attempts to match socioeconomic status do not cause the higher Negro delinquency and premarital intercourse rates to disappear.

The author and two colleagues recently completed a study of the social mobility of white former patients of a child guidance clinic which demonstrated that whether these children did or did not rise above their fathers' occupational levels, as adults, was highly related to their rate of juvenile police records.[9] Children with juvenile police records had low occupational achievement as adults both because they had completed very few years of school (60 percent of the juvenile delinquents failed to complete even elementary school) and because they had poor employment records as adults. One would infer from these findings that minority groups whose children have a high rate of social problems will be handicapped in their efforts to improve their socioeconomic status. We also found that parents with a high rate of nonconformity with social norms produce children with a high rate of behavior problems. Therefore, minority groups with a high rate of social problems will presumably hand these problems on to the next generation, which will in turn prevent the upward social mobility of the second generation. Social problems, in short, tend to be self-perpetuating: those who have them fail to rise, and produce children who will also demonstrate a high rate of social problems and fail to rise.

Low social status then is probably, in part, a consequence of social problems. But it is also probably a factor in the production of social problems. The effect of social status in producing nonconformity is nicely illustrated by a recent study of lower-class children attending high schools that are predominantly lower-class as compared with children of equally low status attending high schools that are predominantly middle-class.[10] The lower-class children in a lower-class high school environment showed a higher rate of juvenile delinquency than those in a middle class environment. This study seems to indicate that exposure to a lower-class milieu fosters social problems.

Our best estimate at the present time of the nature of the relationship between social class and social problems appears to be that low socioeconomic status and social problems form a vicious circle: the presence of nonconforming behavior prevents rising into middle-class status, and low socioeconomic status with its associated economic strains, greater opportunities for association with nonconforming individuals, and low self-esteem tends to encourage the perpetuation of social problems.

SOCIAL MOBILITY

Our study on social mobility, which indicated that childhood problem behavior occurs in the offspring of antisocial fathers and prevents their upward mobility, was carried out on an all-white population. We do not yet know whether the same pattern exists for Negro populations, but it would seem highly probable that it does. Negro students from intact homes are found to test higher on school achievement tests in New York [11] and to rank higher on the Iowa Test of Educational Development in Florida [12] than do those from broken homes. These findings suggest that the pattern of family desertion so often described for the Negro father does predict school problems in Negro children just as it did in our study of white children. That conforming behavior among Negro children predicts upward social mobility is suggested by studies of middle-class Negro society.[13] The middle-class Negro is reported to be highly conforming and to look with severe distaste on the lower-class Negroes' failure to conform to middle-class standards. We do not have any systematic information as to whether middle-class

Negroes adopted these highly conforming attitudes after they achieved middle-class status or before. But with the exception of the few free Negroes who at the time of Reconstruction had already attained the status of artisans, those who reached middle-class status did so through professions and businesses which are strongly associated with controlled, conforming behavior: undertakers, ministers, doctors. It is probable that their rise depended on their having exhibited conforming behavior while youngsters in a lower-class environment.

This approach to the issue of minority groups and their high incidence of social problems suggests that it may be possible to break into this vicious circle at one of two points: either by making upward social mobility easier or by reducing the incidence of social problems at the current socioeconomic level.

Little is known at the present time about methods of reducing the incidence of social problems. The causes, outside of the probable effects of socioeconomic status, are little understood. If the causes were known, we might be better able to suggest remedies. Predisposing factors that have been offered as explanations for the high incidence of social problems in lower-class Negro populations include a set of values that emphasizes current pleasures rather than the postponement of gratifications; a lack of tradition of male responsibility for child-support and child-rearing; a lack of positive feelings toward one's own ethnic group with resultant self-hate as a member of that group; psychological damages resulting from being discriminated against that may interfere with judgment and aggressiveness in the business world; feelings of isolation and disorganization resulting from moving from a small rural community to the large city. Although all these explanations seem plausible, no effort has been made to establish which are valid and which important. All are hypotheses which are susceptible to testing by comparing the rates of social problems in Negroes with and without the hypothesized values, traditions, feelings, and psychological damage. It would seem important to undertake research to investigate factors predisposing to social problems before investing great efforts in reducing them through current techniques of counseling and psychotherapy.

INTERRELATIONSHIP OF SOCIAL PROBLEMS

A point to consider in planning attacks on social problems is that social problems themselves tend to be highly interrelated. Those who suffer from one are likely to suffer from others. Those problems for which high correlations are known to exist include financial dependency, crime, divorce, chronic unemployment, alcoholism, low educational achievement, marital infidelity and desertion, feelings of alienation from society, certain diseases (particularly tuberculosis), and suicide. A recent study of a consecutive series of parolees, probationers, and "flat timers" is one of many that have demonstrated that a population picked for one index of problem behavior (crime) shows a high rate of many other kinds of problem behavior (in this case, alcoholism, divorce, unemployment, and drug use).[14] Therefore, when we think in terms of methods of preventing or ameliorating social problems, it is not necessary to plan an attack on one type of problem at a time, any more than it is necessary to give separate pills for each symptom of pneumonia. Presumably, nonconformity is a global phenomenon, on which a successful attack should eventuate in alleviating a whole set of interrelated problems. This is not to say that it is necessarily a mistake to tackle one accessible area at a time. Cutting into the deviant pattern at one level may tip the total balance in favor of conformity. For instance, if the alcoholic can be persuaded to stop drinking, he may then be able to hold a job, which will in turn reduce marital strife, reduce his need to procure money illegally, and improve his opinion of himself and society. If he is then able to afford to move into an area where his children are less subject to pressures toward delinquency, for him and his heirs the vicious circle of deviance and lower-class status may be broken. But it is also commonly believed that if marital strife is the point at which change is effected for the alcoholic, a similar chain of favorable results may be started. Much more knowledge is necessary before we can specify precisely where in a constellation of social problems intervention will create a widening circle of change and where it creates only a temporary relief of a circumscribed problem.

However, the interconnectedness of social problems does mean that a solution that promises to alleviate a single social problem should be evaluated in terms of the probability of this solution's setting up other favorable changes. For instance, curing tuberculosis in Skid Row bums, while certainly of value in itself as a humanitarian act, is very unlikely to change their total pattern of life adjustment.

What the points of leverage are at which the heavy concentration of social problems among the Negroes can be attacked is still unsolved. If the high rate of social problems is at least partially determined by prejudice, which is reinforced by the public's interpretation of observed problems as symptoms of underlying inferiority, it may be important to change appearances along with attempting to change the real incidence of problems. It may, therefore, be worthwhile to persuade newspapers to refrain from reporting race in crime reports while encouraging the reporting of race in stories that redound to the credit of the newsworthy person. If a public impression of financial success is important in reducing prejudice, the Negro's emphasis on the more visible signs of a high standard of living—good clothes and an expensive car—may not be so misguided as middle-class whites tend to feel.

THE NEGRO GHETTO

If it is difficult to know the underlying causes of the high incidence of social problems among Negroes and how to intervene in reducing them, the second alternative, improving the social status of the Negro, suggests a clearer path to the goal, even though attaining it may be highly problematical. To improve opportunities for social mobility, we need to increase the education of the Negro and to open a greater variety of jobs to him, particularly those at skilled and white-collar levels. But with the current pattern of elementary schools, in which each school serves a neighborhood, materially raising the educational level requires dispersal of the Negro ghetto. So long as urban Negroes continue to attend almost exclusively Negro schools, the level of competition and stimulation from fellow pupils will remain low enough and the amount of school time devoted to discipline will remain high enough that Negro graduates of a *de facto* segregated school system will not have training comparable to that of graduates of an all-white or mixed school system. A study of the allocation of teacher's time to educational versus administrative and disciplinary tasks in an all-Negro as compared with an all-white school in New York City succintly demonstrates how many hours are devoted to discipline and how few to teaching in the Negro school.[15] Negro children who do not themselves exhibit behavior problems get less teaching per school-hour attended because their contemporaries have a high rate of behavior problems. As they learn less, their chances of qualifying for higher education, and simultaneously their opportunities to hold higher status jobs, diminish. Not only do Negro children stay in school fewer years because of financial need and little pressure from parents to acquire a higher education, but the years spent in school are less profitable. In a mixed school, pressure from peers to excel can largely compensate for the lack of stimulation at home, but when the peers all come from the same sort of impoverished intellectual environment and have a high rate of behavior problems, the most dedicated teacher has difficulty in setting high standards of achievement.

Although dispersal of the Negro ghetto appears highly desirable for the improvement of Negro education and subsequent upward mobility, recent studies of factors influencing interracial housing point more to difficulties than successes.[16] To summarize briefly some of the findings:

1. Although attitudes toward Negroes in general as well as toward particular Negroes become less hostile where whites have had the experience of living in mixed neighborhoods or in interracial housing projects, feelings are never positive *enough* that most whites *prefer* interracial housing. Even after forced exposure to Negroes with a consequent increase in friendly feelings, whites prefer all-white neighborhoods and housing projects.

2. White neighborhoods appear to have a limited tolerance for Negro infiltration. Once the number of Negroes passes a certain proportion (which varies with the city and neighborhood, but has been reported as between 30 percent and 60 percent), whites move out and the neighborhood becomes all-Negro.

3. The tendency for whites to abandon a mixed neighborhood is higher if (a) it is adjacent to an all-Negro neighborhood; (b) real estate salesmen pressure the white residents into leaving by soliciting their houses for sale and showing houses in the neighborhood only to Negro prospective buyers; (c) banks refuse mortgages to white purchasers of property in a "changing" neighborhood; (d) it is a neighborhood of young families with school-age children.

4. Whether or not whites are prejudiced against Negroes makes little long-run difference in their decision to move out. Even the most unprejudiced whites believe they will lose money on their houses if Negroes move in and dislike the idea of being a member of a minority in a predominantly Negro neighborhood or having their children members of a minority group in the school.

5. Neighborhoods which are most likely to stay mixed are those where homes are so expensive that the Negro market for them is very small and where there is no adjacent Negro neighborhood.

These findings indicate that the white neighborhoods into which Negroes are *most* likely to move are just those which are least likely to remain mixed. The greatest pressure from the Negroes has been on white neighborhoods immediately adjacent to Negro neighborhoods, particularly those where rents are cheap. In such neighborhoods they find housing they can afford while remaining close to friends and relatives, and to public facilities that they can use without fear of discrimination. At the present time, the only obvious solution to ever-widening Negro ghettos spreading outward from the center of the city appears to be strong governmental action in the form of laws requiring a quota of scattered nonwhite housing in all new subdivisions in which prices are below a fixed level; tax reductions to mixed areas where proportions of Negroes to whites do not climb beyond a fixed limit; supports to selling prices of white-owned housing in mixed neighborhoods; and severe penalties if evidence can be shown that municipalities are dragging their feet in approving permits and providing utilities for planned interracial housing. Whether such laws could conceivably be passed or enforced seems doubtful at the present time, but without them it is hard to imagine how dispersal of the Negro ghetto will occur in an open market. Without dispersal, other ways of equalizing proportions of Negroes in schools will have to be sought. The extensive use of school buses to transport pupils is one method which has been tried despite its obvious disadvantages in terms of wasted time and expense. Dispersed housing would, of course, have values to the Negro beyond that of equalizing educational opportunities, since Negroes in all our major cities are now in dilapidated and overcrowded housing for which they are paying excessive rents.

Improving Negro opportunities for upward social mobility by opening more skilled and clerical jobs to Negroes is also difficult to execute. Progress in this area has, however, been much greater than in housing dispersal. It may be instructive to compare the progress of the Negroes with that of the Jews, who have had a phenomenal degree of movement into professional and executive jobs within a very short time. Not only have the Jews stressed education, which has hastened their learning of the manners, speech, and skills appropriate to upper-level occupations, but they have had a high concentration in small independent businesses. Negroes who have risen into the middle class have done so primarily as professionals and entertainers. The great distadvantage of the professional over the shopkeeper is that his success provides few ancillary jobs to other Negroes. Since the doctor, minister, and social worker need few assistants, few job opportunities are opened for skilled workers and salesgirls, who could have found jobs if the middle-class Negro had been a small manufacturer or merchant. Easing the procurement of capital for investment in small enterprises might make an important contribution to the Negro's opportunities to rise, if the risk of failure, which currently plagues the small independent businessman, can be reduced.

In discussing the relationship between social problems and social status, we pointed out that the presence of social problems is an important deterrent to rising. Obviously then, even if economic opportunities were equalized, Negroes might still be found to have a somewhat higher rate of social problems than white urban populations and a somewhat lower rate of social mobility. However, by allowing the potential risers to rise, the target population for whom more is needed than simple economic opportunity will be more clearly delineated. It then remains to be seen whether we will be skillful enough to change values, family patterns, or whatever the underlying causes of the propensity for social problems may be in this residual group.

Notes

[1] Edward W. Bakke, *The Unemployed Worker* (New Haven: Yale University Press, 1940).

[2] William H. Key, ''Rural-Urban Differences and the Family,'' *The Sociological Quarterly*, 11:1 (January 1961), pp. 49–56.

[3] Davis McEntire, *Residence and Race* (Berkeley: University of California Press, 1960).

[4] A part of the educational advantage of the urban over the rural Negro may result from the fact that Negro migration out of the rural South, unlike the migration of whites, is selective of the better educated. See Horace C. Hamilton, ''Educational Selectivity of Net Migration from the South,'' *Social Forces*, 38:1 (October 1959), pp. 33–42.

[5] Paul Lemkau, C. Tietze, and M. Cooper, ''Mental Hygiene Problems in an Urban District,'' *Mental Hygiene*, 26 (January 1942), pp. 110–119.

[6] ''Mortality from Selected Causes by Age, Race, and Sex: United States, 1953,'' Vital Statistics Special Reports, National Summaries, 42, No. 7 (September 12, 1955).

[7] William Bates, ''Social Stratification and Juvenile Delinquency,'' *American Catholic Social Review*, 21:3 (Fall 1960), pp. 221–228. See also Bernard Lander, *Towards an Understanding of Juvenile Delinquency* (New York: Columbia University Press, 1954).

[8] Ira Reiss, ''Sexual Codes in Teen-Age Culture,'' AAAPSS, 338 (November 1961), pp. 53–62.

[9] Lee Robins, Harry Gyman, and Patricia O'Neal, ''The Interaction of Social Class and Deviant Behavior,'' *American Sociological Review*, 27:4 (August 1962), pp. 480–492.

[10] Albert J. Reiss, Jr., and Albert Lewis Rhodes, ''The Distribution of Juvenile Delinquency in the Social Class Structure,'' *American Sociological Review*, 26:5 (October 1961), pp. 720–732.

[11] Martin Deutsch, *Minority Group and Class Status as Related to Social and Personality Factors in Scholastic Achievement*, Monograph No. 2, Society for Applied Anthropology, 1960.

[12] Raymond E. Schultz, ''A Comparison of Negro Pupils Ranking High with those Ranking Low in Educational Achievement,'' *Journal of Educational Sociology*, 31:7 (March 1958), pp. 265–270.

[13] E. Franklin Frazier, *The Black Bourgeoisie* (New York: Free Press of Glencoe, 1957).

[14] Samuel B. Guze *et al.*, "Psychiatric Illness and Crime," *Journal of Nervous and Mental Diseases*, 134:6 (June 1962) pp. 512–521.

[15] Deutsch, *op. cit.*

[16] Beverly Duncan and Philip M. Hauser, *Housing a Metropolis* (New York: Free Press of Glencoe, 1960); see also Daniel M. Wilner, Rosabelle P. Walker, and Stuart W. Cook, *Human Relations in Interracial Housing* (Minneapolis: University of Minnesota Press, 1955). See also McEntire, *op. cit.*

Foundations of Urban Planning

F. STUART CHAPIN, JR., *is Professor of Planning and Director of the Urban Studies Program at the University of North Carolina. An active city and regional planner, he has been engaged in various phases of planning with the Tennessee Valley Authority and was Director of Planning for the City of Greensboro. He has several times held office in the American Institute of Planning.*

As long as the human species has been in possession of a faculty for reasoning, man has sought to influence the course of events. Early he learned that foresight in the exercise of this power provided a means for achieving certain predetermined objectives. When man utilizes such a means-end mechanism, he is engaging in "planning." By this definition, planning, then, has something of the quality of universality about it. As a professional group, planners acknowledge that they are dealing with the elements of a concept that many fields utilize. They make no exclusive claim to the concept, but since the whole of their effort both in theory and practice is with the study and application of planning in the pursuit of specific needs and problems of human existence, they have come to have a very direct and consuming interest in many facets of planning.

While we might take various paths, for example, we might study planning in the framework of "resource planning" or "regional planning," in this discussion we are concerned with "urban planning," the application of foresight to achieve certain preestablished goals in the growth and development of urban areas. In making urban planning our subject, we are immediately specifying a locus for the study and practice of planning. We are identifying a specific kind of locale, with a particular economic life, political context, and social organization. We are making this entire microcosm a subject for study, but focusing attention on particular choices in the kind of living environment and the means for achieving each that assures the best possible accommodation of the residents' goals of urban life. It should not be surprising, then, to find that the theory and practice of urban planning as it is evolving in this country has a means-ends flavor. Thus, we see American effort in planning theory and research tending to focus on (1) "the planning process" and (2) "urban structure and form," and at the practicing level, attention centering around (1) planning administration and (2) the "comprehensive plan." This discussion will have an emphasis on the first pair of fundamentals and will make only passing reference to the pair cast in the practicing framework. Throughout, our concern is with contemporary emphases of planning. The development of planning thought extending back to the literature on social action and utopias is a large and significant part of the field which is omitted from this paper.

"Foundations of urban planning," accordingly, is pursued in the following three parts. First, we begin with some distinguishing characteristics of the field as a background to understanding its orientations as they have evolved to date. Second, we focus on the *process* orientations, and thirdly, we examine the *structure-form* orientations of the field.

THE NATURE OF PLANNING

Urban planners work in a three-dimensional world and, along with a concern for the city as an economic entity and a social system, possess a direct and absorbing interest in the physical make-up of the city and its visual form—not only how the city functions but also how the city affects man's senses and thereby slips into his consciousness, and how, in turn, this affects his living experiences or, more basically, his values and his behavior. We will come to the urban planner's concern with the functional aspects of the city and the perceptional aspects in the last part of this paper.

To understand more fully the nature of planning, we may look at planning first as a field that is a supradiscipline in the sense that it takes a transdisciplinary view of urban phenomena. Next, we may view planning as a field having a central concern for innovation. Finally, we may view planning as a focus for the conjunction of the sciences and the arts. These ways of viewing urban planning suggest the basis for the differentiation of this field from all others that may be concerned in one way or another with urban phenomena.

TRANSDISCIPLINARY CHARACTER OF PLANNING

The supradisciplinary aspect of urban planning springs from a basic preoccupation the field has with the relatedness of many phenomena in the urban scene. This is in contrast to other fields. Among other things, the economist is concerned, for example, with the market process as an element of the urban economy, the political scientist, with the process of public policy formulation, and the sociologist, with the social control processes. Each discipline essentially has a prior claim on the indicated subject area in the sense that it has developed through the years special knowledge and skills to deal with it. Each discipline to an extent may seek out and draw from another discipline where knowledge and skills join or overlap. But as the market process, the public policy formulating process, social control processes, or other processes associated with other fields interact in multisystem frameworks, there develops a science for the study of the relatedness of these processes which no one of the component fields is fully equipped or disposed to undertake. So, to deal with related aspects of processes that cross into several discipline areas, new fields of specialization emerge. Planning, operations research, and regional science are examples. Planning was the first strong specialization of this kind to develop and assume the characteristics of a distinct field, and urban planning is the most firmly established option today in this field.

Urban planning deals with another kind of relatedness. We have been using a "means" orientation to illustrate the role that planning plays in studying interrelationships among the different "process" systems functioning in the urban milieu. We might also use a "place" concept as the counterpart of an "ends" orientation to examine relatedness of urban phenomena in space. In the same way that each discipline may use the notion of "process," each for its own special reasons may examine the spatial dispositions of phenomena under study and seek to understand their distribution in space. When the interrelationships of these spatial configurations are examined in the framework of over-all urban structure and form, they become of special interest to the field of urban planning. In both the process and structure-form orientations, "relatedness" is of special interest to planning researchers. In the practice of planning, its counterpart is "coordination," which is a way of insuring relatedness in efforts at modifying structure-form elements in the city's make-up.

INNOVATIONAL ASPECT OF PLANNING

Now, if we add to this view of planning a second view, the innovational aspect, we have another basis for differentiating planning from many of its related fields. Social scientists normally apply their knowledge to a means-ends framework in a kind of clinical manner, that is, they may propose different means and ends in a hypothetical framework to test theories or models or they might take a "what would happen if" approach and reason out the consequences of their means-ends schema in the real world. The planning researcher is no less experimental in his research and study, but the ultimate application of his knowledge involves an innovational aspect, that is, it involves the use of the planning process as a means and certain forms of spatial organization in the urban environment as ends in fulfillment of certain defined community goals.

Planning seeks knowledge not for knowledge's own sake but for its applications to the needs of man. In this sense, it is constantly modifying the very phenomena it seeks to study. Thus, the innovational feature of planning gives it a "science plus" aspect, with the end being sought not simply a dispassionate study of "what is," but also "what could be" and "what should be." To put it another way, planning is a combination of the descriptive, projective, and prescriptive. Pure science seeks to understand the nature of phenomena, how it functions and what laws govern its make-up and its transformations. Science will also seek to project the observed behavior of the subject under study to discover "what could be" under specific assumptions governing the projections. But when value judgments enter the picture, as in prescriptive approaches, the "plus" or innovational feature comes into prominence. This, of course, is not unique to planning but is generally characteristic of the professions that apply science to achieve particular ends.

CONJUNCTION OF THE SOCIAL SCIENCES AND THE ARTS

We see urban planning in its broadest usage when we look at it as a field in which the social sciences and the arts coalesce. What may be loosely referred to as "basic planning," on the one hand, and what increasingly is referred to as "urban design," on the other, have long been recognized as related components of urban planning. However, in American planning practice, urban design has been in eclipse for some time, and planning programs have not often accorded urban design studies more than token consideration in the plan preparation stage. Thus, in the normal course of events, urban planning practitioners have commissioned or undertaken economic studies, demographic analyses, housing investigations, thoroughfare studies, etc., and they have applied these findings to the organization and use of space in preparing a general plan for growth and development of the urban area. But, until very recently, few planning programs have undertaken basic design analyses as an essential part of the preparation of a land development plan. The city plans developed in the recent past have been criticized as being a somewhat sterile and mechanistic conception of the future city, often insensitive to the visual and "the human scale." Perhaps because of this imbalance in urban planning, the complementing aspect of planning as a science and planning as an art has been slow to become recognized. One explanation for the imbalance persisting as long as it has may be found in the widely held notion that design is entirely an intuitive field and not researchable. In the last ten years, however, there has been a general swing away from this position, and there has been a steadily increasing interest in urban design research, and even in the application of social science research techniques to the study of urban design.

While the method of approach to research employed by the design researcher can never be fully likened to that of the social science researcher, both follow a system of reasoning backed by well-established principles and tenets. However, the social scientist seeks a product that meets different tests than those the designer uses as his tests. For example, frequently the social scientist will strive for a result that can be replicated, one that can be replicated with number-perfect precision. The designer seeks another kind of universal. He seeks a universal that in some situations will achieve uniqueness in the result rather than exact duplication. While the practicing designer who applies these universals always must rely on a mixture of intuition, artistic creativity, and experience-tempered judgment, which preclude any likelihood of replication, the design researcher is now seeking to bring to him approaches that combine social science and design knowledge.

Post–World War II developments in the planning field have brought these two ancestral trails of planning into a closer relationship. Current thought seeks a conjunction of these two paths through research and, at the practicing level, through improved procedures and defined information flows in the course of a planning study. Conceptual developments in planning thought reflect the growing area of relationship. Of particular interest in this respect is the shift from a "unitary approach" in planning (emphasis on the single, detailed, and invincible scheme) to an "adaptive approach" (emphasis on an evolutionary scheme which is based on a firm set of development policies embodied in a general plan but which is progressively adapted to recognize unpredictable elements of change and technology).[1] Under the adaptive approach, urban design can be continuously brought into play in translating the basic plan concepts of urban structure into urban forms that have visual meaning on the site. In this sense, in the same way that basic planning analyses must be continuously investigating new considerations brought to light by science and technology, urban design must be continuously prescribing changes in urban form in adaptation to changes uncovered in basic planning analyses. These information flows may proceed in steady progression or occur in feedback sequences. Thus, in the long pull, urban analyses may lead to an urban design expression which feeds back a behavioral impact that modifies the analytical requirements and calls for a somewhat modified emphasis in a new design expression. The affinity of these two traditionally separated areas of learning is especially clear in the field of urban planning. We will return to urban design again in the last part of this paper.

As must be evident from the foregoing discussion, planning has parallels with other fields, but it also has distinctive features. Three of these features that differentiate planning from other fields are: (1) its multidisciplinary ties, (2) its innovational bias, and (3) its joint identification with the sciences and the arts. We may now go on to examine two rather fundamental orientations to urban planning. In some respects these orientations constitute areas of specialization in the field. To the extent that researchers must have a focus, these offer two focal areas in which to achieve some depth in their investigations. To the extent that practitioners utilize both orientations as integral parts of one profession, the separation implied in the term "orientations" is artificial.

PROCESS ORIENTATIONS

Process is an old chestnut of the social sciences, but because of its dynamic quality it continues to offer a useful approach to the study of certain phenomena. Every field has introduced refinements into the literature on the nature of process in applying dynamic features of the concept to its own needs. So, it is not surprising to find *planning process* a source of frequent searching commentary in the urban planning field.

The concept of process has both a technical and a behavioral usage in the field. The technical usage generally relates to stages of planning in some defined work program of the planning agency. Thus, we see reference to the establishment of a work program which proceeds from a specification of what is needed to how a study is to be done and in what order the work is to be executed. The planning agency might, therefore, establish a work program for the preparation of a land development plan and specify the elements as an economic study, a population study, and a land use study. It might then proceed to the scheduling of specific analyses to be undertaken—say, an input-output analysis as a means of testing economic growth assumptions; a population forecast as a means of studying the implications of the economic growth assumptions; and a holding capacity analysis of open land adaptable for various uses as a means of estimating the implications of the economic and population assumptions for land development patterns. Once the work program is specified, the technical process of planning then proceeds to data collection, analysis, and the preparation of plans, cost analyses, and recommendations. This kind of technical application of the concept constitutes one specific meaning of process within the planning field.

The behavioral usage of process in planning literature is in a tradition not unlike that found in the social sciences generally. In current planning thought, this usage of the *planning process* has to do with a *sequence of action* which begins with establishing certain goals, involves certain decisions as to alternative ways of achieving these goals and eventually takes the form of steps for carrying out decisions, followed by evaluation and perhaps a new sequence of action. It is this usage which will be followed in the discussion below. The sequence falls into these stages:

Goal specification stage
Decision-making stage
Plan execution, evaluation,
and reorientation stage

In discussing these stages, we will take the view that these three stages occur in cycles which proceed in a circular rather than a straight-line sequence, with one sequence of action moving into a second, and a second into a third, and so on. Throughout, our concern will be with *process,* reserving *content* or substance of goals, decisions, and follow-through for consideration in the final section of the discussion.

Before examining these stages of the planning process, we need some kind of differentiation between the various actors and the roles they portray throughout the three stages of the sequence. In other words, goals, decisions, execution, and evaluation each involve the questions, "by whom" and "for whom." Who specifies the goals? Who decides among the specified goals? Who follows through on decisions? And who evaluates the consequences? Moreover, for whom are goals, decisions, follow-through, and evaluation made—for what group? The residents? The leaders? Or the officialdom of the city?

Clearly, these actors can be cast in a number of different role combinations, multiplying the complexities of the ways in which the planning process can be studied many times. For purposes of this discussion, we shall give officialdom the center of the stage and cast other actors as "walk-ons" who interact with city officials as the planning process progresses through the three-act sequence we have noted above. To simplify things still further, the spotlight will most frequently focus on the urban planner to observe how he takes part in the planning process in relation to other city officials, civic leaders and the general public. Along the lines of the following Daland-Parker nomenclature, we will need to be aware that at each stage the role or combination of roles the planner assumes under any particular set of circumstances may vary according to whether he is functioning in an *institutional role* as an administrative official in local government, in a *professional role* as a practitioner of the precepts of the planning profession, in a *political innovation role* as he relates his actions to political channels and the political "influentials" in the community, or in an *educational role* as he relates his actions to the grass roots citizenry of the community at large.[2]

GOAL SPECIFICATION

With these differentiations as to actors and roles, let us now direct our attention to the dynamic aspects of the planning process, the sequence of action through the three stages of the process. Goal specification is a logical point of entry into the circular sequence we have identified with the planning process. At the outset, it might be observed that while goals of planning have been in the forefront of planning thought since the early literature on utopias, only in relatively recent times has the identification of goals been made an integral part of the technical work of planning. This spotlighting of goals bids well to be a characteristic of the sixties, not alone in planning, but pervading many fields. (Witness the work of the President's Commission on National Goals in 1960.)

Until relatively recently, goals specified in the course of the planning process were identified on the basis of the planner's perception of community goals. His sources for these goal statements were, in part, a combination of observation and experience in his contacts with the public, with civic groups and with pressure groups of all kinds and, in part, his own intuitive view of what the goal content should be. The intuitive approach to the definition of goals is a hold-over from the design origins of the field. While the design aspect of the field must always draw on the intuitive creativity of the artist, particularly when proposals for achieving goals are translated into design expressions, the identification of community goals need no longer be an intuitive matter.

What constitutes a valid basis for the identification of the goals of a populace? The nebulousness of identifying goals that have one and the same meaning to both the average urbanite and the decision maker is difficult enough, but how are goals to be arrayed and given meaning in combinations that have never been articulated or viewed before by the general public or even the decision maker in any goal form of physical development? Though the problems are difficult, research is beginning to shed some light on these questions, and effort is being directed toward the identification and measurement of group goals, that is, widely held goals, and the intensity with which goal concepts are held by groups of city residents.

Contemporary thinking on the identification of planning goals is increasingly turning to the use of survey research methods in the study of attitudes. Except for Branch's early experiment in a public opinion poll, the application of these methods to goal identification for planning has been very recent.[3] Wilson's work offers an illustration of the directions in which research is currently moving.[4] One of several planning research studies at the University of North Carolina concerned with the identification of goal perceptions with respect to the living qualities of cities, this study experiments with a series of devices for getting at attitudes. It uses direct questions to probe for responsiveness on physical features of goal forms that are associated with "livability" in the city, and in a complementary line of questioning it seeks to get at past behavior that might also shed light on goals. Thus, questions are asked on reasons for past choices in the selection of the hometown. Similarly, residents are queried on reasons for choosing the neighborhood in which they settled in the one or more communities that had been picked as hometowns, and questions are asked that indicate the intensity of satisfaction with respect to these past choices. As an indirect approach, game techniques are used to induce respondents to simulate their choices and thus divulge what their current satisfactions are likely to be with respect to goals. At the Massachusetts Institute of Technology, Lynch has experimented with other approaches.[5] In some home interview experiments, he has respondents take imaginary trips through their city and comment on features in the community that they consider to be noteworthy. On other occasions he actually makes trips through parts of the city with respondents using tape-recorded interviews to obtain on-the-spot responses of residents as they pass through their community.

One important distinction between public opinion polls and attitude surveys might be borne in mind here. Without getting into the specifics of definitions, we might remember that polls seek direct measures of satisfaction and dissatisfaction with widely recognized problems or issues. Attitude studies frequently focus on less obvious and sometimes hidden problems which are not fully understood or perhaps may not even be recognized by the general public. In this connection, it is interesting to speculate on the political overtones of any attempt to use poll findings or even the results of attitude surveys as a basis for public forum and a "popular vote" on goals. If the public views a survey as a "vote," conflict may be intensified, or created, where none existed before. Thus, the solicitation of opinion on goals may lead to conflicting expectations among a populace which are politically irreconcilable and potentially a source of widespread dissatisfaction. On the other hand, attitude studies devoid of hoop-la and taken simply as one of an array of aids to decision making, may be politically innocuous.

Even though the older value-laden approaches to goal identification are being superseded, the act of selecting the goal combinations to be introduced into the planning process is still a subjective matter. The establishment of standards to be used in determining how widely held a goal must be before it is given prominence in a goal combination requires a value judgment. To devise goal combinations meaningful to decision makers and at the same time bracket the many divergent planning goals that are held by residents, also unquestionably involves an exercise of judgment. More importantly, when the planner identifies a series of "goal forms," (say, a "nucleated form," a "diffused form," and a "compact form" of urban development) as alternative approaches to satisfying goal preferences of the general public, he is imputing to these goal forms certain living qualities that match up with public goal preferences. Here again value judgments are involved.

Ex post facto, correspondence between goals and goal forms can be demonstrated, but when correspondence is sought ahead of time, it is necessary for the planner to make a judgment. In other words, whereas survey research methods may assist in goal identification, they are not likely to be very helpful in eliciting any meaningful response on design forms with which respondents have had no direct experience. Some kinds of preferences can be inferred or forecast from choices made in areas of questioning where there has been direct experience, but as yet techniques have not been devised which can predict with any great reliability what respondent reactions will be to new and unfamiliar design forms. Thus, it is still necessary for the planner to use value judgments in making up the goal combinations and in devising alternative goal forms from which decision makers can make a choice. Moreover, the designer must still depend upon his design ingenuity and the sales appeal of a new idea in securing acceptance of new and unique design expressions.

The specification of goal combinations in the form of alternatives often involves a variety of other goals. Thus, for example, to implement a general goal of revitalizing the central business district, established as an objective in the local planning effort, the planning agency may put before city council another set of goal alternatives—a choice between maintaining the central business district as a single strong center or promoting the development of a series of decentralized satellite centers.

In addition to ramifications of one goal leading to others, the specification of goal forms in terms of alternatives means greater complexity in the entire sequence of action in the planning process.[6] That is to say, any particular goal combination obviously involves several successive investigative cycles of action before a choice is made. Such systems of linked investigative actions bear a resemblance to what will be recognized from decision-making theory as "decision chains."

Another order of complexity may be introduced by varying the actors and by varying the roles taken in the specification of goals. If we put the spotlight on the urban planner alone and vary the roles he may be disposed to play, there can be considerable variation in the way goals are presented. For example, in a political innovation role the urban planner may be sensitive to the tipping point at which decision makers will tend to act or not act. He may, therefore, specify goal forms entirely with reference to the tipping point. If he functions solely as a professional, he may present choices without consideration of the political feasibility of his goal forms. On the other hand, where the goal has no policy ramifications and where no issue is involved, role may be relatively less important, and goal specification can be quite perfunctory, direct, and uncomplicated. So, we may conclude that goal specification is very complexly interwoven into the action sequence, sometimes varying according to the policy implications behind the goal, sometimes varying with the actors dominating a particular issue at a particular time, and sometimes varying with the political climate prevailing at that time.

At this juncture we begin to note that "goal specification" is a somewhat elusive term, and when too much emphasis is given to it as a "stage," it has a slightly static ring. Clearly, from the above discussion, goal specification consists of many linked frames in the film of action we are inspecting, and to get at the dynamic aspect of the action sequence, for all practical purposes, we cannot attach too great importance to stages as such. Indeed, stages as used here are really only convenient labels for breakpoints in the action sequence which we have introduced in order to observe some of the variables of the planning process.

DECISION MAKING

Let us now inspect a breakpoint in the action sequence which will give us some insight into the dynamics of the decision-making stage of the action sequence. This is the stage in which alternative courses of action for the fulfillment of goals are considered and evaluated, and a selection is made. For purposes of this discussion, while keeping the urban planner near the front of the stage, we will focus the spotlight on the city council as the decision-making unit and consider the role of the urban planner only in relation to the city council in this setting.

Using Simon's three-part sequence of steps to decision making, and the Meyerson-Banfield adaptation of it, we may think of this stage in the planning process as involving: (1) consideration of all action alternatives within the framework of conditions that prevail and goals sought; (2) evaluation of the consequences following from the pursuit of each action alternative, including the change of conditions predicted and the extent of goal achievement anticipated; and (3) selection of the alternative that in the light of consequences and in consideration of goals is the most preferable course of action.[7]

Now, let us assume that a decision must be made on how to maintain the central business district as a single strong center. Our first step is to examine the action alternatives. Although additional alternatives or other combinations of alternatives might be proposed, the following are adequate for purposes of illustration:

First Action Alternative: Hold-the-Line Approach. A program emphasizing more efficient use of the existing street system through strategic traffic engineering solutions (one-way streets, removal of on-street parking, etc.) and the provision of off-street parking under self-liquidating projects, coupled with a concerted effort to get downtown property owners to undertake a face-lifting and general refurbishing of their properties.

Second Action Alternative: Rehabilitation Approach. A program providing for limited strategic revisions in street layout (street closings, new connecting links, etc.) and the provision of public off-street parking, coupled with the introduction of a mall, open squares, or shopping courts worked into a unifying design for the organization of space and circulation in the central area.

Third Action Alternative: Redevelopment Approach. A program providing for some reallocation of uses between central and outlying centers, the reorganization of uses and circulation systems within the central business district and a general renewal of the central area by a public redevelopment program and private action of downtown property owners according to a unifying and balanced design.

Of course, a fourth alternative would be no action, that is, do nothing. In this connection, it may be noted that inaction as well as action may produce additional actions in the decision chain.

While very general in their meaning, these action alternatives obviously are arrayed in an ascending order of the involvement of local government and in the extent of capital outlay commitment. They also constitute a gradation in the decisiveness with which they go at the problem. If backed up with supporting data, action alternatives can be compared as to costs and benefits; they can be compared in terms of the nonmonetary aspect of the choice, that is, the extent of satisfaction each alternative offers or how close each solution comes to achieving the goal. The city council theoretically can proceed to make a rational decision.

Prevailing policies and even the absence of policy may have an important bearing on the outcome of a decision. We may note also that the outcome can be governed by policy considerations of both a higher and lower order. If we view policies as tending to fall into a hierarchical array that range from the topmost strategic kind of consideration on down to those that constitute more detailed and specific kinds of considerations that follow from previous higher order policies, we must recognize that in making a choice between two or more action alternatives at any intermediate point in the hierarchy, decision makers, consciously or unconsciously, are making higher order commitments as well as involving themselves in additional decisions that must subsequently be made down the line.[8] Thus, implicit in a decision on any one of the above choices is a prior, higher order policy decision that a single strong center is to be actively promoted in the future growth and development of the metropolitan area. Whether or not this policy was deliberated on, a decision on any one of the action alternatives listed above constitutes a commitment in the allocation of resources for many years to come to a kind of transportation system that must be able to accommodate very large numbers of people, bringing them into the central area with a minimum of delay and a maximum of comfort. Whether consciously considered or not, a commitment to a single strong center is a rejection of a different kind of transportation system, one which seeks to bring relatively smaller numbers of people to several centers. Down the hierarchy, implied are decisions on particular implementing schemes of vastly different scope and differing amounts of capital outlay. Thus, every decision has reference points to a broad array of policies of higher or lesser order.

Of course, what has been said about decision making in the action sequence is greatly simplified. First, it might be noted that the alternatives submitted to the city council are not fixed alternatives and often are modified in form and content in the course of the decision-making sequence. It is a prerogative of decision makers, often a consciously exercised prerogative, to restrict, extend, or otherwise modify the scope of their decision area. This can happen when the staff, which is involved in specifying the alternatives and the implications of each, is not in possession of all of the relevant political information. Secondly, and related to this consideration, are the underlying behavioral variables to decision making. There is a whole body of literature on political behavior dealing with leadership and role playing in decision making and how, in turn, the impact of these vary with the issue being decided upon and the alignment of pressure groups. No less important, there are the background variables deeply embedded in the attitudes and value systems of each actor. Finally, it should be noted that we have used illustrations assuming a situation where no other units of local government are involved and where no special authorities exist. The dynamics of intergovernmental decision making and the inter-jurisdictional aspects of decision making in a ''fractionalized'' metropolitan governmental situation of course add tremendously to the complexities of this and other stages of the action sequence.

PLAN EXECUTION, EVALUATION, AND REORIENTATION

Continuing with our stage framework and breaking into the action sequence at another point, we come to the post–decision making stages consisting of what we have termed the execution, evaluation, and reorientation stage of planning. The steps in this stage coalesce to a considerable degree from the time one is initiated until the last is completed, and since the follow-through on one decision is the take-off for the next, we shall treat all of them together.

Plan execution may be any one or a combination of several of the following measures. It may be a public improvement—a new water plant, a school expansion program, or an extension to the expressway system. It may be clearance of a slum and carrying out a redevelopment plan. It may be accomplished through regulatory measures—the adoption of a minimum housing standards ordinance or a revision of the zoning ordinance. However, from the moment a decision is made evaluation begins, and eventually a new or modified view of the intended action may emerge. The evaluation of the effects of a decision may result in reorientation and may subsequently involve take-off on a new action sequence. Evaluation by the city council reflects consideration of the unanticipated side effects as well as repercussions from the anticipated effects of their earlier decision. Perhaps no new action sequence ensues directly related to the previous one and the planning process substantially achieves the goal for which action was initiated in the original instance. On the other hand, the dynamics of the situation may produce a new sequence, with a change of goals, a change of action alternatives, and a change of decisions. The featured actors and the walk-on actors and their roles may vary, and the new sequence of action may involve additional actors and modified roles from those that were involved in preceding action sequences.

In summary, it may be observed that the process orientations of urban planning have a distinct behavioral emphasis and involve the applications of knowledge of human behavior to the study of man's actions in adapting his environment to his living needs. The planning process is the means mechanism used in achieving adaptation. Although greatly simplified in order to give an overview of the process orientation in planning, the urban planning process consists of a sequence of stages which tend to proceed from goal specification to decision making to execution, evaluation, and reorientation. It is now appropriate to turn to the substance with which this process is concerned, namely, the urban environment, particularly its spatial structure and form.

URBAN STRUCTURE AND FORM

To the social scientist who views urban planning only in the context of the foregoing process orientation, the field may seem to be a little more than a behavioral science specialty in public administration. Exclusive preoccupation with process, and thus the means of planning, overlooks the application of this process to the ends of planning which deal with the structure and form of the city. Of course, when the architect or the urban designer approaches city planning purely in terms of design expressions, he in turn may overlook the crucial importance of the means by which his design concepts may be brought into reality. It is important to recognize the essential relatedness of both aspects of the means-ends rationale.

There is another kind of relatedness appropriate to the orientations of this final part of the discussion, and this has to do with the relatedness of analytical and design aspects of urban structure and form. In this discussion, *urban structure* refers to the spatial organization of key functional areas and essential service facilities of the city in response to certain fundamental living needs and activities of human society, and *urban form* refers to the visually perceptive features of the city which this structure produces, both the two-dimensional and three-dimensional forms created by surfaces, spaces, structures, and circulatory systems in a defined natural setting. ''Goal form'' as we have been using the term is an abstraction referring to the general character and form of the land development pattern of an urban area which has been structured to fulfill certain defined goals. While structure-form concepts are thus interrelated, each ties back into precepts of its derivative discipline area: in the one case, a science, and in the other, an art. Thus, a study of the disposition of the structural elements in space follows the tenets of a science, but proposals for organizing or reorganizing these elements and translating them into new spatial forms in harmony with forces regulating structure follow the tenets of an art. In this framework, there is no schism to these approaches and, as indicated earlier, urban planning unites the tenets of both in one rationale.

In a generic sense the study of urban spatial structure and form as it is developing in the planning field draws from a wide variety of fields. Indeed, planners seek the continuing participation of fields related to planning through a kind of ''sustained yield'' philosophy of self-interest. The strands that make up the fabric of knowledge in urban studies are many. At the risk of narrowing the discussion too abruptly without recognizing the many contributions of these fields to present-day knowledge of urban structure and form, we will turn directly to work which is central to structure-form orientations of the planning field. Structure-form concepts are taken up in the first part of the discussion, followed by a brief examination of models on urban spatial structure, with urban form taken up last. Since structure-form concepts are difficult to separate, no clear-cut division of subject matter is feasible or attempted here.

STRUCTURE-FORM SYSTEMS OF THOUGHT

It is of interest to note that the most significant work in this area is very recent—of the past ten years. While it is, perhaps, premature to classify this work into discrete schools of thought, certain discernible trends in the emphases of research are useful to note in this discussion. Each student of the city, of course, views these trends somewhat differently. For example, Wingo, addressing himself to work on urban spatial structure alone, has classified work into *ad hoc* approaches, potential models, and economic models.[9] In examining work in both urban structure and urban form in studies at the University of North Carolina, we have suggested a somewhat broader basis of grouping: goal-oriented approaches, function approaches, and behavioral approaches.[10] But overlapping is inevitable, and to force systems of thought into any classification system may not only result in interpretations not intended, but could also obscure some of the intended interpretations. In the present discussion, we will refer to work that has been carried to the point where a statement of theory, a schema, or a rationale has been advanced. Where models have been proposed as an outgrowth of a schema, these will be examined in the next part of the discussion.

Lynch and Rodwin have developed a theory of urban structure and form that integrates the goal emphasis of a normative approach with the function emphasis of an analytical approach.[11] Under their approach, structure and form of the city are evaluated in the framework of a defined series of basic goals for urban development. Somewhat like the more purely function type of approach discussed below, the schema views urban structure and form in terms of use activities (''adapted space'') and flows of people, goods, and messages (''flow systems''). Subcategories in the analytical system are *typology* of space and flows; the *quantity* of these spaces and flows; their *density,* that is, the intensity with which spaces and channels fill a unit area; what the authors call *grain,* which takes into account differentiation and separation in space of the major activity and flow elements of the city; *focal organization,* or the spatial arrangements of key points as they relate to one another and the whole urban pattern (for example peaks of population density or key traffic intersections), and *space distribution,* or the gross pattern of space arrangements.

The schema calls for the definition of a pattern of use activities and flow systems which have relevance for a predetermined set of goals, with the analytical framework employing various combinations of the six factors noted above to make a bridge to proposals for the form of the city. Under this particular approach, goals are used as an integral part of the theoretical construct. This is in contrast to other approaches below where goals are external to the theory formulation. In effect, this schema is saying: "if we insert these goals, assuming these values, into the analytical framework, planning action will organize space and flows in the city with this effect." In passing, it might be noted that the schema provides a singularly clear-cut illustration of an integrated use of social science and design systems of thought which, as noted earlier, is an essential characteristic of the urban planning field.

Lynch has drawn on his studies of urban form perceptions of city residents to illustrate types of goal forms that might be utilized as prototypes by the urban designer in applying results from an analysis using such a schema in any particular urban area.[12] His prototype forms are the "dispersed sheet," the "galaxy," the "core," the "star," and the "ring." As implied in the nomenclature, each emphasizes a particular pattern or form that urban development might take.[13]

While also possessing elements of the more purely function emphasis, Webber has developed another conceptual system for classifying spatial patterns of activities that has a goal-oriented aspect.[14] He identifies three dimensions of urban spatial structure and form: the interaction component, the activity component, and the physical component. Within the context of a particular set of goals for a particular urban area, he would use six paralleling spatial variables for each dimension to identify optimal spatial arrangements among use activities. Webber conceives of the application of his schema to urban form in much the same manner as Lynch and Rodwin, that is, he views goal forms as an integral element in the analytical sequence of the schema, with the full application of his system of thought resulting in specific goal forms applicable to a particular situation in the real world.

In his interaction component, Webber places considerable emphasis on the extraspatial ramifications of a theory of urban spatial structure and form and, in this respect, of special interest is his concept of "urban realms," which are spheres of activity defined by patterns of communications and other forms of human interaction. With changing technology, he stresses the increasing "placelessness" of patterns of human interaction in the random way in which networks of interaction spread over the face of the earth. This portends, he predicts, some changes in urban form that may well go beyond our present-day perceptions of urbanity.

Meier has had a notable influence on Webber's thinking with respect to the interaction component. Using communications as a measure of human interaction, Meier has proposed a theory of urban growth in terms of social accounting procedures.[15] While he does not view his schema at this juncture as leading to specific prescriptive end products in urban form, he sets forth an intriguing schema for achieving new insights in urban spatial structure. He proposes to measure the production and flow of information in the form of communications in the framework of a social accounting system and, through an assessment of these findings, to examine the growth, structure, and culture of cities. In a predictive context, he utilizes what he calls an urban time budget to establish time allocations to likely activities and thus identify future patterns of human interaction and their intensity in the pursuit of these activities.

The purer forms of function theory of urban structure and form are constructs that are analytically or synthetically built from systems of relationships that can be derived from the analysis of certain key functions of the city. This emphasis in theory generally focuses on space or location concepts of urban activities (land use), intensity of development (density), and flow systems (people, goods, or communications). Mitchell and Rapkin first opened up this route to the study of urban spatial structure by classifying and organizing land use and traffic concepts according to functions served by different systems of uses and movements.[16] As noted above, Lynch and Rodwin draw on these same elements in their schema, as does Webber. Guttenberg's rationale is an illustration of the function approach without the goal-form emphasis.[17] Components of his schema are what he refers to as the "distributed facility," the "undistributed facility," and transportation as the function elements of urban structure, with "physical density" and "economic density" as variables in this framework. With a central objective of overcoming distance between people and facilities in metropolitan areas, he indicates that basic steps to overcome distances are made by the structural organization of space, and residual improvements in overcoming distance are made by adjustments in urban form.

Approaches to urban structure by economists offer perhaps the purest form of the function approach. Isard's work in spatial economics has had a significant effect in organizing the conceptual systems from this line of approach.[18] He has done much to bring classical theory of land value and rent and the contributions of the German schools of thought on spatial economics to a point where others could propose specific models on urban spatial structure. The application of economic thought to urban spatial structure is illustrated in Wingo's work which applies elements of equilibrium theory and basic concepts of rent and spatial economics to the functioning of transportation as a variable in urban spatial structure.[19]

The behavioral emphasis in planning thought on urban structure and form uses many of the same concepts noted in other approaches above but seeks explanations in terms of human behavior. Work at the University of North Carolina has both a function and a behavioral emphasis.[20] In essence, under our approach, function concepts are used to set forth regularities in space-flow relationships, and behavioral concepts are used to determine conditions under which these space-flow relationships will vary.

The schema views urban spatial structure as a product of a myriad of individual actions (households), private actions (firms and institutions), and public actions (government), developing out of varying motivations such as livability satisfaction, profit maximization, the public interest considerations, and other bases of action. Some are "priming actions" and some are "secondary actions." Tending to occur in particular related behavioral sequences, the priming actions are said to have a structuring effect on the spatial make-up of the city. Illustrative of these actions are highway location decisions, industrial location decisions, and public policy decisions relative to such services as water, sewers, or schools. Under this rationale, priming actions trigger the secondary actions: first, actions by real estate developers, builders, and investors, and then a flood of actions by the individual families, merchants, institutions, etc., which, taken together, account for the broad, massive settlement pattern of the city.

In a loose and general sense, the intervening variables in this analytical framework which function between the decisions, on the one hand, and the end product urban spatial structure, on the other hand, are such structure-function elements as land use, density, and flow systems, with key decisions being conditioned to some extent by these elements at the same time that decisions, in turn, are making their influence felt in modifying the structure and form of the city. Growth multipliers are implicit in the prediction aspects of such a schema. Thus, it is expected that under a specified magnitude of growth, assuming a particular combination of public and private actions known to have a structuring effect on urban development, this schema will enable policy makers to estimate the impact that any particular set of decisions will have on urban structure.

Urban form is introduced into the rationale by linking particular action combinations with particular goal forms. Given a set of alternative goal forms, a magnitude of growth, and particular action alternatives for achieving these goal forms and accommodating this growth, the schema provides a basis for identifying the particular combinations of priming and secondary actions that tend to produce the spatial characteristics of each of the desired goal forms. Once it is known that the consequences of a particular set of actions will tend to produce a particular goal form, that goal form can be translated into a design proposal. In the context of process orientations of planning covered earlier in this discussion, at this point urban design produces specific alternative design proposals for decision and follow-through in the planning process.

MODELS OF URBAN SPATIAL STRUCTURE

When systems of thought of the kind we have just been examining are put into more formal and mathematically expressed constructs, they assume the form of "models." Some of the constructs that are beginning to appear in experimental form in planning and related fields are analytic models in the sense that structured relationships or interactions are "analyzed down" into their components as they occur in the real world; some are synthetic, in the sense that components are put together, that is, are synthesized into the end result of these relationships and interactions without going through the real world; and some are *ad hoc*, in the sense that they are borrowed constructs from physics, mathematics, or statistics, used in limited ways to test the significance of relationships in an otherwise general statement of theory.

To illustrate the analytic type of model, we may refer to two recently advanced land development models. Lowry's model for forecasting land development in the Pittsburgh region proposes to build future land use activities in aggregate or mass patterns.[21] Using the locations of centers of employment as given, with levels of activity at these centers exogenously determined, the model generates a household population and distributes it on the basis of access to employment, with residential development constrained by the availability of land suitable for residential use and by set, maximum density levels; and it distributes retail and service trade activities in the aggregate on the basis of access to markets, in this case households, but constrained by a specified minimum market size. In contrast, a model for residential development proposed by Herbert and Stevens for the Penn-Jersey Transportation Study seeks to forecast development by aggregating the expected behavior of individual households in the urban land market.[22] The model examines the size of household budget in relation to cost of the house type, the amenity and size of the house site, and the travel patterns which are sought in the market, and then, through linear programing techniques, seeks to distribute households to locations where they can maximize their aggregate rent-paying ability. Clearly, both models deal with selected aspects of urban spatial structure, but as experience with analytic models applied to this kind of problem increases, we can expect more refined models to develop.

Synthetic models are a very recent development and have become possible through the use of the modern computer. Garrison's proposal to simulate what he calls urban systems, that is, a variety of linked frameworks for the study of urban phenomena, is an example of this new trend in model building.[23] In studies of urban spatial structure at the University of North Carolina, Donnelly is preparing to "build" cities by a randomizing procedure on the computer, modified to recognize structuring influences.[24] Using analyses we have been making as to how priming actions structure the pattern of land development in cities, we plan to develop measures of the attractiveness for urban development at various locations on a piece of terrain. By successive passes on the computer, a large number of cities can be "built" over and over again on this given piece of terrain with its given measures of attractiveness. We hope to put together a model of the real world by experimentation with priming actions and measures of attractiveness until an average pattern of the simulated city approaches the real city, within defined limits of confidence. Such a model can be tested in any given situation by taking, say, the 1950 city and "predicting" the 1960 city. If the range of error seems to be unreasonably high, investigations would be made to discover other hidden structuring variables that need to be introduced to modify our measures of attractiveness.

Ad hoc constructs for testing particular aspects of the kinds of systems of thought discussed earlier are illustrated by the gravity model and by various statistical models. The gravity model utilizes that familiar Newtonian gravity principle which holds that the attraction between two bodies is directly proportional to their masses and inversely proportional to some function of the distance between them. Many variations on this model are in experimental usage today after the earlier work of Stewart, Zipf, and others.[25] Stewart and Clark both provide an application of the model to population densities and their distribution in urban areas, and Duncan, in the context of human ecology uses as components of the model, manufacturing employment densities and land occupied per establishment as well as population density.[26] While Lowry's model as presented above is an analytic model, the model utilizes the gravity principle in distributing retail and service activities in relation to households that compose the market.[27] Similarly, Hansen, in still another model, uses the gravity principle as a means of representing accessibility in his model for forecasting the distribution of residential growth.[28]

Our work at the University of North Carolina illustrates the application of statistical techniques in tests of urban spatial structure concepts.[29] We have used the circular normal distribution as a "template" for the analysis of growth patterns of cities. The hatlike surface of this three-dimensional distribution represents the intensity of development expected in a city on a flat plain where growth occurs in concentric form outward from a given point on the plain. For any particular city being studied, the deviation of the actual or observed intensities (as obtained by land use surveys) from the expected intensities of development (as determined from the template) may be attributed to some combination of structuring factors, what we have called priming actions. Through interviews with resident planners, city engineers, and city managers, such factors as highway location, location of employment centers, and service areas of the water and sewerage systems can be identified as possible explanations of the observed deviations. Using deviations from the expected intensity of development as the dependent variable, multiple regression analysis can be made of these factors. Through this kind of statistical model and standard statistical tests, it is possible to evaluate parts of a theoretical schema.

CREATIVE DESIGN AND URBAN FORM

While these advances have been unfolding in the science of city growth, new developments are occurring in the art of urban design. There is a new concern for urban esthetics, and urban design generally is experiencing a renaissance of significant proportions. A word on the background is relevant here. As so often happens with movements, an excess in one direction is often followed by one in another direction. Thus, the great public interest in "city beautiful" that was heralded in by Chicago's first great world's fair in the nineties, was followed subsequently by a strong emphasis on solving practical problems. Part of the explanation for the swing in the pendulum was the somewhat limited and often surface interest that developed in city appearance, with much of it focused on civic centers, facade treatment of individual building groups, and other schemes of isolated and limited conception. Emphasis on the practical took hold in the depression of the thirties and extended well into the fifties. By the fifties, the lack of success in dealing with the urban development in its visual aspects had become a source of concern in many quarters. More planners were entering the field and more from design disciplines were coming into planning, but manpower and designers were not providing a solution to the problem. The need for a new field of specialization became increasingly evident. So, in response to the deepening interest in urban design and the need for special training in this specialized field, we see today several new graduate study programs being offered to give people from design fields special training in urban design.

There are other emphases emerging from this reawakening of interest in the visual aspects of the living environment. For the first time, the designer is turning to social science to help him devise techniques to get a deeper insight into human responses to physical surroundings. Thus, the new thinking on urban form seeks to find leads for the design task from investigations of a much broader range of factors than ever before, and it is groping for a theory of design which combines knowledge from both design and the social sciences.

There are at least three areas of investigation that promise to give the urban designer deeper insights into his design subject. One concerns the study of significant historical values that have influenced the growth of the city. The study of urban form in any particular city is deeply rooted in its culture of the past as well as in the functions it serves in the present. The student of urban form gets important cues for the design task in the history of the city as well as in the values of the people who live there today. Once he has a grasp of how the physical environment of the city came to be as he sees it today, he has two other research tasks. One is a study that seeks to understand and interpret the values of the city's residents relating to the urban environment, and the other is a survey of the perceptual features of this environment. We have already noted such recent developments as attitude surveys in an attempt to get at widely held feelings of residents about important environmental features. Such surveys help to establish qualities about the city that are a source of pleasure or satisfaction and qualities that are a source of irritation. Much more needs to be done in this area of study, and to relate value systems to the surface responses obtained in the form of attitudes will involve a very complex kind of research.

The third kind of investigation of importance in the study of urban form is one which systematically records and evaluates the features and qualities of the physical environment which are so fundamental to the design task. Early in his urban form studies, Lynch recognized the importance of identifying such recordable qualities of the urban environment as size, density, grain, outline or shape, and the internal pattern of the city as features that affect the pleasantness of city living.[30] In his interviews on childhood memories that sought to learn from people born and raised in the city what aspects of their surroundings were most vividly recalled,[31] Lynch found these perceptual features to be so dominant that he set about to develop and test a survey approach to assessing the visual resources of the community which coupled with sampling interviews would supply the urban designer with an image of the city and the features to be synthesized in his design.[32] Working in this same area, Williams also developed an approach for classifying and recording land forms and man-made features added to the site.[33] In addition to these basic features of urban form, Williams' survey records significant ''paths'' and vantage points from which the city can be seen by residents of the community, noting the panorama, the skyline, the vista, and the urban open space, and recording the visual experience of the individual in motion during the daily journey to work, on shopping trips, and in other movements he makes in and around the urban area.

In their investigations of the historical features of the city and the role of urban design in conserving significant elements in its cultural heritage, Jacobs and Jones have developed still another visual classification system.[34] The system consists of three main categories of observation: (1) what the authors call sensory material, which has to do with such visible surface qualities as color, texture, pattern, shape, and rhythm; (2) forms and whether they are isolated forms or part of a related series of forms; and (3) ''expressions,'' which have historic significance or symbolic importance for present-day activities. They seek to systemize the evaluation of results by establishing levels of satisfaction through the use of indifference curves in relation to supply and demand for particular objects of historic or cultural significance and by introducing sketch representations of various features of the city to get at what they call a scale of relevance.

These three emphases in work on urban form along with the work being done on urban structure promise to supply the urban designer with information never before so complete. Accordingly, the prospects are bright for an urban design approach to planning that can achieve design in the city that relates much more closely to goals of residents and at the same time gives more complete recognition to the realities of urban growth processes and the structural elements of the city. All of this work, of course, in no way alters the important role that the talented designer must play in the planning process and the use of his developed sense of intuition for translating these concepts and this information into a creative design that achieves both order and convenience but also captures the "sense of the city"—the glimpse of the skyscraper, the unfolding street vista, the press of crowds, the peace of the backyard garden, the carnival spirit of shopping areas, or the many other ways in which the city slips into the consciousness of its residents.

In retrospect, this view of the foundations of urban planning can be brought into sharp focus by observing that the structure-form orientations of the field seek to provide more perfect information for the process orientations, but, at the same time, that the planning process is a mechanism that seeks the decisions necessary to achieve a certain structure and form to the urban area that will bring the city alive for its residents as a pleasant, rewarding, and exciting place in which to live. But if these dreams about the city are to be realized, we come back to the all-important place of the actors in this production. Only where the principal actors possess that sixth sense—both *a vision of the city in the round* and how to achieve a more livable environment, and *a sense of timing,* a knack for picking the right moment in time to act—can these promising developments in urban planning realize their full potential.

Notes

[1] I am indebted to Donald L. Foley for this nomenclature which he developed in a session at the Urban Studies Seminar, Chapel Hill, August 14, 1961.

[2] Robert T. Daland and John A. Parker, ''Roles of the Planner in Urban Development,'' in F. Stuart Chapin, Jr., and Shirley F. Weiss, eds., *Urban Growth Dynamics* (New York: John Wiley & Sons, Inc., 1962).

[3] Melville C. Branch, Jr., *Urban Planning and Public Opinion: National Survey Research Investigation* (Princeton: Bureau of Urban Research, September 1942). See also *Urban Planning Public Opinion: A Pilot Study* (Princeton: Bureau of Urban Research, February 1942).

[4] Robert L. Wilson, ''Livability of the City: Attitudes and Urban Development,'' in Chapin and Weiss, eds., *Urban Growth Dynamics.*

[5] Kevin Lynch, *The Image of the City* (Cambridge: The Technology Press and Harvard University Press, 1960).

[6] Some planning agencies identify only one goal form, i.e., one scheme for the physical development of the urban area, and subsequently follow up in the decision-making stage with recommendations based on the one goal choice. However, increasingly planning agencies are considering goal forms in terms of alternatives before a decision is reached on a single goal form.

[7] Herbert A. Simon, *Administrative Behavior* (New York: The Macmillan Company, 1957), p. 67. Martin Meyerson and Edward C. Banfield, *Politics, Planning and the Public Interest* (New York: The Free Press of Glencoe, 1955), p. 314.

[8] For a fuller discussion, see F. Stuart Chapin, Jr., *Urban Land Use Planning* (New York: Harper & Row, Publishers, 1957), pp. 267–273.

[9] Lowdon Wingo, Jr., *Transportation and Urban Land* (Washington, D.C.: Resources for the Future, Inc., 1961), pp. 11–18.

[10] F. Stuart Chapin, Jr., George C. Hemmens, and Shirley F. Weiss, ''Patterns of Land Development in the Piedmont Industrial Crescent,'' an Urban Studies Research Paper, Institute for Research in Social Science, Chapel Hill, University of North Carolina, December 1960, mimeo. Material in this section of this paper draws from a part of the author's contribution to this document.

[11] Kevin Lynch and Lloyd Rodwin, ''A Theory of Urban Form,'' *Journal of the American Institute of Planners,* 24:4 (Fall 1958).

[12] Kevin Lynch, "The Pattern of the Metropolis," *Daedalus*, 90:1 (Winter 1961).

[13] Some of the alternative long-range growth patterns for the Washington metropolitan area under various policy combinations bear a close resemblance to Lynch's abstractions of urban form. See National Capital Planning Commission and National Capital Regional Planning Council, *A Policies Plan for the Year 2000: The Nation's Capital* (Washington, D.C.: Government Printing Office, 1961).

[14] The only available published references to Melvin Webber's schema are in "Studies in Metropolitan Form," A Graduate Student Report, Department of City and Regional Planning, Berkeley, University of California, January 1960. These concepts will appear in a forthcoming symposium to be published by Resources for the Future, Inc.

[15] Richard L. Meier, *A Communications Theory of Urban Growth* (Cambridge: Technology Press, M.I.T., and Harvard University Press, Nov. 1, 1962).

[16] Robert B. Mitchell and Chester Rapkin, *Urban Traffic: A Function of Land Use* (New York: Columbia University Press, 1954).

[17] Albert Z. Guttenberg, "Urban Structure and Urban Growth," *Journal of the American Institute of Planners*, 26:2 (May 1960).

[18] See Walter Isard, *Location and Space-Economy* (New York: John Wiley & Sons, Inc., jointly with Technology Press, M.I.T., 1956). See also his *Methods of Regional Science* (New York: John Wiley & Sons, Inc., jointly with Technology Press, M.I.T., 1960).

[19] Wingo, *op. cit.*

[20] F. Stuart Chapin, Jr., and Shirley F. Weiss, "Land Development Patterns and Growth Alternatives," in Chapin and Weiss, eds., *Urban Growth Dynamics*.

[21] An unpublished work paper by Ira S. Lowry of the staff of the Economic Study of the Pittsburgh Region prepared for the Pittsburgh Regional Planning Association, September 1960.

[22] John D. Herbert and Benjamin H. Stevens, "A Model for the Distribution of Residential Activity in Urban Areas," *Journal of Regional Science*, 2:2 (Fall 1960).

[23] William L. Garrison, "Toward a Simulation Model of Urban Growth and Development," *Proceedings of the Symposium on Urban Research* (Lund, Sweden: C. W. K. Gleerup, 1961).

[24] Thomas G. Donnelly's work is described in F. Stuart Chapin, Jr., and Shirley F. Weiss, *Factors Influencing Land Development* (Chapel Hill, N.C.: Institute for Resarch in cooperation with the Bureau of Public Roads, U.S. Department of Commerce, 1962).

[25] John Q. Stewart, "Suggested Principles of Social Physics," *Science*, 106:2747 (August 1947), and "Demographic Gravitation: Evidence and Applications," *Sociometry*, 11:1–2 (February–May 1948); George K. Zipf, *Human Behavior and the Principle of Least Effort* (Reading, Mass.: Addison-Wesley Publishing Company, 1949).

[26] John Q. Stewart and Warren Warntz, "Physics of Population Distribution" *Journal of Regional Science*, 1:1 (Summer 1958); Colin Clark, "Urban Population Densities," *Journal of the Royal Statistical Society*, Serial A, 114:4 (1959); and Otis Dudley Duncan, "Population Distribution and Community Structure," *Cold Spring Harbor Symposia on Quantitative Biology*, XXII (1957).

[27] Lowry, *op. cit.*

28 Walter G. Hansen, "How Accessibility Shapes Land Use," *Journal of the American Institute of Planners,* 25:2 (Spring 1959).

29 Chapin and Weiss, eds., *Urban Growth Dynamics.*

30 Kevin Lynch, "The Form of the City," *Scientific American,* 190:4 (April 1954).

31 Alvin K. Lukashok and Kevin Lynch, "Some Childhood Memories of the City," *Journal of the American Institute of Planners,* 22:3 (Summer 1956).

32 Lynch, *The Image of the City.*

33 Sydney H. Williams, "Urban Aesthetics," *The Town Planning Review,* 25:2 (July 1954).

34 Stephen W. Jacobs and Barclay G. Jones, "City Design Through Conservation," unpublished ms., Department of City and Regional Planning, Berkeley, University of California, 1960.